Angular Projects

Build nine real-world applications from scratch using Angular 8 and TypeScript

Zama Khan Mohammed

BIRMINGHAM - MUMBAI

Angular Projects

Commissioning Editor: Pavan Ramchandani
Acquisition Editor: Karan Gupta
Content Development Editor: Aamir Ahmed
Senior Editor: Martin Whittemore
Technical Editor: Jane Dsouza
Copy Editor: Safis Editing
Project Coordinator: Manthan Patel
Proofreader: Safis Editing
Indexer: Rekha Nair
Graphics: Alishon Mendonsa
Production Designer: Jyoti Chauhan

First published: September 2019

Production reference: 1130919

Published by Packt Publishing Ltd.
Livery Place
35 Livery Street
Birmingham
B3 2PB, UK.

ISBN 978-1-83855-935-9

www.packt.com

I dedicate this book to my family, my wife, my parents, and my son, who was born during the writing process. I would also like to give a special dedication to my friends Saad Ather, Mohammed Abdul Kareem, and Ruman ul Hassan, who kept me motivated and helped me along the way.

– Zama Khan Mohammed

Subscribe to our online digital library for full access to over 7,000 books and videos, as well as industry leading tools to help you plan your personal development and advance your career. For more information, please visit our website.

Why subscribe?

- Spend less time learning and more time coding with practical eBooks and Videos from over 4,000 industry professionals

- Improve your learning with Skill Plans built especially for you

- Get a free eBook or video every month

- Fully searchable for easy access to vital information

- Copy and paste, print, and bookmark content

Did you know that Packt offers eBook versions of every book published, with PDF and ePub files available? You can upgrade to the eBook version at www.packt.com and as a print book customer, you are entitled to a discount on the eBook copy. Get in touch with us at customercare@packtpub.com for more details.

At www.packt.com, you can also read a collection of free technical articles, sign up for a range of free newsletters, and receive exclusive discounts and offers on Packt books and eBooks.

Foreword

As a core contributor to popular Angular modules, Zama is an active member of the community. Together we've collaborated on several projects related to improving the accessibility of Angular apps. With his work, Zama has demonstrated his strong expertise in the ecosystem, and his practical user-centric approach demonstrates his exceptional professionalism.

In this book, you'll find a series of examples that will let you look at Angular from different perspectives. Each chapter introduces a new app that will allow you to explore the framework in depth and understand how to quickly get a project with a rich user interface up and running.

I'm excited to see *Angular Projects* getting published! I hope it helps you build fantastic Angular apps!

Minko Gechev, August 2019

Angular Team Engineer at Google

Contributors

About the author

Zama Khan Mohammed is a software architect, building enterprise web applications, with more than 7 years of experience. He has a master's degree in computer science and has loads of experience in software development using technologies such as Angular, React, and AWS. He has a keen interest in software development as well as machine learning, and he is passionate about teaching his interests to others and mentoring.

About the reviewers

Anand Narayanaswamy works as a freelance writer and reviewer based in Thiruvananthapuram. He has published articles on leading print magazines and online tech portals. He was the recipient of the Microsoft MVP award from 2002 to 2011. He is currently a Windows Insider MVP and also part of the prestigious ASPInsiders group.

Anand has worked as a technical editor and reviewer for several publishers. Anand also authored *Community Server Quickly* for Packt Publishing. Anand contributes content to Digit Magazine and Manorama Year Book.

Anand works as Unacademy educator and also runs his own blogs, Netans and Learnxpress. Anand is active on social media and can be reached at `@visualanand` on Twitter and `@netanstech` on Instagram.

Sajeetharan Sinnathurai is a cloud solution architect and an enthusiast in cloud and web development with over 9 years of experience in the ICT industry. He currently works at Microsoft as a Cloud Solution Architect. His skills in web application architecture, the cloud, and more has seen him become a Microsoft MVP in Developer Technologies, and a Google Developer Expert in Web Technology. He is also the top contributor on Stack Overflow in Sri Lanka and he ranks among the top 10 contributors in the world on Angular, Cosmos DB, and more. He now focuses on channeling his knowledge into open source projects and sharing it with the community by mentoring, creating POCS, running workshops, and writing blogs to help make the world a better and more developed place.

Packt is searching for authors like you

If you're interested in becoming an author for Packt, please visit `authors.packtpub.com` and apply today. We have worked with thousands of developers and tech professionals, just like you, to help them share their insight with the global tech community. You can make a general application, apply for a specific hot topic that we are recruiting an author for, or submit your own idea.

Table of Contents

Preface

Angular is one of the best frameworks, not only to build web applications with but also to build applications on other platforms such as Native, desktop, and so on. It is packed with amazing tools that allow developers to become more productive and have a more joyful experience doing what they do.

Angular Projects aims to take you on a journey of developing and building applications using the Angular framework. As the title of the book implies, we will develop a series of projects using Angular, learning different concepts and supporting different use cases of building applications. We'll do so in an orderly way, starting from the very beginning by setting up the development environment and covering fundamental topics that we'll revisit throughout the rest of the book. Each chapter that follows will expand on the basics, allowing for a gentle progression curve that will allow almost any user to follow along. Each chapter will cover a new application, a new capability, by using a different set of component libraries, and thus can be conceived as an independent unit, letting you tackle it separately from the others if you are already proficient in the other topics.

We'll first introduce you to the basics of Angular and its tools, which will help you develop and debug Angular applications. You will then learn how to create a single-page application using the Angular Router, and optimize it by code splitting and preloading routes. We will then look at building a form-heavy application and make forms reactive by using reactive forms. After that, we will look into making a progressive web app, a server-rendered app, and a monorepo app. Furthermore, we will also dive into mobile apps using Ionic and NativeScript. We will then end the book by creating a component library for our application using the Angular CDK and testing Angular apps.

Who this book is for

Angular Projects is aimed at any JavaScript developers who want to start with Angular and become an expert in all the tools and the various use cases that they might deal with as an Angular expert. Whatever the case, a basic understanding of Angular is a plus but is not required. You should know the basics of developing web applications and have experience working with ES6 or TypeScript.

What this book covers

Chapter 1, *Setting Up the Development Environment*, starts off the book by setting up the development environment, and covering the basics of TypeScript, the Angular CLI, and other tools required for this book and for the effective development of Angular applications.

Chapter 2, *Building a Flashcard Game Using Angular*, is aimed at novice Angular developers, going through basic concepts regarding Angular components, services, and some other fundamental concepts such as important decorators, template-driven forms, observables, and change detection.

Chapter 3, *Building a Personal Blog Using Angular Router and WordPress*, shows how you can create multi-environment systems, communicate with APIs, create multiple routes, and optimize an application using lazy loaded routes and different prefetching strategies.

Chapter 4, *Building an Inventory Application Using Reactive Forms*, covers building complex forms using reactive forms and introduces you to using third-party Angular component libraries. We will also learn how to optimize a bundle by first analyzing it and optimizing it if possible.

Chapter 5, *Building a PWA E-Commerce Application Using Angular Service Worker*, introduces **Progressive Web Apps (PWA)** and then goes through building an application, adding to PWA capabilities by adding Angular service workers, and other PWA capabilities.

Chapter 6, *Building an Auditing Application Using Angular and Ionic*, introduces Ionic Framework to build native applications. You will develop apps with Firebase and ngx-formly for real-time communication and creating dynamic JSON forms, respectively.

Chapter 7, *Building a Server-Side Rendering Application Using Angular*, takes the personal blog app we created and renders it on the server side to optimize the application for performance and search engine optimization.

Chapter 8, *Building an Enterprise Portal Using Nx, NgRx, and Redux*, introduces you to using Nx to create an enterprise portal as a monorepo application. We will convert an app developed using the Angular CLI, upgrade it to an Nx workspace, add a new admin portal, and use NgRx to handle the whole authentication flow using it. Lastly, we'll use ngx-charts to add D3 visualization.

Chapter 9, *Building a Multi-Language NativeScript Application with Angular*, goes over creating a native app using NativeScript Angular, introducing the different layouts available, and then using an Angular module and a NativeScript module. The ngx-translate Angular module will allow you to add multiple language support to the application.

Chapter 10, *Building a Component Library Using Angular CDK and Elements*, teaches how you can create a reusable component library with a component that is accessible by using the Angular CDK and then publish it to npm. You will also learn about Angular elements and how to use them in any JavaScript non-Angular application.

Chapter 11, *Testing an Angular Application Using Jasmine, Jest, and Protractor*, covers testing strategies a developer can use to test applications and teaches different testing strategies by writing tests for components, services, and pipes. We will also look at how we can mock HTTP calls for Jasmine tests using Jest, snapshot testing, and end-to-end testing, and learn about test coverage and error handling.

To get the most out of this book

You will need to have a version of Angular installed on your computer—the latest version, if possible. Most of what we will cover in this book should work on different Angular versions, but we recommend 8.3.0 or higher in order to have the latest features installed.

Prior knowledge of Angular is not a must, but having some working experience with it will help you to enjoy a smoother experience throughout the book. While no Angular skills are required, you are required to have knowledge of JavaScript and experience using HTML, CSS, and JavaScript.

Download the example code files

You can download the example code files for this book from your account at www.packt.com. If you purchased this book elsewhere, you can visit www.packtpub.com/support and register to have the files emailed directly to you.

You can download the code files by following these steps:

1. Log in or register at www.packt.com.
2. Select the **Support** tab.
3. Click on **Code Downloads**.
4. Enter the name of the book in the **Search** box and follow the onscreen instructions.

Once the file is downloaded, please make sure that you unzip or extract the folder using the latest version of:

- WinRAR/7-Zip for Windows
- Zipeg/iZip/UnRarX for Mac
- 7-Zip/PeaZip for Linux

The code bundle for the book is also hosted on GitHub at `https://github.com/PacktPublishing/Angular-Projects`. In case there's an update to the code, it will be updated on the existing GitHub repository.

We also have other code bundles from our rich catalog of books and videos available at `https://github.com/PacktPublishing/`. Check them out!

Download the color images

We also provide a PDF file that has color images of the screenshots/diagrams used in this book. You can download it here: `https://static.packt-cdn.com/downloads/9781838559359_ColorImages.pdf`.

Conventions used

There are a number of text conventions used throughout this book.

`CodeInText`: Indicates code words in text, database table names, folder names, filenames, file extensions, pathnames, dummy URLs, user input, and Twitter handles. Here is an example: "TypeScript has a special keyword called `interface`, which doesn't exist in ECMAScript."

A block of code is set as follows:

```
interface ICar {
    make: string;
    model: string;
    year: number;
    vin?: string;
}
```

When we wish to draw your attention to a particular part of a code block, the relevant lines or items are set in bold:

```
@Component({
    ...
})
export class AppComponent {
    ...

    handleToggleCard(id: number) {
        const flash = this.flashs.find(flash => flash.id === id);
        flash.show = !flash.show;
    }
}
```

Any command-line input or output is written as follows:

```
> yarn add bootstrap-scss
```

Bold: Indicates a new term, an important word, or words that you see onscreen. For example, words in menus or dialog boxes appear in the text like this. Here is an example: "Afterward, we need to go to the **Audits** tab in developer tools, as follows."

 Warnings or important notes appear like this.

 Tips and tricks appear like this.

Get in touch

Feedback from our readers is always welcome.

General feedback: If you have questions about any aspect of this book, mention the book title in the subject of your message and email us at customercare@packtpub.com.

Errata: Although we have taken every care to ensure the accuracy of our content, mistakes do happen. If you have found a mistake in this book, we would be grateful if you would report this to us. Please visit www.packtpub.com/support/errata, selecting your book, clicking on the Errata Submission Form link, and entering the details.

Piracy: If you come across any illegal copies of our works in any form on the Internet, we would be grateful if you would provide us with the location address or website name. Please contact us at copyright@packt.com with a link to the material.

If you are interested in becoming an author: If there is a topic that you have expertise in and you are interested in either writing or contributing to a book, please visit authors.packtpub.com.

Reviews

Please leave a review. Once you have read and used this book, why not leave a review on the site that you purchased it from? Potential readers can then see and use your unbiased opinion to make purchase decisions, we at Packt can understand what you think about our products, and our authors can see your feedback on their book. Thank you!

For more information about Packt, please visit packt.com.

Setting Up the Development Environment

1

In this book, we will be covering different kinds of projects, from the basic Angular app to a server-rendered one, and a native app for Android and iOS. We will also look at how to create a component library for our enterprise applications and start testing our components. We will be using different Angular component libraries and tools and get a holistic view of Angular Framework and its capabilities.

Angular apps are written using web technologies. In order to run Angular apps, we need to install Node.js on our machine, which is what we will be doing in this first chapter.

Angular is a framework for building mobile and web applications. It uses TypeScript, which is a superscript of ECMAScript. It adds support for types in JavaScript, which makes the development of Angular apps easier at compile time. We will look into some basic concepts of TypeScript in this chapter, which will explain some of the syntax that we will be using in this book.

Another tool we will look at is Angular CLI, the command-line interface program that the Angular team has created to help with the development and maintenance of Angular apps.

We could write Angular apps using a simple text editor, but to get full productivity out of building our Angular application, we will be using VS Code. Instead of being an **Integrated Development Environment (IDE)**, it's a code editor with rich extension support. In this chapter, we will use VS Code and install the required extensions to make Angular development faster.

The following topics will be covered in this chapter:

- Installing Node.js
- Understanding the basics of TypeScript
- Introducing Angular CLI
- Introducing Angular Console
- Installing VS Code and installing various extensions
- Installing Augury and looking at various sections that help us debug our application

Installing Node.js

If you don't have Node.js installed on your machine, make sure you go to `https://nodejs.org/en/` and follow the instructions for the installation of Node.js on your machine.

To make sure you have Node.js installed on your machine, run `node --version`. If you have Node.js installed, the version of the installed Node.js environment is printed. The most recent version at the time of writing is **v12.10.0.**

Make sure that your version is above **v8.0.0**. If it's not, then please update your version of Node.js.

 You may also want to install **Node Version Manager (NVM)** so that you can manage multiple Node.js versions on your machine in the future. To install NVM, follow the instructions at `https://github.com/creationix/nvm`.

Introducing TypeScript

TypeScript is a superset of the JavaScript language that was built by Microsoft. It adds the functionality of being able to add types to JavaScript code and transpiles the TypeScript code into JavaScript. The advantage that we get by using TypeScript is that since it's a compiled language that compiles to JavaScript, we get failure information (if there is any) at compile time. This means that we don't find errors after the JavaScript code gets to run on the browser.

TypeScript adoption has been increasing since 2016. One of the reasons for its adoption in the JavaScript ecosystem has been Angular. Angular is built entirely using TypeScript, and so is almost all of the community's Angular modules and the applications using it.

TypeScript not only supports most of the features from ECMAScript, such as classes, arrow functions, template literals, import/export, and so on, but also transpiles them to equivalent ES5 JavaScript code so that you don't have to worry about supporting browsers that don't support specific ECMAScript features.

Let's cover a few of the important concepts of TypeScript, interfaces, decorators, and access modifiers.

Interface

TypeScript has a special keyword called `interface` that doesn't exist in ECMAScript. Interfaces fill the role of naming the types in TypeScript and is used to describe the contracts within the code:

```
interface ICar {
    make: string;
    model: string;
    year: number;
    vin?: string;
}
```

Here, we have an `interface` for `Car` called `ICar`; we have added `I` before `Car` to describe it as an `interface`. In our `ICar` interface, we have `make` and `model` as `string` types, and `year` as a `number`. We also have an optional `vin` in our object shape with the type of `string`, it is optional is represented by `?`.

To use this `interface`, we assign the `ICar` interface to the `car` variable, as follows:

```
const car: ICar = {
    make: 'Chevrolet',
    model: 'Malibu',
    year: 2019,
};
```

This is how TypeScript helps you to assign different types and also use interfaces to define types of an object.

Class and property decorators

Decorators can be used as wrappers around code, such as classes, functions, or even properties, as well as getters and setters. They are used to add an additional feature to that piece of code.

The Angular team wanted to use decorators in JavaScript—in fact, the Angular team first proposed this by creating a superset of TypeScript called AtScript, which was later merged into TypeScript. Decorators have been proposed as a feature for future JavaScript. The following code shows examples of class and property decorators:

```
@Component({
    selector: 'app-cars',
    templateUrl: './cars.component.html',
    styleUrl: './cars.component.css'
})
class CarsComponent {
    @Input() cars: ICar[]; // Array of ICar type
    // property sameMake takes type boolean explicitly here because of
        the assignment
    private sameMake = true;
    /*
        Function updateCarYear takes parameter car of type ICar,
        and doesn't returns anything(void)
    */
    public updateCarYear(car: ICar): void {
        car.year = car.year + 1;
    }
}
```

In this example, we are using a couple of decorators: `@Component` and `@Input`. `@Component` is a class decorator that's defined by Angular which takes the configuration of the component as an object, whereas `@Input` is a property decorator that makes the `cars` property the input for the component.

We see how these simple decorators can add a lot of capabilities to the classes or class properties. Next, let's learn about access modifiers.

Access modifiers

In the preceding example regarding decorators, we can also see the use of access modifiers (`public` and `private`). If the property is going to be used by any class that extends this class or if the property is going to be used in a template (in terms of Angular), then it should be marked as `public`; otherwise, it should have the access modifier marked as `private`.

If the access modifier is not added, like the `cars` property in `CarsComponent` in the preceding example, the default `public` access modifier is assigned to the property.

Now that we understand some basics of TypeScript, let's also get familiar with Angular CLI, a command-line interface tool developed by the Angular team to develop Angular applications.

Introducing Angular CLI

Angular CLI is the command-line interface tool that helps you kickstart new projects and maintain your application using best practices while you're creating different components of Angular, and also lets you test these practices. It also allows you to build for production and serve the application for development with its live reloading capability, along with the ability to lint, test, and run **end-to-end (e2e)** test cases. This project is open source and is maintained by the Angular team. Because of its wide use in the Angular community—apart from making life easier while developing an application—if you were to encounter a new Angular app that uses Angular CLI, it would follow the same shape. We will be using Angular CLI to create Angular applications and add additional functionality as and when required.

Installing Angular CLI

To install Angular CLI, make sure that you have installed Node 8 or above. Then, run the following command in the terminal:

```
> npm install -g @angular/cli
```

Alternatively, you can use npx instead of installing Angular CLI globally in order to avoid updating it in the future. In this book, we will not be using npx to run Angular CLI commands.

To make sure that @angular/cli has been installed, and to check the version of the CLI that you have, run the following command:

```
> ng version
```

Here, ng is the command of Angular CLI, and version is one of the commands in Angular CLI which will give you the global version as well as the local project's Angular CLI version. Global version is the version of Angular CLI installed using npm on the machine, whereas the local version is specific to the project. It will also describe all the different @angular packages that are being used in the project folder.

Now that Angular CLI is available on your local machine, you can use it for various purposes:

- Scaffolding a new Angular app
- Updating existing Angular app to newer version of Angular
- Generating new files
- Serving the application
- Building the application
- Testing the application

And many more.

Let's look at the capabilities of Angular CLI next.

Scaffolding a new Angular app

Angular CLI lets you create a basic application with all the required setup to develop a professional/enterprise application. Now that we have installed Angular CLI, let's generate a new Angular project. We can do that by running the following command:

```
> ng new angular-project-name
```

This command creates a folder called angular-project-name and all the files that are required for a basic Angular application.

You can use ng new command with the flag enableIvy to use Ivy Rendering in the application, that will make your Angular application faster and smaller without any breaking changes. In Angular 9, Ivy Rendering would be enabled by default for all projects created using Angular CLI.

If you peek into the folder, you will see that it consists of the following files:

- `angular.json`: This is a configuration file for the Angular CLI application. It consists of all the application's descriptions and the configurations for those apps. If you need to add projects, add global assets/styles/scripts, or add some configurations, you can make a change to this file.
- `tsconfig.json`: This file consists of the TypeScript configuration for the project.
- `tslint.json`: This file consists of all the linting rules for this Angular app. If you peek into the file, you will see that it extends codelyzer, which is a custom TypeScript linter. This adds more Angular-specific rules to `tslint` configurations.
- `src`: This folder consists of application-related files. Some of these are as follows:
  - `styles.css`: This file is a global CSS file that will be used in the application.
  - `polyfills.ts`: This file has polyfills for the application to make the app run on older browsers.
  - `browserlist`: This file consists of browser versions that the app supports. This file is used by autoprefixer to add vendor prefixes based on the browser's support in this file.
  - `main.ts`: This is the main TypeScript file for the application. It bootstraps `AppModule`.
  - `app/app.module.ts`: This is the Angular's app module, also known as the root module for the application. It initially has the declaration of `AppComponent`. The files related to `AppComponent` can be found in the `app` folder.
- `e2e folder`: This folder consists of all the end-to-end testing files that use Protractor.

Now that we know how to scaffold a basic Angular app, let's learn about the other actions that Angular CLI can perform.

Updating your Angular application

Angular has adopted semantic versioning, which includes major, minor, and patch releases. A major release is updated when breaking changes or substantial changes are introduced in the framework; a minor release is updated when there is a new feature being introduced in the framework; and patch releases are to fix bugs. These help users find out the potential impact of updating. Every six months, Angular releases a major update, and around 1-3 minor updates and patches every week.

With this comes the difficult task of updating the application to the latest version every six months. The Angular CLI makes this easier to update. To update Angular, run the following command in your angular application folder in the terminal.

```
> ng update @angular/cli @angular/core
```

You can also use flags such as `--all` and `--next` to update all the available updates in all the Angular schematics packages installed, and update it to the latest available version of the packages.

For more detailed help about upgrading, please visit `http://update.angular.io`. On it, you can select different options about your current state of the application and to what version you want to upgrade, and get a checklist of stuff you might need to update for a successful update.

Generating files

Generating different files for things such as components, directives, pipes, and so on, can be tedious for some people, as it requires adding multiple files and some boilerplate code every time we create them. The Angular CLI has a command called `generate` that generates different kinds of files. It allows you to generate components, which are the basic building blocks of Angular apps. It generates TypeScript files, CSS files, HTML files, and a spec file. It reduces the effort of manually creating the files and then writing the initial boilerplate for the integration of those files.

To find out what files the Angular CLI can generate, please visit `https://angular.io/cli/generate`.

Serving an Angular app

To serve an Angular app using development settings, run `ng serve` or `npm start` in your Terminal and open `http://localhost:4200/` in your browser. You will see that a minimalistic Angular app has been created by the Angular CLI:

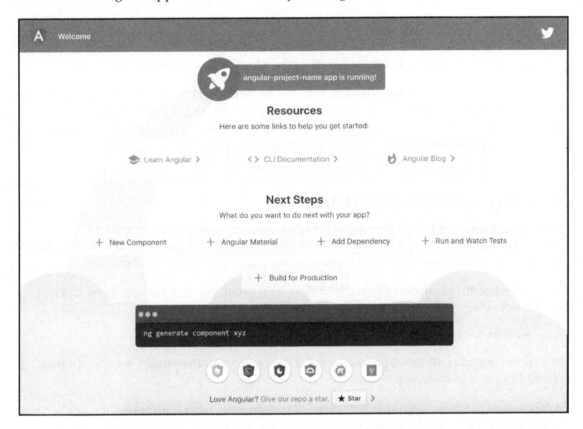

We served the application so that we can develop and see the changes of our code change in the browser. Now when we are ready for our application to be deployed to production, we need to optimize the application by building and bundling our application. Let's look at it next.

Building the application

If you want to deploy your application to production, we need to first build our application and deploy the files generated after the build to the required server. To build the application for deployment, run the following command:

```
> ng build --prod
```

This command will create a `dist` folder, where you will be able to see all the files of the build app. You could serve this application using a local server such as `http-server`.

The `prod` flag in the preceding command creates an optimized bundle of the application. It does **Ahead of Time (AOT)** compilation using the `ngc` (the Angular compiler), which is built on top of the TypeScript compiler, to create highly optimized code. This will make the application smaller and faster.

Adding CLI extensions

Angular CLI makes it to add new capabilities to your application via the use of CLI extensions. There are many CLI extensions available; some of them have been built by the Angular team, but many have been created by the awesome Angular community.

Let's say you want to add the Progressive Web App capability to your app—you can just run the following command:

```
> ng add @angular/pwa
```

This command adds all the dependencies and file changes to the project, which will make it a basic Progressive Web App.

In this section, we have seen that Angular CLI can do a lot, from scaffolding the application to generating files, serving the application, building the application, and so on, with a lot of different options. This can become overwhelming for beginners to remember. In the next section, we will see another tool that can help new Angular developers to use Angular CLI without remembering all the different commands.

Introducing Angular Console

The Angular Console is a **graphical user interface (GUI)** tool for the Angular CLI that was built by the **Narwhal Technologies (Nrwl)** team. It makes it easier for a beginner who is not familiar with all the Angular CLI commands and with the different options available for each command to use the Angular CLI effectively and learn about different commands along the way. Now, let's learn how to download Angular Console and configure it:

1. Download Angular Console from `https://angularconsole.com` and complete the step-by-step installation.
2. When you open Angular Console, you will be given the option to either add a new project or use a current Angular CLI application. Let's go ahead and create a new application:

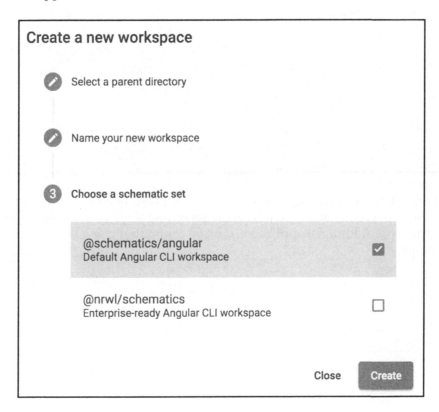

First, select the parent directory where the project will reside and then name the workspace for the project before selecting a schematic. Angular CLI uses schematics to provide you with different commands and functions that you can use for an application. Here, we are given the choice of using **@schematics/angular**, which is a default schematic that comes with Angular CLI, and **@nrwl/schematics**, which is an enterprise-ready monorepo schematic that was built by the Nrwl.io team:

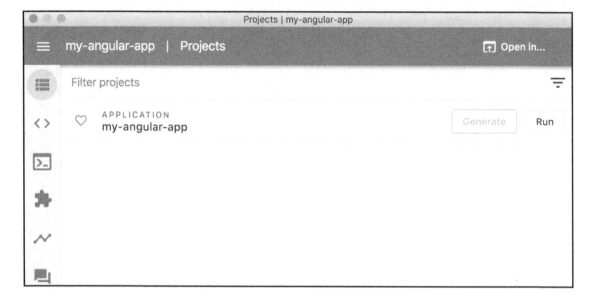

Once the project has been created, you are taken to the **Projects** page. On this screen, you will see all the applications in the project. In the preceding screen, we can see one project: one is the main app. Additional applications can be configured using the `angular.json` file in the project.

We also have the **Run** button, and when you click it, it opens up a dropdown with **Build**, **Serve**, **Test**, **Lint** and **E2e** end-to-end test command. Once you click on **Serve** on the **Projects** page, you will be taken to the commands detail page. Here, you can add/change different fields, which are categorized into two buckets: **Important** and **Optional**. You can see this in the following screenshot:

You can change the fields and click on the **Run** button at the top to serve the application:

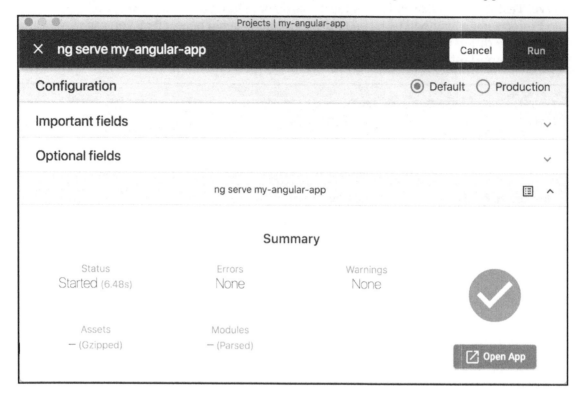

Once the build is complete, just click on the **Open App** link in the task output to open the application in the browser.

You can close this command execution window by using the close icon in the top left and continue to use other features of Angular CLI using this GUI tool. Angular Console also allows you to add additional Angular CLI extensions. You can navigate to this option using the left menu on the **Projects** page.

Angular Console is a great tool for those who are beginners to Angular CLI as well as those who cannot keep up with all the commands and their options. Now that we have Angular Console installed, let's install the editor we will be using in this book, VS Code, and configure it for working with Angular projects.

VS Code

VS Code is a code editor that was built by Microsoft. It's currently the most popular code editor for JavaScript projects. The best part about VS Code is its support for TypeScript projects and rich extensions. You can find so many useful extensions that support Angular development, which makes it the most used editor by Angular developers. You can use any text editor to develop Angular applications, but in this book, we will be using VS Code.

Installing VS Code

To install VS Code, go to `https://code.visualstudio.com/`. Download the latest stable version or the insiders version. VS Code releases new stable version every month, whereas the insiders version receives updates as soon as new changes are added to VS Code.

Installing extensions

In this section, we will install some important extensions for VS Code that will help us in the development of Angular applications.

To go to **EXTENSIONS** in VS Code, find the **Extensions** tab on the left bar:

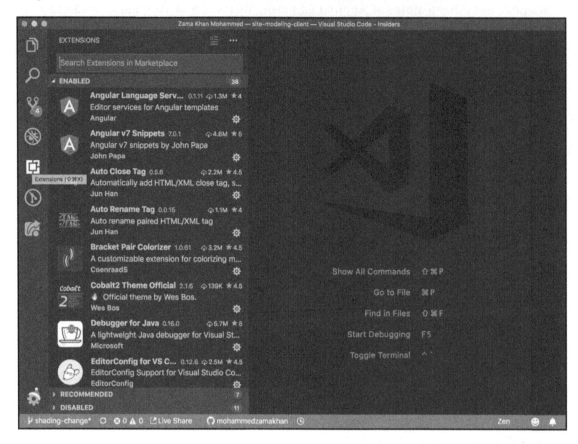

You can also find the extension you are looking for by using *Ctrl + Shift + P* on Windows or *command + Shift + P* on macOS, typing View: Show Extensions, and then searching for the extensions from the large VS Code extensions library and installing them. Let's go over some of the essential Angular extensions that are available and should be installed:

- **Angular Essentials**: This is an extension pack for VS Code that consists of various extensions that will be helpful for Angular development. These extensions include **Angular Language Services**, **Angular v7 Snippets by John Papa**, **EditorConfig**, **TSLint**, and **Prettier**.
- **Angular Language Services**: This extension provides a rich editing experience in internal as well as external HTML templates, such as auto-completion, go to definition, and quick info:

- **Angular Snippets**: This is a snippet extension that has shortcuts to different useful snippets for all the different file types, that is, HTML, CSS, and TypeScript.
- **TSLint**: Following a strong coding practice is important, and that's where linting comes into the picture. TSLint is a linter for TypeScript code and helps projects follow strong guidelines. If you use this extension, you will get real-time errors and warnings in your editor that will help you resolve code formatting or code errors.
- **Prettier**: Prettier is a very opinionated code formatter that supports multiple languages, including TypeScript, HTML, and CSS. This extension allows you to auto fix any formatting issues based on the Prettier settings of the project.
- **Angular Console**: This extension adds Angular Console directly to VS Code.

Other extensions that I use for Angular development are **Bracket Pair Colorizer**, **angular2-switcher**, **angular2-inline**, **Path Intellisence**, **Git Blame**, **Git History**, and **GitLens**.

Now that we have our extensions installed, let's look at how we can control them using VS Code settings.

VS Code settings

VS Code settings is a powerful way to VS Code at a granular level. Some of the settings are in-built with VS Code, such as `tabSize`, `fontSize`, and so on, and some of them are added after you add extensions to your VS Code editor, such as TSLint.

These are some of my settings that help me while developing Angular applications, which you can reach by *Ctrl + Shift + P* and then searching for `Preferences: Open Settings (JSON)` and adding all these settings:

```
{
    ...
    "editor.tabSize": 2,
    "editor.fontFamily": "Fira Code",
    "editor.fontLigatures": true,
    "editor.fontSize": 15,
    "editor.minimap.enabled": false,
    "stylelint.enable": true,
    "tslint.autoFixOnSave": true,
    "javascript.updateImportsOnFileMove.enabled": "always",
    "editor.codeActionsOnSave": {
        "source.organizeImports": true
    },
    ...
}
```

Here, I have set various editor options, such as `tabSize`, `fontSize`, `fontFamily`, `fontLigatures`, and disabled the `minimap` that shows up on the right side of the code editor when a file is open. We have set the `fontFamily` to `Fira Code`, which is one of the best open source fonts available. You can install it from `https://github.com/tonsky/FiraCode`. We have also enabled `stylelint`, which will give linting errors in your styling (CSS, SCSS, or LESS), and we enabled autofix on save for the TSLint errors, which will be helpful for us because the editor can autofix some of the errors for us. You can check more settings that you can customize to your likings by searching in the command palette for `Preferences: Open Default Settings (JSON)`. This Default Settings file is not editable and should only be used to check what are the different settings available for us to change and check the default values for them.

Now that we have our VS Code all set up, let's install a new tool in our browser that will help us debug Angular applications, Augury.

Debugging Angular applications using Augury

Augury is an application inspection tool and is one of the most commonly used developer tool extensions for Angular apps. It was built in collaboration with Rangle and Google and makes debugging and profiling Angular applications simpler during development by creating component tree visualizations and visual debugging tools.

Augury supports both Chrome and Firefox. To install it, either go to Chrome Web Store/Firefox Add-ons and search for Augury. Alternatively, you can go to `https://augury.rangle.io/` and find the appropriate links for the respective extensions.

Once installed, go to an Angular application that's served using the development environment (that is, without prod mode enabled), open developer tools, find **Augury** in the tabs, and navigate to it:

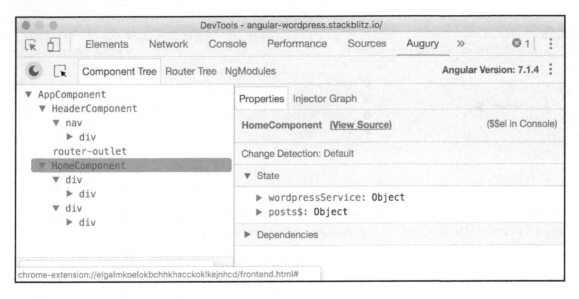

In the top right-hand corner, you will find the Angular version that the application is being served with. The preceding screenshots show that the **Angular Version** that's being used in the app is **7.1.4**.

On the top, we have three tabs,

- **Component Tree**: The Angular Component Tree structure is similar to the **Elements** panel, but with Angular components. We can also select the components and see more details about them in the right-hand panel.
- **Router Tree**: Used to visualize all the available routes in the application.
- **NgModules**: Lists all the modules in the application with all their dependencies.

You should also be able to see that the **Component Tree** tab is selected by default. Here, you can see the whole component tree, select different components, and view more details about its current state. Once a component has been selected in the **Component Tree** on the left, you can use $$el to access the component in the console. You will also find a link to **View Source** for that specific component, which is handy.

You can also select the **Router Tree**, where you can see all the routes that are being used in the application:

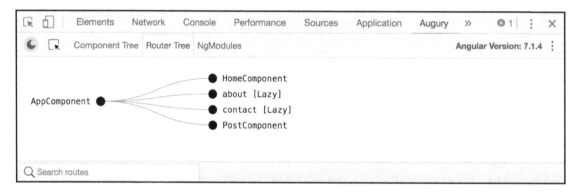

In this view, you can also see which routes are being **Lazy** loaded. We will talk about Lazy routes in more detail in Chapter 3, *Building a Personal Blog Using Angular Router and WordPress*.

The last tab in Augury is **NgModules**:

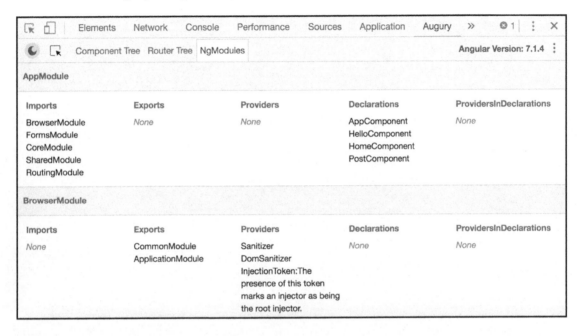

This shows all the different components that make up the Angular modules that are used in the application.

Summary

In this chapter, we have covered the basics tools that are required for building an Angular application. We installed Angular CLI, Angular Console, VS Code, and Augury to make our developer experience better. These tools will be used in the rest of the chapters to develop exciting projects.

In the next chapter, we will build a complete basic Angular app. This will be a flashcard application that displays a list of the available flashcards and also can add/edit/remove flashcards.

2
Building a Flashcard Game Using Angular

In this chapter, we will develop a basic Angular app for a flashcard game. We will also introduce some of the built-in attributes and structural directives in the Angular framework and create a basic template-driven form so that we can add/edit the flashcards. We will be introduced to observables and learn how to use the `async` pipe to get observable data on the page. We will also create a basic `FlashService` to perform all the operations related to adding, editing, and deleting flashcards.

The following topics will be covered in this chapter:

- Creating a new Angular project and a component
- Introducing template-driven forms
- Introducing services
- Introducing observables

Technical requirements

This chapter's code can be found in this book's GitHub repository at `https://github.com/PacktPublishing/Angular-Projects`, under the `Chapter02` folder. This code has been provided so that whenever you are stuck, you can verify whether you've done something differently and play around with it.

Creating a new project and a component

Let's start by creating a new project using Angular Console and name it `ng-flashcards`. As this is our first chapter, we will use Angular Console to run Angular CLI commands, rather than using terminal to run them.

We will be using Bulma for this project. Bulma is a CSS framework that provides CSS for different styled elements and components. You can find more information about Bulma at `https://bulma.io/`. Let's get started:

1. Let's first add Bulma CSS to our application. To add Bulma CSS, we will need to install it using `npm` by going to the projects folder in Terminal:

   ```
   > npm install bulma
   ```

2. In order to include the Bulma CSS file globally in the project, which is an external CSS file, we will have to update the `angular.json` file. Let's open the project in VS Code, open the `angular.json` file, and update the `styles` array that's present in the project:

   ```
   ...
   "styles": [
       "src/styles.css",
       " node_modules/bulma/css/bulma.min.css"
   ],
   ...
   ```

3. Now, we can simply include the link to the Font Awesome font icons (`https://fontawesome.com/start`) that Bulma uses in the `index.html` file:

   ```
   <link rel="stylesheet"
   href="https://use.fontawesome.com/releases/v5.6.3/css/all.css"
   integrity="sha384-
   UHRtZLI+pbxtHCWp1t77Bi1L4ZtiqrqD80Kn4Z8NTSRyMA2Fd33n5dQ8lWUE00s/"
   crossorigin="anonymous">
   ```

4. Let's serve our application, by clicking **Run** and then selecting **Serve** on the Angular Console's Project page, so that we can see the changes we will be making in the browser. The browser will automatically reload after a change is made. Now let's close the running task using the **X** at the running commands header.

5. Click on the **Generate** tab on the side menu and select **Component**. On the **Generate** page, enter `flash` for the component name, and click **Generate**. You will see that a folder called `flash` has been created with four files: an HTML file, a CSS file, a `.ts` file, and a `.spec.ts` file, respectively.

6. Let's add a card component from Bulma's documentation (`https://bulma.io/documentation/components/card/`) and modify it so that it has a question in the header, an answer in the content area, and four buttons; that is, a check mark, a cross mark, an edit icon, and a trash icon:

```
<div class="card">
    <header class="card-header">
        <p class="card-header-title">{{flash.question}}</p>
        <a class="card-header-icon" href="javascript:void(0)" aria-
        label="more options">
            <span class="icon"><i class="fas fa-angle-down" aria-
            hidden="true"></i></span>
        </a>
    </header>
    <div class="card-content">
        <div class="content">{{flash.answer}}</div>
    </div>
    <footer class="card-footer">
        <a class="card-footer-item" href="#"><i class="fas fa-
        check"></i></a>
        <a class="card-footer-item" href="#"><i class="fas fa-
        times"></i></a>
        <a class="card-footer-item" href="#"><i class="fas fa-
        edit"></i></a>
        <a class="card-footer-item" href="#"><i class="fas fa-
        trash"></i></a>
    </footer>
</div>
```

Here, we have added angular interpolation, `{{}}`, to bind the data from `FlashComponent` to our HTML.

7. Next, let's add the `flash` property as `Input` to our flash component:

```
import { Component, Input } from '@angular/core';
import { IFlash } from './../flash.model';

@Component({
    selector: 'app-flash',
    templateUrl: './flash.component.html',
})  styleUrls: ['./flash.component.css']
export class FlashComponent {
    @Input() flash: IFlash = {
        id: 1,
        question: 'React to Angular',
        answer: 'No Reaction :)',
        show: false,
    };
}
```

8. We also need to make sure that we add the `IFlash` interface to our application. Let's create `flash.model.ts` in our `app` folder:

```
export type IFlash = {
    question: string;
    answer: string;
    show: boolean;
    id: number;
    remembered?: 'correct' | 'incorrect';
}
```

9. Now, we need to add some styles to our `card` element. Since we don't want them to span the whole width, let's give it a `width` and a `margin`:

```
.card {
    width: 300px;
    display: inline-block;
    margin: 10px;
}

.card-header {
    cursor: pointer;
}
```

10. Let's use this component in our app. Go to `app.component.html` and use the component we just created, by replacing the existing HTML in the file:

```
<div class="flashs">
    <app-flash></app-flash>
</div>
```

11. Let's use flexbox for the `flashs` class, which is a wrapper for the flash component:

```
.flashs {
    display: flex;
    flex-wrap: wrap;
}
```

Now, you should be able to see one flashcard in the browser:

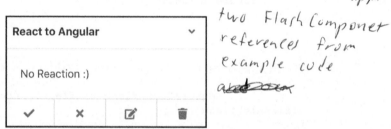

must include in app.module.ts two Flash Componet references from example code al~~kdl~~or

A simple card will be displayed with a question in the header and an answer in the card body. You should also see that the header has a toggle icon, and that the footer has four different action buttons. The first button has a check icon, which will be clicked if the user remembers the answer to the question. The second button, which has a cross icon, will be clicked if the user doesn't remember the answer, the edit icon allows the user to edit the flashcard, and the trash icon allows the user to delete the card.

Now, let's create an array of flashes in our app component and render all of them:

1. Add the following `flashs` property and `getRandomNumber` function to `AppComponent` in `app.component.ts` file:

```
...
function getRandomNumber() {
    return Math.floor(Math.random() * 10000);
}
...
export class AppComponent {
    flashs: IFlash[] = [{
        question: 'Question 1',
```

```
        answer: 'Answer 1',
        show: false,
        id: getRandomNumber(),
    }, {
        question: 'Question 2',
        answer: 'Answer 2',
        show: false,
        id: getRandomNumber(),
    }, {
        question: 'Question 3',
        answer: 'Answer 3',
        show: false,
        id: getRandomNumber(),
    }];

    trackByFlashId(index, flash) {
      return flash.id;
    }
  }
}
```

2. Now, in `app.component.html`, we will add a `for` loop directive called `*ngFor`:

```
<app-flash *ngFor="let flash of flashs; trackBy: trackByFlashId"
[flash]="flash"></app-flash>
```

This will display three different flashcards on the screen:

Always remember to add `trackBy` in `ngFor`, even though they are optional. This helps Angular keep the list performant when it comes to the addition or removal of objects from the list. By default, Angular tracks these objects using a reference. So, if we provide the `trackBy` property, some identifier in the item, such as `id` in the preceding example, Angular knows how to update the list performantly.

3. Now, let's add a simple click action to the toggle icon in the header:

```html
<header class="card-header" (click)="toggleCard()">
    <p class="card-header-title">{{flash.question}}</p>
    <a class="card-header-icon" href="javascript:void(0)" aria-
    label="more options">
        <span class="icon"><i class="fas fa-angle-down" aria-
        hidden="true"></i></span>
    </a>
</header>
```

As you can see, we have added `(click)="toggleCard()"`, where `()` signifies an output/event, and `toggleCard` is the name of the member function that we will add to the `FlashComponent` class.

4. Let's add the following `toggleCard` method, which will emit the `onToggleCard` `EventEmitter` as follows:

```typescript
import { Component, Input, Output, EventEmitter } from
'@angular/core';
@Component({
    ...
})
export class FlashComponent {
    ...
    @Output() onToggleCard = new EventEmitter();
    toggleCard() {
        this.onToggleCard.emit(this.flash.id);
    }
}
```

We have added a couple of things here. First, we have defined the `toggleCard` member function, as well as a property called `onToggleCard` with a value of `EventEmitter()`, which we have added an `Output` decorator to. When you click on the toggle icon, the `toggleCard` function is called. Rather than toggling the card in the component itself, I am calling `this.onToggleCard.emit(this.flash.id)` and passing the value of the flash ID to its parent component.

5. Now, let's wire this up in `app.component.html`:

```
<app-flash
    *ngFor="let flash of flashs; trackByFlashId"
    [flash]="flash"
    (onToggleCard)="handleToggleCard($event)"
></app-flash>
```

6. Here, we have added the `onToggleCard` output of `FlashComponent`, which calls the `handleToggleCard` function in `AppComponent`, which we will define next, and passes `$event`, which is the value emitted to `onToggleCard` in `FlashComponent`:

```
@Component({
    ...
})
export class AppComponent {
    ...

    handleToggleCard(id: number) {
        const flash = this.flashs.find(flash => flash.id === id);
        flash.show = !flash.show;
    }
}
```

7. Now that we have our `show` property changing when the toggle icon is clicked, we will add the functionality of showing and hiding the card body and footer, using the `*ngIf` directive:

```
<div class="card">
    <header class="card-header" (click)="toggleCard()">
        <p class="card-header-title">{{flash.question}}</p>
        <a class="card-header-icon" href="javascript:void(0)" aria-
          label="more options">
            <span class="icon"><i class="fas fa-angle-down" aria-
              hidden="true"></i></span>
        </a>
    </header>
    <div *ngIf="flash.show">
        <div class="card-content">
            <div class="content">{{flash.answer}}</div>
        </div>
        <footer class="card-footer">
            <a class="card-footer-item" href="#"><i class="fas fa-
              check"></i></a>
            <a class="card-footer-item" href="#"><i class="fas fa-
              times"></i></a>
```

```
        <a class="card-footer-item" href="#"><i class="fas fa-
          edit"></i></a>
        <a class="card-footer-item" href="#"><i class="fas fa-
          trash"></i></a>
    </footer>
  </div>
</div>
```

8. Similarly, let's go ahead and add events to all the other buttons in the footer of the flashcard. Let's update the `flash.component.html` file:

```
<footer class="card-footer">
    <a href="#" class="card-footer-item" (click)="markCorrect()">
        <i class="fas fa-check"></i>
    </a>
    <a href="#" class="card-footer-item" (click)="markIncorrect()">
        <i class="fas fa-times"></i>
    </a>
    <a href="#" class="card-footer-item" (click)="editFlash()">
        <i class="fas fa-edit"></i>
    </a>
    <a href="#" class="card-footer-item" (click)="deleteFlash()">
        <i class="fas fa-trash"></i>
    </a>
</footer>
```

9. We also need to update the `FlashComponent` class and emit new `EventEmitter`:

```
export class FlashComponent {
    ...
    @Output() onDelete = new EventEmitter();
    @Output() onEdit = new EventEmitter();
    @Output() onRememberedChange = new EventEmitter();
    ...
    deleteFlash() {
        this.onDelete.emit(this.flash.id);
    }
    editFlash() {
        this.onEdit.emit(this.flash.id);
    }
    markCorrect() {
        this.onRememberedChange.emit({
            id: this.flash.id,
            flag: 'correct',
        });
    }
```

```
        markIncorrect() {
            this.onRememberedChange.emit({
                id: this.flash.id,
                flag: 'incorrect',
            });
        }
    }
```

10. Now, let's wire this up in `app.component.html`:

```
<app-flash
    *ngFor="let flash of flashs; trackBy trackByFlashId"
    [flash]="flash"
    (onToggleCard)="handleToggleCard($event)"
    (onDelete)="handleDelete($event)"
    (onEdit)="handleEdit($event)"
    (onRememberedChange)="handleRememberedChange($event)"
    ></app-flash>
```

11. Lastly, let's update `AppComponent`:

```
@Component({
    ...
})
export class AppComponent {
    ...
    editing = false;
    editingId: number;
    flash = { question: "", answer: "" };
    handleDelete(id: number) {            FindIndex
        const flashId = this.flashs.indexOf(flash => flash.id ===
        id);
        this.flashs.splice(flashId, 1)
    }
    handleEdit(id: number) {
        this.editing = true;
        this.editingId = id;
        // TODO: We will add editing logic after adding the form
    }

    handleRememeberedChange({id, flag}) {
        const flash = this.flashs.find(flash => flash.id === id);
        flash.remembered = flag;
    }
}
```

Now, if you click on the Delete icon, you will see that the flashcard is removed. Since we don't have a form, we will look into adding and editing functionality in the next section.

12. We will end this section by using the `remembered` flag in our `flash.component.html` file:

```
<header class="card-header" (click)="toggleCard()"
[ngClass]="flash.remembered">
    <p class="card-header-title">{{flash.question}}</p>
    <a class="card-header-icon" href="javascript:void(0)" aria-
    label="more options">
        <span class="icon"><i class="fas fa-angle-down" aria-
        hidden="true"></i></span>
    </a>
</header>
```

The value of `flash.remembered` can be either `correct` or `incorrect`, so our `card-header` can get either of those classes.

13. Let's add some style so that our users can differentiate between the two cards:

```
.card-header.correct {
    background: #51be51;
}

.card-header.incorrect {
    background: red;
}

.correct .card-header-title,
.incorrect .card-header-title {
    color: white;
}
```

Let's look at how our application works when we click on the various buttons. By default, all the flashcards are closed, and when you open them, if your guess was correct, you can click on the checkmark, and if it was wrong, then you can click on the cross mark. When you click on the checkmark, the flashcard's header turns green, and if you click on the cross, the flashcard's header turns red, as shown here:

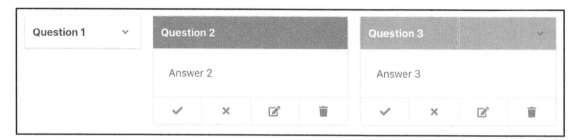

Now the only functionality left to implement is to create an editing form for completing our application, which we will cover in the next section, when we discuss template-driven forms.

Introducing template-driven forms

Angular provides you with two different ways to add forms to an application. A very easy way of creating forms is to use templates, which Angular calls template-driven forms. By using these templates, we can add some directives to form elements as well as functionality such as value accessing and validations. In this section, we will be creating one of these forms. Let's get started:

1. Let's add a simple HTML form so that we can add/edit the flashcards at the top of the `app.component.html` file:

```
<form>
    <h1 class="is-size-3">Add New Flash Card</h1>
    <div class="field">
        <label class="label" for="">Question</label>
        <div class="control">
            <input required class="input" type="text"
             name="question">
        </div>
    </div>
    <div class="field">
        <label for="" class="label">Answer</label>
        <div class="control">
            <input required class="input" type="text"
```

```
            name="answer">
        </div>
    </div>
    <button class="button is-primary" type="submit">Submit</button>
    <button class="button clear-btn">Clear</button>
</form>
```

2. Then, we will add some CSS in the `app.component.css` file:

```
form {
    margin: 10px;
    width: 300px;
}

.clear-btn {
    margin-left: 10px;
}
```

As you can see, we have added two fields: one for the question and another for the answer. We also have two buttons at the end of the form: one for submitting the form and one for clearing it.

3. Now, we need to be able to get the data that we enter in the form back to our component. Angular provides a directive called `ngModel` to get data into the input fields. Since Angular uses one-way data binding, in order to get data out of the input field when you update the value in the DOM, we need output such as `keyup` or `change`:

```
<input required class="input" type="text" name="question"
[ngModel]="flash.question" (keyup)="handleQuestionKeyup()">
```

4. Instead of adding both `input` and `output` for control, Angular provides a syntax called *Banana in a box*, which does both things at once:

```
<input required class="input" type="text" name="question"
[(ngModel)]="flash.question">
```

Now, whenever you change the value in the input field, the flash.question property is automatically updated. This syntax makes it look like Angular supports two-way data binding, like in Angular (the previous framework before Angular was created by the Angular team).

5. ngModel also provides additional functionality. It not only binds our controller properties to the fields but also stores the state of the input field. As you can see, our input field has a required attribute, which adds a validation rule that states that this field shouldn't be left empty. To get information regarding whether the input field is valid or not, we can use access input using a local variable, which can be created by using #variable in the template itself, as follows:

```
<input required class="input" type="text" name="question"
[(ngModel)]="flash.question" #question="ngModel" [ngClass]="{'is-
danger': quesiton.invalid && !question.pristine}">
```

In the preceding code, we added a local variable called question by using # and assigning the value to ngModel. Now, the question variable has the state of the input field.

We also added a directive called ngClass, which is used to dynamically add classes to our elements. In this example, we have passed an object with one property; that is, is-danger. Here, the is-danger class will be added if the value of question.invalid && !question.pristine is true; that is, if the question field is invalid and if it's not pristine (that is, the user hasn't changed the value since it was displayed in this form).

6. Let's wire this thing up in our form:

```
<form #flashForm="ngForm">
    <h1 class="is-size-3">Add New Flash Card</h1>
    <div class="field">
        <label class="label" for="">Question</label>
        <div class="control">
            <input required class="input" type="text"
            name="question" #question [(ngModel)]="flash.question"
            [ngClass]="{'is-danger': question.invalid &&
            !question.pristine}">
        </div>
    </div>
    <div class="field">
        <label for="" class="label">Answer</label>
        <div class="control">
            <input required class="input" type="text" name="answer"
            #answer [(ngModel)]="flash.answer" [ngClass]="{'is-
            danger': answer.invalid && !answer.pristine}">
```

```
        </div>
      </div>
      <button class="button is-primary" type="submit"
        (click)="handleSubmit()">Submit</button>
      <button class="button clear-btn"
        (click)="handleClear()">Clear</button>
    </form>
```

Along with adding `ngModel` and `ngClass`, we have added click events to our `Submit` and `Clear` buttons. We have added a local variable on the form element called `flashForm` and assigned it as `ngForm`. This means that the `flashForm` variable has the status of the whole form.

While developing, whenever you want to check a value quickly, we can use `<pre>{{ flashForm.value | json }} </pre>`. The `json` pipe is used to display objects in the UI, and the `pre` tag shows it in a nice format in the browser.

The form will look as follows in the browser:

7. Now, let's wire up the logic of the `submit` buttons in `AppComponent`:

```
import { Component, ViewChild } from '@angular/core';
import { NgForm } from '@angular/forms';

@Component({
  ...
})
export class AppComponent {
  @ViewChild('flashForm', {static:true}) flashForm: NgForm;
  ...
  handleSubmit(): void {
    this.flashs.push({
      id: generateId(),
```

handleSubmit(): void {
  this.flashs = [
    ...this.flashs, {
    ...this.flash,
  show: false,
  id: getRandomNumber(),
}]
}

```
            ...this.flash,
      })
      this.handleClear();
}
```
(handwritten margin note: this. handle Clear ();)

```
    handleClear() {
        this.flash = {
            question: '',
            answer: '',
        };
        this.flashForm.reset();
    }
}
```

We have used `ViewChild` to query and to get access to the local variable `flashForm`, that we created in the template.

8. Let's wrap up this section by adding the edit functionality, which we always want to add once we have the form in place. Our `handleEdit` method is changing the `editing` property's value to `true`. We will use that in our HTML file to update the form title from `Add New Flash Card` to `Update Flash Card`, and we'll use the `Update` and `Cancel` buttons instead of the `Submit` and `Clear` buttons so that we can update the flash and cancel the update:

```
<form #flashForm="ngForm">
    <h1 class="is-size-3">{{editing ? 'Update' : 'Add New'}}
    Flash Card</h1>
    <div class="field">
        <label class="label" for="">Question</label>
        <div class="control">
            <input required class="input" type="text"
            name="question" #question[(ngModel)]="flash.question"
            [ngClass]="{'is-danger': question.invalid &&
            !question.pristine}">
        </div>
    </div>
    <div class="field">
        <label for="" class="label">Answer</label>
        <div class="control">
            <input required class="input" type="text" name="answer"
            #answer [(ngModel)]="flash.answer" [ngClass]="{'is-
            danger': answer.invalid && !answer.pristine}">
        </div>
    </div>
    <button *ngIf="editing; else submitBtn" class="button is-
     primary" type="submit"
```

```
        (click)="handleUpdate()">Update</button>
        <ng-template #submitBtn>
            <button class="button is-primary" type="submit"
            (click)="handleSubmit()">Submit</button>
        </ng-template>
        <button *ngIf="editing; else clearBtn" class="button clear-btn
         (click)="handleCancel()">Cancel</button>
        <ng-template #clearBtn>
            <button class="button clear-btn"
            (click)="handleClear()">Clear</button>
        </ng-template>
    </form>
```

Now, let's click on Edit on one of the existing flashcard. You should see that the form is updated, as shown:

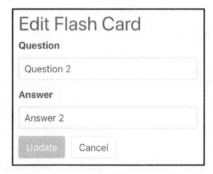

9. Now, let's add the definitions for the `handleEdit`, `handleUpdate`, and `handleCancel` methods that we are using in the template:

```
@Component({
    ...
})
export class AppComponent {

    handleEdit(id: number): void {
        this.editing = true;
        this.editingId = id;
        const flash = this.flashs.find(flash => flash.id === id);
        this.flash.question = flash.question;
        this.flash.answer = flash.answer;
    }

    handleUpdate() {
        const flash = this.flashs.find(flash => flash.id ===
        this.editingId);
```

```
            flash.question = this.flash.question;
            flash.answer = this.flash.answer;
            this.handleCancel();
        }

        handleCancel() {
            this.editing = false;
            this.editingId = undefined;
            this.handleClear();
        }
    }
```

10. Let's now disable the **Submit** button and the **Update** button if the form is invalid, using the `disabled` attribute as follows:

```
<button *ngIf="editing; else submitBtn" class="button is-primary"
type="submit" (click)="handleUpdate()"
[disabled]="flashForm.invalid">Update</button>
<ng-template #submitBtn>
    <button class="button is-primary" type="submit"
(click)="handleSubmit()"
[disabled]="flashForm.invalid">Submit</button>
</ng-template>
```

Now when the form is invalid, you should see that the **Submit** or the **Update** button will be disabled, as shown:

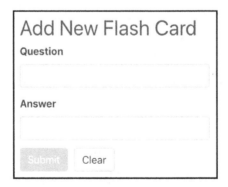

Now the user will be able to add a new flashcard and edit the existing flashcard.

This should complete our simple application. In the next two sections, we will try to improve our application by removing all the logic from `AppComponent` and adding the login to service in the next section.

Introducing services

Angular allows you to create services, which are classes that are created for a single purpose. In our project, we have added all of our logic for `flash` in AppComponent. Suppose we wanted the flash data deep down in the component tree—we would have to pass it down from one component to another. Services make communication between multiple components easier and reduce the logic inside them.

Let's use the Angular Console to generate a `service` by going to the **Generate** tab in the side menu, and select **Service**, and name it as `flash` and click **Generate**.

This should create two files: `flash.service.ts` and `flash.service.spec.ts`, respectively.

Let's transfer all the logic for `flash` in the service:

```
import { Injectable } from '@angular/core';
import { IFlash } from './flash.model';

function getRandomNumber() {
    return Math.floor(Math.random() * 10000)
}

@Injectable({
    providedIn: 'root'
})
export class FlashService {
    flashs: IFlash[] = [{
 question: 'Question 1',
 answer: 'Answer 1',
 show: false,
 id: getRandomNumber(),
 }, {
 question: 'Question 2',
 answer: 'Answer 2',
 show: false,
 id: getRandomNumber(),
 }, {
 question: 'Question 3',
 answer: 'Answer 3',
 show: false,
 id: getRandomNumber(),
 }];

addFlash(flash: IFlash) {
```

flash: {question: string, answer: string} (handwritten annotation; `IFlash` crossed out)

```
this.flashs.push({
...flash,
show: false,
id: getRandomNumber(),
});
}

toggleFlash(id: number) {
const flash = this.flashs.find(flash => flash.id === id);
this.flash.show = !this.flash.show;
}

deleteFlash(id: number) {
const index = this.flashs.findIndex(flash => flash.id === id);
this.flashs.splice(index, 1);
}

rememberedChange(id: number, flag: string) {
const flash = this.flashs.find(flash => flash.id === id);
flash.remembered = flag;
}

updateFlash(id, updatedFlash: IFlash) {
const flash = this.flashs.find(flash => flash.id === id);
flash.question = updatedFlash.question;
flash.answer = updatedFlash.answer;
}

getFlash(id: number) {
const flash = this.flashs.find(flash => flash.id === id);
return flash;
}
}
```

Handwritten annotations: "'correct' | 'incorrect'" above flag: string; "{question: string, answer: string}" above IFlash

We will update `AppComponent` so that it uses the service accordingly:

```
import { FlashService } from './flash.service';

export class AppComponent {
    flashs;

    constructor(private flashService: FlashService) {
        this.flashs = this.flashService.flashs;
    }

    handleSubmit(): void {
        this.flashService.addFlash(this.flash);
        this.handleClear();
```

```
    }

    handleClear() {
        this.flash = {
            question: '',
            answer: '',
        };
        this.flashForm.reset()
    }

    handleToggleCard(id) {
        this.flashService.toggleFlash(id);
    }

    handleDelete(id) {
        this.flashService.deleteFlash(id);
    }

    handleEdit(id) {
        this.flash = this.flashService.getFlash(id);
        this.editing = true;
        this.editingId = id;
    }

    handleUpdate() {
        this.flashService.updateFlash(this.editingId, this.flash);
        this.handleCancel();
    }

    handleCancel() {
        this.editing = false;
        this.editingId = undefined;
        this.handleClear();
    }

    handleRememberedChange({ id, flag }) {
        this.flashService.rememberedChange(id, flag);
    }
}
```

We have injected the `FlashService` by specifying a constructor `flashService` variable with the dependency type.

Now that we have all the logic transferred from a component to a service, let's look at observables in the next section, and see how they can be used in our application to optimize our components.

Introducing observables

Observables are a proposed feature for ES7 and are used for creating a continuous communication channel for various kinds of events. They add that communication channel by passing messages between publishers and subscribers. The unique thing about observables is that they are declarative—that is, once they are defined, they do not emit values unless they are subscribed to. One way of creating observables is by using `subject`. Let's see how it works by creating a new `Subject`:

```
const subject = new Subject();

// emitting two values before subscribing
subject.next(1);

// subscribing
subject.subscribe(value => console.log(value));

// emitting value after subscribing
subject.next(2)
```

In the preceding example, we have created a new instance of `subject` and then emitted a value using the `next` method. Then, we subscribed `subject` to listen for new values and then emit a value after doing so. Since we emitted 1 before subscribing, we won't see 1 in the console; we will see 2 because it was emitted after it was subscribed.

Another feature of observables is that there are more than 100 different operators available that we can pipe our observables to. The values that are passed to `subscribe` are passed through all the pipes first before they end up in `subscribe`. Here's an example:

```
import { Subject } from 'rxjs';
import { filter, tap } from 'rxjs/operators';

let numbers = [];
const subject = new Subject();

// subscribing
subject
    .pipe(
        filter(value => value !== 1),
        tap(value => console.log(value)),
    )
    .subscribe(value => numbers.push(value));

// emitting values 1, 2, 3
subject.next(1);
```

```
subject.next(2);
subject.next(3);

console.log(numbers); // [2, 3]
```

Here, we have used a couple of pipes that are provided by rxjs in the rxjs/operators package. We used a pipe called filter so that subscribe shouldn't get a value of 1. Then, we used the tap operator, which is really helpful for debugging or performing operations before a subscription runs. These are just two of the operators that are available. For more information on all the available operators, please visit https://rxjs.dev/.

We will be using BehaviorSubject in our service. BehaviorSubject is a subject that has had an initial value passed as a parameter to it.

Additionally, we will update all our methods so that they don't mutate the flash array. Before we speak about why we should not mutate objects/arrays in JavaScript, let's try and understand what immutability is, and why is it important. To answer this question, let's first look at the following block of code:

```
function newPersonWithSameAge(p, name) {
    p.name = name;
    return p;
}

const person = {
    name: 'Micheal Smith',
    age: 21,
}

const newPerson = newPersonWithSameAge(person, 'John Doe');

console.log(newPerson.name); // 'John Doe'
console.log(person.name); // 'John Doe'
```

Here, we have the newPersonWithSameAge function, which is supposed to return a new person with the same age, but with a new name. However, when we check the name value of person and newPerson, we can see that they are both the same. In JavaScript, both objects and arrays are mutable, which can add bugs to our code if not properly used. To avoid this problem, we always return a new object and a new array and never mutate. This means that we need to use concat() over push(), map() and reduce() over for loops, spread over Object.assign, and so on.

Let's go ahead and use BehaviorSubject in our service for our flash, and also update the methods so that we don't mutate our flash array:

```
import { Injectable } from '@angular/core';
import { IFlash } from './flash.model';
import { BehaviorSubject } from 'rxjs';

function getRandomNumber() {
    return Math.floor(Math.random() * 10000)
}

@Injectable({
    providedIn: 'root'
})

export class FlashService {
    flashs: IFlash[] = [{
        question: 'Question 1',
        answer: 'Answer 1',
        show: false,
        id: getRandomNumber(),
    }, {
        question: 'Question 2',
        answer: 'Answer 2',
        show: false,
        id: getRandomNumber(),
    }, {
        question: 'Question 3',
        answer: 'Answer 3',
        show: false,
        id: getRandomNumber(),
    }];
    flashs$ = new BehaviorSubject<IFlash[]>(this.flashs);
    addFlash(flash: IFlash) {
        this.flashs = [
            ...this.flashs, {
                ...flash,
                show: false,
                id: getRandomNumber(),
            }
        ];

        this.flashs$.next(this.flashs);
    }
    toggleFlash(id: number) {
        const index = this.flashs.findIndex(flash => flash.id === id);
        this.flashs = [
            ...this.flashs.slice(0, index),
```

```
                    {
                        ...this.flashs[index],
                        show: !this.flashs[index].show
                    },
                    ...this.flashs.slice(index + 1),
                ];
                this.flashs$.next(this.flashs);
            }
    deleteFlash(id: number) {
        const index = this.flashs.findIndex(flash => flash.id === id);
        this.flashs = [
            ...this.flashs.slice(0, index),
            ...this.flashs.slice(index + 1),
        ];
        this.flashs$.next(this.flashs);
    }

    rememberedChange(id: number, flag: string) {
        const index = this.flashs.findIndex(flash => flash.id === id);
        this.flashs = [
            ...this.flashs.slice(0, index),
            {
                ...this.flashs[index],
                remembered: flag
            },
            ...this.flashs.slice(index + 1),
        ];
        this.flashs$.next(this.flashs);
    }

    updateFlash(id, flash: IFlash) {
        const index = this.flashs.findIndex(flash => flash.id === id);
        this.flashs = [
            ...this.flashs.slice(0, index),
            {
                ...this.flashs[index],
                ...flash,
            },
            ...this.flashs.slice(index + 1),
        ];
        this.flashs$.next(this.flashs);
    }

    getFlash(id: number) {
        const index = this.flashs.findIndex(flash => flash.id === id);
        return this.flashs[index];
    }
}
```

Here, we have created an observable called `flash$`, which we can subscribe to in our component in order to get data from the service:

```
import { Component, ViewChild, OnInit, OnDestroy } from '@angular/core';

...

export class AppComponent implements OnInit, OnDestroy {
    ...
    constructor(private flashService: FlashService) { }

    ngOnInit() {
        this.subscription = this.flashService.flashs$.subscribe(flashs => {
            this.flashs = flashs;
        });
    }

    ngOnDestroy() {
        if (this.subscription) {
            this.subscription.unsubscribe();
        }
    }
    ...
}
```

Whenever we subscribe to an observable, we have to make sure that we clean it up when it's not required. In our case, we know that once `AppComponent` is destroyed, we should clean it up.

Angular provides multiple life cycle hooks for us so that we know what phase our component life cycle is in. The `OnInit` life cycle hook is called once the view is mounted, and upon the component's destruction, the `OnDestroy` life cycle hook is called. That's why we subscribed to our observable in the `OnInit` life cycle and unsubscribed to the observable in our `OnDestroy` life cycle.

Angular provides a pipe called `async`, which is a better way to subscribe and unsubscribe to observables, without the need for a template.

The preceding component code changes to this after using observables:

```
import { Component, ViewChild, OnInit, OnDestroy } from '@angular/core';
import { Observable } from 'rxjs';

...

export class AppComponent implements OnInit {
    ...
    flash$: Observable<IFlash[]>
```

```
    ...
    constructor(private flashService: FlashService) { }

    ngOnInit() {
        this.flash$ = this.flashService.flashs$
    }
    ...
}
```

Now, we will use the `async` pipe in our template, as follows:

```
<app-flash
    *ngFor="let flash of flashs$ | async; trackBy id"
    [flash]="flash"
    (onToggleCard)="handleToggleCard($event)"
    (onDelete)="handleDelete($event)"
    (onEdit)="handleEdit($event)"
    (onRememberedChange)="handleRememberedChange($event)"
></app-flash>
```

The `async` pipe takes care of subscribing and unsubscribing to the observable. Now that we are using immutability, and not mutating our array and objects, we can use the `OnPush` change detection strategy to improve the performance of our application where we feel that it's laggy.

We only have one component in this application. We won't be able to see any performance issues right now, but if we did observe some lag, then we can try to add a change detection strategy to `FlashComponent`, like so:

```
import { Component, Input, Output, ChangeDetectionStrategy } from
'@angular/core';
@Component({
    ...,
    changeDetection: ChangeDetectionStrategy.OnPush,
})
export class FlashComponent {
    ...
}
```

The `OnPush` change detection strategy will make your components much faster as it will only run change detection on components if the inputs to the components are updated or changed.

Summary

In this chapter, we have successfully created a flashcard app where you can add/edit/delete flashcards and also create a service to manage the business logic related to flashcards. In the end, we used observables in our services, which makes it easier to manage the state of an application. We also used immutability to improve performance by using the `OnPush` change detection strategy.

In the next chapter, we will create a **single-page application** (**SPA**) personal blog using the WordPress API and make some performance improvements to the application.

Questions

- What are the different ways of adding external stylesheets/scripts to our project?
- What are inputs and outputs in a component?
- What is the *Banana in a box* syntax?
- How can we display array/map/set data in our Angular templates?
- How do you use `*ngIf else` in Angular templates?
- What are observables?
- What is the difference between `Subject` and `BehaviorSubject`?
- Where do you unsubscribe observables in Angular components?
- What is the importance of the `async` pipe?

Further reading

The following reading material will provide with you more information about Angular basics, template-driven forms, and observables:

- Attribute directives: `https://angular.io/guide/attribute-directives`.
- Structured directives: `https://angular.io/guide/structural-directives`.
- Architecture devices: `https://angular.io/guide/architecture-services`.
- Template-driven forms in Angular: `https://angular.io/guide/forms`.
- Observables: `https://angular.io/guide/observables`.

3

Building a Personal Blog Using Angular Router and WordPress

In this chapter, we will create a personal blog using Angular. We will create it as a **single-page application (SPA)** using Angular Router. SPAs have the benefit of loading most of an application on their initial load, which is crucial when you are browsing a website. When going from one page to another, an SPA doesn't have to download the whole page; instead, it requests the required API for the page, which is way faster. You will also learn how to configure multiple environments for the project, optimize the SPA using lazy loading routes, and animate routes and elements in Angular applications.

The following topics will be covered in this chapter:

- Setting up a WordPress server
- Setting up an Angular project with the Angular CLI
- Adding multiple routes to our application
- Calling the WordPress API
- Implementing the lazy loading route
- Introducing pre-loading strategy
- Adding animations

Technical requirements

This chapter's code can be found in this book's GitHub repository at `https://github.com/PacktPublishing/Angular-Projects`, under the `Chapter03` folder. This code has been provided so that whenever you are stuck, you can verify whether you've done something differently and play around with it.

Understanding SPAs

In this section, we will learn about SPAs and why have they become de facto in the creation of applications using client-side libraries. An SPA is an app that's built on one page. For example, you will have one `index.html` file in the application, but this app will still have different routes/links to different pages. Let's understand how this works.

In your `index.html` file, you will create one HTML empty element, for example:

```
<div id="root"></div>
```

Then, you will load the whole application using JavaScript. All the HTML that gets rendered in that element will be rendered using JavaScript. We will also be changing the routes, but it will just be this HTML file that's going to be used. Suppose you have a home page (`www.example.com`) and an about page (`www.example.com/about`). When you land on any of these pages, you will load the same `index.html` file, and then the JavaScript will render the respective content based on the URL. The benefit that we get here is that we don't have to download any extra HTML, CSS, or JavaScript files when going to other pages after the initial page load. The only thing that might be required is to load the dynamic JSON data onto the other page if any dynamic data has to be displayed.

However, while SPAs provide you with faster page transfers, it means that the initial load will load every page of the application, which could slow down the application considerably. Later in this chapter, we will lazy load some of the JavaScript when going to other pages so that we don't load all the JavaScript for all the pages at once.

Now that we understand what SPAs are compared to traditional websites, let's quickly look at an overview of the project we will be building in this chapter.

Project overview

WordPress is one of the best frameworks for building blogs, but since it's built using PHP and not JavaScript, it would be challenging to convert blogs into an SPA. WordPress has a great REST API that can be used in our Angular application to show blog posts.

In this chapter, we will be creating a personal blog using the WordPress REST API and using Angular Router to create and link to multiple pages. Initially, we will bundle the whole application in one JavaScript file and then move to lazy loading the JavaScript when required. We will use a pre-loading strategy for this, which will make our application faster on its initial load.

The following screenshot shows our **Home** page for the blog:

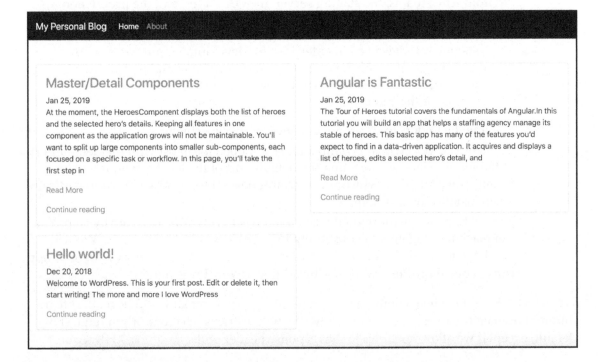

Now that we have had an overview of the project, let's get started with it.

Setting up a WordPress server

To get a WordPress website to run on our local machine, first, we need to install a PHP server on our local machine:

1. If you are using macOS/Linux, install MAMP (`https://www.mamp.info`). If you are using Windows, install WampServer (`http://www.wampserver.com`).

2. Download WordPress files from their website: `https://wordpress.org/download/`.

3. Unzip the folder and put the files from it in the `applications/mamp/htdocs` folder for the MAMP server and the `wamp/www` folder for the WampServer. For more details, follow the respective documentation: `https://documentation.mamp.info/en/MAMP-Mac/` and `http://www.wampserver.com/en/..`

4. Duplicate this folder three times so that we can simulate three different environments; that is, the staging server, the QA server, and the production server.

 A staging server is used in enterprise for development purposes, a QA server is used after the development of a feature is completed and we want the quality assurance team to test the changes, and the production server is for the end users.

5. Rename the folders to `staging`, `qa`, and `prod`, respectively.

6. Start your server (MAMP/WampServer) and open localhost with the default port of the server. Since we are using the default port of the local server, it will be running on port `8080`, which is the default port set for local servers automatically when installed on a system.

7. Now, let's go to the individual websites and set up WordPress, step by step. You can reach the staging server by going to `localhost:8080/staging`. We will also have to enable CORS for `localhost:4200`, which is where our Angular app runs to our WordPress websites, by adding a WordPress plugin.

We get a CORS issue when a domain (`example abc.com`), is making a XHR request to a different domain (`example xyz.com`). Browsers will restrict such cross-origin request by default, except if we allow `abc.com` in the response header of the `xyz.com` XHR request.

For this book, we don't need to know how to add/configure WordPress plugins, and so we can bypass CORS by using the browser's extensions. One such extension is called *Allow-Control-Allow-Origin: **, which can be installed from `https://chrome.google.com/webstore/detail/allow-control-allow-origi/nlfbmbojpeacfghkpbjhddihlkkiljbi`.

If you want to skip the installation of WordPress altogether, then I have created mock responses of the WordPress APIs that we require in this chapter. For the dev environment, QA and prod let us use the following hosts where the mocked responses will be available on `/posts` and `/post/{id}`:

- Development: `http://demo5683935.mockable.io/`.
- Prod: `http://demo8034777.mockable.io/`.
- QA: `http://demo7831153.mockable.io/`.

Now that we have the APIs ready, let's get started with our Angular app.

Setting up an Angular project with the Angular CLI

In this section, we will start with scaffolding a simple Angular application with routing enabled using the Angular CLI and use some Angular generation schematics to create modules and components.

Let's get started and build a simple Angular application with routing and SCSS by using the Angular CLI. Here, we will use the prefix of pb so that our component tags are pb-root, pb-post, and so on:

```
> ng new personal-blog --routing --style scss --prefix pb
```

The ng new command is used for creating a new Angular app:

- personal-blog is the name of the project, and so we will create a folder called personal-blog and include all the application files in it.
- *manual(* The routing flag is used to create an application with routing capability enabled. The routing flag creates an extra module called AppRoutingModule, which can be found in app-routing.module.ts.
- The style flag can be used to select what you want to select for application styles. In the preceding command, we have selected SCSS for styles.
- *manual(* prefix is used for the selectors within the project. In the preceding command, we have used pb as the prefix, so the selector for our AppComponent will be pb-root instead of the default app-root.

If you want to save the application in a different folder, you can use the directory flag. You can check out the other options that the Angular CLI provides for the ng new command by going to https://angular.io/cli/new.

Let's use Bootstrap CSS to style our application. Since we are using SCSS for this application, we will install the bootstrap-scss package:

```
> yarn add bootstrap-scss
```

Here, I have used yarn to install bootstrap-scss. Yarn is a package manager for node packages similar to npm. It's faster than npm. You can install it by following the steps at https://yarnpkg.com/en/docs/install.

Let's include some of the styles from `bootstrap` in `styles.scss`:

```scss
@import "~bootstrap-scss/bootstrap"
```

This includes the whole Bootstrap CSS file, which has a lot of different components. If you just want to include the components that you are including in the project, then import the specific SCSS files:

```scss
// Base SCSS files
@import "~bootstrap-scss/functions";
@import "~bootstrap-scss/variables";
@import "~bootstrap-scss/mixins";
@import "~bootstrap-scss/root";
@import "~bootstrap-scss/reboot";
@import "~bootstrap-scss/type";

// Include specific SCSS components that is used in our application
@import "~bootstrap-scss/nav";
@import "~bootstrap-scss/navbar";
@import "~bootstrap-scss/card";
```

Now, let's structure our application so that it uses a couple of *shared* modules and a *core* module. Angular provides modules that can hold a set of Angular modules, components, services, pipes, and so on. In our application, a shared application would hold all the reusable components of the application, whereas the core module's purpose would be to hold all the singleton services and modules. To generate these modules, let's use the `generate` command that's provided by the Angular CLI:

```
> ng generate module shared --module app
> ng g m core -m app
```

Both of the preceding commands are identical, and so both of them create a module. The only difference between them is that the second command uses shorthand syntax that's provided by the Angular CLI. Shorthand commands are really easy to remember and also make it easier to generate code.

Here, we will be calling the WordPress REST API, and hence we will need to use an HTTP call (AJAX calls). To make HTTP calls, Angular provides us with a module called `HttpClientModule`. Since it will be used throughout the application and we only need one instance of the `HttpClient` service, we will include this module in our `CoreModule`, which we just generated:

```typescript
import { NgModule } from '@angular/core';
import { CommonModule } from '@angular/common';
import { HttpClientModule } from '@angular/common/http';
```

```
@NgModule({
    imports: [
        CommonModule,
        HttpClientModule,
    ],
    declarations: [],
    providers: []
})
export class CoreModule { }
```

We will be using `HttpClient` later in our WordPress service.

Let's also add `RouterModule` to our `SharedModule` so that we can use routing directives in our shared components:

```
import { NgModule } from '@angular/core';
import { CommonModule } from '@angular/common';
import { RouterModule } from '@angular/router';

@NgModule({
    declarations: [],
    imports: [
        CommonModule,
        RouterModule,
    ]
})
export class SharedModule { }
```

Now, let's add our home and about components for our home page and about page, respectively:

```
> ng g c home -m app
> ng g c about -m app
```

The preceding two commands are shorthand commands, where g stands for generate and c stands for component. This creates two folders, home and about, with four files each (an HTML file used for components templates, an SCSS file used for component styles, a TS file used for component logic, and a spec file used for the testing component).

Now that we have our components, let's use them to configure multiple routes in the next section.

Adding multiple routes to our application

Now, let's use `HomeComponent` and `AboutComponent` and use them in configuring the routes to these pages in `AppRoutingModule`:

```
import { NgModule } from '@angular/core';
import { Routes, RouterModule } from '@angular/router';
import { HomeComponent } from './home/home.component.ts';
import { AboutComponent } from './about/about.component.ts';

const routes: Routes = [
    { path: '', pathMatch: 'full', redirectTo: 'home' },
    { path: 'home', component: HomeComponent },
    { path: 'about', component: AboutComponent },
    { path: '**', component: HomeComponent },
];

@NgModule({
    imports: [RouterModule.forRoot(routes)],
    exports: [RouterModule]
})
export class AppRoutingModule { }
```

Here, we added four different routes:

- The first path is an empty string, which will redirect to the `'home'` route. So, if someone lands on `https://example.com`, we would redirect them to `https://example.com/home`.
- The second route is the `home` route, which will load `HomeComponent`.
- The third will load `AboutComponent` if you go to the `https://example.com/about` page.
- The last one is a wildcard route, which has a path of `**`, which means that if anyone puts a random URL in the browser, such as `https://example.com/random-path`, then it will load that component. We have assigned `HomeComponent` here, so it should load up `HomeComponent`.

If you check your `app.component.html` file, you will find the following:

```
<router-outlet></router-outlet>
```

Use the snippets that we installed in Chapter 1, *Setting Up the Development Environment*; that is, **Angular Snippets** by John Papa. It provide a lot of helpful snippets, like the one you can use to write the routes that we generated in the preceding code. When you start typing the name of a snippet like a-route-path-default, a-route-path-404, or a-route-path-eager, VS Code will allow you to select it and get the whole snippet.

Now, serve the application. We will get the following output:

Figure 1: Screenshot of the application

At the bottom of the screen, you can see **home works!**, which is the content of the home.component.html file. If you check the route of the browser, you will see http://localhost:4200/home, and if you manually change the URL to http://localhost:4200/about, you will see the **about works!** content.

Now, let's remove all the content of `app.component.html`, except for `router-outlet`, and add a `header` component:

```
> ng g c shared/header —m shared
```

The preceding command is used for creating a component in the `shared` folder, and we want it to be included in `SharedModule`. In addition to it being included in the imports of `SharedModule`, it would be better to also include some exports:

```
import { NgModule } from '@angular/core';
import { CommonModule } from '@angular/common';
import { RouterModule } from '@angular/router';
import { HeaderComponent } from './header/header.component';

@NgModule({
    declarations: [HeaderComponent],
    imports: [
        CommonModule,
        RouterModule,
    ],
    exports: [HeaderComponent]
})
export class SharedModule { }
```

Let's edit the `header.component.html` file so that it includes the Bootstrap navigation:

```
<nav class="navbar navbar-expand-lg navbar-dark bg-dark">
    <a class="navbar-brand" href="#">My Personal Blog</a>
    <button class="navbar-toggler" type="button" data-toggle="collapse"
     data-target="#navbarSupportedContent" aria-
     controls="navbarSupportedContent" aria-expanded="false" aria-
     label="Toggle navigation">
        <span class="navbar-toggler-icon"></span>
    </button>
    <div class="collapse navbar-collapse" id="navbarSupportedContent">
        <ul class="navbar-nav mr-auto">
            <li class="nav-item active">
                <a class="nav-link" href="#">Home</a>
            </li>
            <li class="nav-item"><a class="nav-link" href="#">About</a>
            </li>
        </ul>
    </div>
</nav>
```

Let's add some styling to our `header.component.scss` file:

```scss
.bg-dark {
    background: #000;
}
```

Let's add the `header` component to our `app.component.html` file:

```html
<pb-header></pb-header>
<div class="route-container">
    <router-outlet></router-outlet>
</div>
```

We also need to add some CSS to `app.component.scss`:

```scss
.route-container {
    margin: 16px;
    margin-top: 50px;
}
```

Now, let's link all the links in our navigation; currently, it's using the `href` attribute. When using Angular Router, instead of using `href`, we use a directive called `routerLink`.

Let's update the code with it:

```html
<nav class="navbar navbar-expand-lg navbar-dark bg-dark">
    <a class="navbar-brand" [routerLink]="['home']">My Personal Blog</a>
    <button class="navbar-toggler" type="button" data-toggle="collapse"
     data-target="#navbarSupportedContent" aria-
     controls="navbarSupportedContent" aria-expanded="false" aria-
     label="Toggle navigation">
        <span class="navbar-toggler-icon"></span>
    </button>
    <div class="collapse navbar-collapse" id="navbarSupportedContent">
        <ul class="navbar-nav mr-auto">
            <li class="nav-item" routerLinkActive="active">
                <a class="nav-link" [routerLink]="['home']">Home</a>
            </li>
            <li class="nav-item" routerLinkActive="active"><a class="nav-
             link" [routerLink]="['about']">About</a></li>
        </ul>
    </div>
</nav>
```

Now, you will be able to go to different pages using the respective links. As you can see, we have also added `routerLinkActive`, which is a directive provided by Angular Router, to add class dynamically to an element. This only happens if the router link on that element or the child element inside that element has `routerLink` currently active. So, if you are on the home page, you will see that the `home` link will have an `active` class, and if you are on the about page, you will see that the `about` link has an `active` class.

Now that we have our basic application structure ready, let's start by creating services that will call the WordPress API, and also configure multiple environments, so that each environment uses its own WordPress API.

Calling the WordPress API

As we mentioned earlier, in the *WordPress setup* section, we have two different WordPress sites: one for staging and one for production. We need Angular to use a staging WordPress site while developing an Angular application and use a production WordPress site while building the application for production.

For this, we will utilize the environment files that Angular provides. By default, Angular provides two environment files: `environment.ts` and `environment.prod.ts`. The `environment.ts` file is imported into the application and used, and then when you build for production, Angular replaces the `environment.ts` file with `environment.prod.ts`. This makes it easier for us to support multiple environments.

Let's edit our `environment.ts` and `environment.prod.ts` files:

```
export const environment = {
    production: false,
    WORDPRESS_REST_URL: 'http://demo5683935.mockable.io/'
};
```

Now, we will add our prod WordPress URL to the `environment.prod.ts` file:

```
export const environment = {
    production: true,
    WORDPRESS_REST_URL: 'http://demo8034777.mockable.io/'
};
```

By default, Angular provides configuration for dev and prod, but we can also configure additional environments using `angular.json`. In `angular.json`, let's add additional configuration for qa, as follows:

```
    ...

    "configurations": {
        ...
        "qa": {
            "fileReplacements": [
                {
                    "replace": "src/environments/environment.ts",
                    "with": "src/environments/environment.qa.ts"
                }
            ],
            "optimization": true,
            "outputHashing": "all",
            "sourceMap": false,
            "extractCss": true,
            "namedChunks": false,
            "aot": true,
            "extractLicenses": true,
            "vendorChunk": false,
            "buildOptimizer": true
        }
    }

    ...
```

Here, we have added configuration that's similar to the production configuration, except that we have updated our file replacement for a new file called `environment.qa.ts`.

Now, let's create a `environment.qa.ts` file in the `environments` folder; that is, `http://demo7831153.mockable.io/`:

```
export const environment = {
    production: false,
    WORDPRESS_REST_URL: 'http://demo7831153.mockable.io/'
};
```

To serve the application with the qa configuration, run the following command:

```
> ng serve --configuration=qa
```

The `--configuration=qa` flag is used to `serve` or `build` the application using the qa configuration.

Create `post.model.ts` based on the response we get from the server in the `src/app` folder:

```
export interface IPost {
    id: number;
    title: {
        rendered: string;
    };
    content: {
        rendered: string;
    };
    excerpt: {
        rendered: string;
    };
    date: Date;
    slug: string;
}
```

Next, let's use this environment configuration in a service that we'll be calling in the WordPress API. Let's call it `WordpressService`:

```
> ng g s core/wordpress
```

This will create `WordpressService` in the `core` folder. Let's update the service with the following code:

```
import { Injectable } from '@angular/core';
import { HttpClient } from '@angular/common/http';
import { of, Subject, Observable } from 'rxjs';
import { tap } from 'rxjs/operators';
import { environment } from '../../environments/environment';
import { IPost } from './../post.model';
const POSTS_URL = 'posts';

@Injectable({
 providedIn: 'root'
})
export class WordpressService {
    posts: IPost[];
    post$:Subject<IPost> = new Subject();

    constructor(private http: HttpClient) { }

    getPosts(): Observable<IPost[]> {
        if (this.posts) {
            return of(this.posts);
        }
        return
```

```
    this.http.get<IPost[]>(`${environment.WORDPRESS_REST_URL}${POSTS_URL}`).pip
e(tap((posts) => this.posts = posts)
        );
    }

    getPost(id: number) {
        if (this.posts) {
            const post = this.posts.find(p => p.id === id);
            if (post) {
                this.post$.next(post);
            }
        }

    this.http.get<IPost>(`${environment.WORDPRESS_REST_URL}${POSTS_URL}/${id}`)
    .subscribe(post => this.post$.next(post));
    }
}
```

Here, we have created two functions, getPosts and getPost, and also added some local caching so that if you land on the posts page (we will have posts on the home page), we have some data from the posts to display that post. However, we will also be calling the API to get an API every time we go to an individual post in case we want to use some new data that we might get from that API. It will also make sure that when we reload the page and don't have data for cached posts, we just get it from the API.

Since the APIs are integrated, let's go ahead and display posts on the Home page. Let's update HomeComponent:

```
import { Component, OnInit } from '@angular/core';
import { WordpressService } from './../core/wordpress.service';

@Component({
    ...
})
export class HomeComponent implements OnInit {
    posts$ = this.wordpressService.getPosts();

    constructor(private wordpressService: WordpressService) { }
    ...
}
```

Here, we have injected the service into the constructor and assigned posts$ to the getPosts method of the service, which returns an observable. Now, let's use our posts$ observable to display the posts in our home.component.html file:

```
<div class="row">
```

```
<div class="col-md-6" *ngFor="let post of posts$ | async">
    <div class="card flex-md-row mb-4 shadow-sm h-md-250">
        <div class="card-body d-flex flex-column align-items-start">
            <h3 class="mb-0">
                <a class="text-dark"
                href="#">{{post.title.rendered}}</a>
            </h3>
            <div class="mb-1 text-muted">{{post.date | date}}</div>
            <p class="card-text mb-auto"
            [innerHTML]="post.excerpt.rendered"></p>
            <a>Continue reading</a>
        </div>
    </div>
</div>
</div>
```

Let's also add `margin-bottom` to our `card` class:

```
.card {
    margin-bottom: 20px;
}
```

Now, you can see the posts being displayed on the **Home** page, as follows:

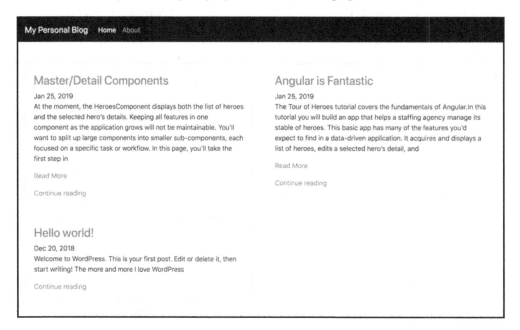

In this section, we have successfully configured multiple routes and displayed blog posts using the APIs. In the next section, we will look at how to create lazy loaded routes so that we do not add more JavaScript to our initial bundle.

Implementing lazy loading route

In this section, we will create another route to this application so that we can view an individual post. This time, however, we will make this route a lazy loaded route. To create a lazy loaded route, we need to add a new module, which is also called as **feature module**. Let's create a `post` module first by using the following command:

```
> ng g m post --routing
```

Now, we will create a component with the `routing` flag, which will also create a `routing` module for this component, and add it to the `post` module:

```
> ng g c post -m post
```

Now that `component` and `module` have been created, it's time to link the route to the post-module, and then post the `routing` module to the post component. A lazily loaded route is defined using `loadChildren`. Let's add the following code to the routes of `app-routing.module.ts`:

```
{
    path: 'post/:id/:slug',
    loadChildren: () => import('./post/post.module').then(m =>
    m.PostModule)
}
```

Instead of importing the component and defining it to the component in the route, we can just use a dynamic `import()` to import the module.

 Support for dynamic imports in `loadChildren` of the router definition was introduced in Angular v8. Before Angular v8, you needed to define a `./post/post.module#PostModule` string to lazy load modules.

The other thing that's new is the `path` string. The other two; that is, `home` and `about`, were straightforward. The `path` string has two parameters: `id` and `slug`. To go to a post page, `id` was enough, but we need `slug` (`slug` is a user-friendly name and the URL-friendly name of the post) in the URL for better **Search Engine Optimization (SEO)**. These parameters can be accessed in the component.

Now, we need to attach our `component` to `PostRoutingModule`. Let's import it and add the following code:

```
...
import { PostComponent } from './post.component';

const routes: Routes = [{
    path: '',
    component: PostComponent
}];

...
```

 Instead of creating a module with routing module, component in the module, and manually configuring the route, we can use a new flag `route` introduced in Angular CLI 8.3.0. So you can now run `ng g m post --route post/:id/:slug --module app`.

Now that our routes are linked, let's go ahead and add the links on our home page, where we display our posts, to go to the individual post page:

```
<div class="col-md-6" *ngFor="let post of posts$ | async">
  <div class="card flex-md-row mb-4 shadow-sm h-md-250">
    <div class="card-body d-flex flex-column align-items-start">
      <h3 class="mb-0">
        <a class="text-dark" [routerLink]="['/post', post.id,
         post.slug]">{{post.title.rendered}}</a>
      </h3>
      <div class="mb-1 text-muted">{{post.date | date}}</div>
      <p class="card-text mb-auto" [innerHTML]="post.excerpt.rendered"></p>
      <a [routerLink]="['/post', post.id, post.slug]">Continue reading</a>
    </div>
  </div>
</div>
```

As you can see, we are passing the `id` and `slug` parameters, along with `'/post'` route.

It's time for us to get `id` and show our individual posts:

```
import { Component, OnInit } from '@angular/core';
import { ActivatedRoute } from '@angular/router';
import { WordpressService } from './../core/wordpress.service';

@Component({
    selector: 'pb-post',
    templateUrl: './post.component.html',
    styleUrls: ['./post.component.css']
```

```
})
export class PostComponent implements OnInit {
    post;

    constructor(
        private route: ActivatedRoute,
        private wordpressService: WordpressService
    ) {
        this.wordpressService.post$.subscribe(data => {
            this.post = data;
        });
    }

    ngOnInit() {
        this.route.params.subscribe(params => {
            this.wordpressService.getPost(params.id);
        });
    }
}
```

Now, let's use the `async` pipe and display the post in `post.component.html`:

```html
<div *ngIf="post">
    <h3 class="mb-0">
        <a class="text-dark" href="#">{{post.title.rendered}}</a>
    </h3>
    <div class="mb-1 text-muted">{{post.date | date}}</div>
    <p class="card-text mb-auto" [innerHTML]="post.content.rendered"></p>
</div>
```

Now, when we click on the post's title on the **Home** page, you should see that it goes to the new page, individual post page `http://localhost:4200/post/1/hello-world`, as shown in the following screenshot:

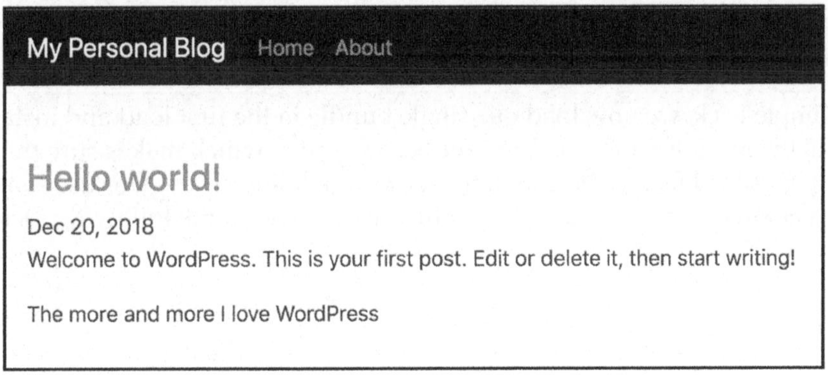

Now that we understand how to lazy load our routes, let's look at some pre-loading strategies that we can apply to our routing, to improve the overall performance of our application.

Introducing pre-loading strategy

Lazy loading will make our application faster and smaller on its initial load. However, we can optimize it even further so that we won't download a JavaScript file on page transition. You may be wondering how we will load that page without its JavaScript. To do that, we pre-load the JavaScript after the initial bundle of the landing page is downloaded, and after the page is rendered, download the JavaScript of other pages when the browser is idle.

In Angular Router, you can define your pre-loading strategy as follows:

```
import { RouterModule, Routes, PreloadAllModules } from '@angular/router';
...

@NgModule({
    imports: [
        CommonModule,
        RouterModule.forRoot(routes, {
            preloadingStrategy: PreloadAllModules,
        }),
    ],
    declarations: [],
    exports: [RouterModule],
})
export class RoutingModule { }
```

In the `forRoot` method of `RouterModule`, pass configurations as the second parameter, where you can set `preloadingStrategy`. Here, we have used one of the strategies that Angular Router provides, called `PreloadAllModules`, which will load all the modules after the page renders initially.

Using this simple trick, we now load our single bundle in the first load and instantly download all the modules after the browser becomes idle, which makes sure that subsequent pages load faster. We can define our pre-loading strategy or use some third party strategies such as `ngx-quicklink`, which we'll cover in the following section.

Adding ngx-quicklink

In this chapter, we will be using one of the Angular community's best pre-loading strategies: ngx-quicklink. Once the page is loaded, this strategy will check whether there are any instances of routerLink on the page and only load those modules since you don't need all of them.

Let's assume that our web app has 20 pages. With no pre-loading strategy, you will just be downloading all the module's code in one bundle and then your page will render. If you use the PreloadAllModule strategy, you will have 20 lazy modules, and when you come to the initial page, it will download that one page's JavaScript and render the page, and then request the other 19 modules. But if you use ngx-quicklink, you will not only download that one page's JavaScript but also only request the modules that are referenced on that page.

To include ngx-quicklink, we need to install it:

```
> npm i ngx-quicklink --save
```

This will replace preloadStrategy:

```
import { QuicklinkModule, QuicklinkStrategy } from 'ngx-quicklink';
...

@NgModule({
    imports: [
        CommonModule,
        QuicklinkModule,
        RouterModule.forRoot(routes, {
            preloadingStrategy: QuicklinkStrategy,
        }),
    ],
    declarations: [],
    exports: [RouterModule],
})
export class RoutingModule { }
```

In this section, we have used a quick link strategy that, instead of downloading all the modules unlike the PreloadAllModules strategy, only downloads the modules for the pages referred from the current page.

If you need a more advanced pre-loading strategy based on the usage of the web app, then consider using Guess.js. Guess.js can use analytics from services such as Google Analytics about the usage of your application and use it to download only essential modules. For more information, check the docs for Guess.js at https://guess-js. github.io/docs/angular.

Next, let's look at how we can add animations to our Angular application using Angular animations.

Adding animations

Animations have become an essential part of web apps as they give meaning to your application in that they inform users about the different states of the application. In this section, we will add three different types of animations that are commonly added in Angular apps. We will also be animating ngIf and ngFor, as well as animating the routes.

Let's start by adding BrowserAnimationModule to SharedModule:

```
import { BrowserAnimationsModule } from '@angular/platform-
browser/animations';

@NgModule({
    imports: [
        ...
        BrowserAnimationsModule,
    ],
    ...
})
export class SharedModule { }
```

Once the module is included, we can add some animations to our list of posts in HomeComponent:

```
...
import { trigger, transition, style, animate } from '@angular/animations';

@Component({
    selector: 'pb-home',
    templateUrl: './home.component.html',
    styleUrls: ['./home.component.css'],
    animations: [
        trigger('postsAnimation', [
            transition(':enter', [
                /* initial */
```

```
              style({ transform: 'translateY(100%)', opacity: 0 }),
              /* final */
              animate('1s cubic-bezier(.8, -0.6, 0.2, 1.5)', style({
              transform: 'translateY(0)', opacity: 1 }))
          ]),
      ])
    ]
  })
export class HomeComponent {
    ...
}
```

Here, we are defining our first animation; that is, `trigger`. We pass our `animations` to the `Component` decorator, and then we call our `trigger` as `postsAnimation`, which we will add to the template next. We have added a `transition` for entering since we know that when we come to the home page, we will be displaying our posts. We could have added a transition for `leave`, but since we aren't removing any posts when on the Home page, we don't need that here. We have started the animation with the `style` in the `initial` comments, and then in `final`, we added `animate`, where we have passed the timing and the `style` we want it to end at.

We can also abstract the whole `trigger` definition in a different file and import it, and then use this animation definition in other places in our application for reuse.

Let's add `trigger` to `home.component.html`:

```
<div class="col-md-6" @postsAnimation *ngFor="let post of posts$ | async">
    ...
</div>
```

Now, when you go to the home page, you should see that all the posts slide up from the bottom.

We will reuse the animation that we used for posts in our individual `post` component. Let's abstract the animation into a separate file. Let's name it `animations.ts` and put it in our `src` folder:

```
import { trigger, transition, style, animate } from '@angular/animations';

export const postsAnimation = trigger('postsAnimation', [
    transition(':enter', [
        /* initial */
        style({ transform: 'translateY(100%)', opacity: 0 }),
        /* final */
        animate('1s cubic-bezier(.8, -0.6, 0.2, 1.5)', style({ transform:
        'translateY(0)', opacity: 1 }))
```

```
    ]),
]);
```

Now, we will import it into two components, `HomeComponent` and `PostComponent`:

```
import { postsAnimation } from './../animations';

@Component({
    selector: 'pb-post',
    templateUrl: './post.component.html',
    styleUrls: ['./post.component.css'],
    animations: [ postsAnimation ]
})
export class PostComponent {
    ...
}
```

Next, we will add the trigger on `ngIf` to `post.component.html`. Now, if you go to the individual post page, you should see the same animation that was being triggered on the **Home** page.

Let's add a route animation in our `animations.ts` file:

```
import { trigger, transition, style, animate, query, group } from
'@angular/animations';

...

export const routerTransition = trigger('routerTransition', [
    transition('* <=> *', [
        query(':enter, :leave', style({ position: 'fixed', width: '100%' })
        , { optional: true }),
        group([
            query(':enter', [
                style({ transform: 'translateX(100%)' }),
                animate('0.5s ease-in-out', style({ transform:
                'translateX(0%)' }))], { optional: true }),
                 query(':leave', [
                style({ transform: 'translateX(0%)' }),
                animate('0.5s ease-in-out', style({ transform:
                'translateX(-100%)' }))
            ], { optional: true }),
        ])
    ])
]);
```

The transition here; that is, * <=> *, defines the start state and end state. Here, * means any state, so the * <=> * transition means that the transition should happen whenever the state changes. We will assign the state in the component that has router-outlet, where the route actually changes. In our case, it is in AppComponent.

Let's add this to app.component.html:

```
<div class="route-container" [@routerTransition]="getOutlet(o)">
    <router-outlet #o="outlet"></router-outlet>
</div>
```

Let's also add the getOutlet method:

```
export class AppComponent {
    getOutlet(o) {
        return o.activatedRouteData.routeState;
    }
}
```

Here, we added routerTransition to the parent of router-outlet to control the animation and passed the outlet, which we get by creating a local variable on router-outlet. Then, in the getOutlet method, we used the outlet to return the new state of the route. Here, we have used routerState. Now, if you try to load the page, you still won't see the animation. That's because the routerState value is not defined anywhere, and thus it's undefined even though the route has changed. Let's add our data in routes:

```
const routes: Routes = [
    { path: '', pathMatch: 'full', redirectTo: 'home' },
    { path: 'home', component: HomeComponent, data: { routeState: 1 } },
    { path: 'about', component: AboutComponent, data: { routeState: 2 } },
    { path: 'post/:id/:slug', loadChildren:
      './post/post.module#PostModule', data: { routeState: 3 } }
    { path: '**', component: HomeComponent },
];
```

If we were to check the app now, we would see that whenever we change our route, the page comes in from the right to the left, which makes it look smoother.

Summary

In this chapter, we successfully created a personal blog as a SPA. We learned how to set up Angular Router, add routes to our application, load the routes lazily, and then use a pre-loading strategy to load our routes ahead of time using both `PreloadAllModules` and `ngx-quicklink`. In the end, we added some animations to our application using Angular animations.

We have learned how to create a SPA using Angular, and improve the performance of our SPA using lazy load routes and pre-loading strategies. We have also learned how to animate the routes and content of our application using Angular animations.

In the next chapter, we will create an application with reactive forms, which is a powerful way to create forms in Angular. In `Chapter 2`, *Building a Flashcard Game Using Angular*, we used template-driven forms, which is good for creating a simple form, but when we have complex forms, reactive forms is the best option.

Questions

Test your knowledge of this chapter by answering the following questions:

- What is a SPA and what are its benefits?
- What are the roles of `CoreModule` and `SharedModule` in an Angular app?
- How do you support different environments in an Angular app?
- How do you create a feature module?
- How do you add a lazy loaded route in Angular?
- What is `PreloadAllModules`? What benefit do we get from using it?
- How do you add Angular animations and use them?

Further reading

The following reading material will provide you with more information about Angular feature modules/core modules/shared modules, routers, lazy loading, and animations:

- Feature modules: `https://angular.io/guide/feature-modules`.
- Shared modules: `https://angular.io/guide/sharing-ngmodules`.
- Singleton services: `https://angular.io/guide/singleton-services`.
- Angular Router: `https://angular.io/guide/router`.
- Angular animations: `https://angular.io/guide/animations`.

4
Building an Inventory Application Using Reactive Forms

In this chapter, we will be creating an application for managing an inventory using one of the third-party component libraries that was created by VMware's team, known as the Clarity component. It follows the Clarity Design System, which has detailed UX/UI guidelines that need to be followed for using the components correctly. It also documents do's and don'ts for using each of the components. You can find the documentation at https://clarity.design.

Throughout this chapter, we will be displaying products and performing **Create**, **Read**, **Update**, and **Delete (CRUD)** operations. In this project, we will also be using reactive forms and creating a complex form via a step-by-step workflow using Clarity's wizard component. We will be using some built-in validations from Angular and will also be creating a custom validator.

The following topics will be covered in this chapter:

- Understanding reactive forms
- Using reactive forms
- Adding built-in and custom validations
- Optimizing the bundle

Technical requirements

This chapter's code can be found in this book's GitHub repository, https://github.com/PacktPublishing/Angular-Projects, under the Chapter04 folder.

The code has been provided for you so that whenever you are stuck, you can verify whether you've done something differently and play with the working project in the repository.

We want you to follow the sections in this chapter in the order in which they appear and learn as much as you can about different aspects of Angular development.

Understanding reactive forms

Angular provides two ways of creating forms. We looked at one of these ways in Chapter 2, *Building a Flashcard Game Using Angular*, using template-driven forms. Template-driven forms are good for creating simple forms using ngModel. If we wish to create any complex forms in a flexible way, we need to use reactive forms. Reactive forms are created in the Component class instead of the templates. We have more control over the definition of the form and can create complex form groups, all of which can have controls, groups of controls, and arrays of controls/groups.

Reactive forms provide three different building blocks, FormControl, FormGroup, and FormArray. All three have one base class called AbstractControl. They share some common methods to get the values, the state of the form elements, and the controlling validations, and some methods are common to that particular building block. You can find all the properties and methods of AbstractClass here: https://angular.io/api/forms/AbstractControl. Some of the most common methods that are used are as follows:

- value: The value of the control
- valid: Whether the form is valid (the opposite property is invalid)
- pristine: true if the user did not interact with that control (the opposite property is dirty)
- touched: true if the user has triggered a blur event on the control (the opposite property is untouched)
- errors: This is an array of all the validation errors on the control
- setValue: set the value of the control
- patchValue: update the value of the control
- hasError: boolean value to check if the control has error or not

Apart from these useful methods, there are others. It also provides two observables, valueChanges and statusChanges, which, as their names suggest, can be subscribed to so that we can get values constantly.

Reactive forms also provide a `FormBuilder`, which can be used to easily create form definitions using the building blocks.

Now that we have understood some basics about reactive forms, let's get started with our project and use Angular reactive forms to create a multi-step complex form.

Project overview

In this section, we will look at what we will be building in this chapter. This is an overview of our project.

We will have a single page in this application. We will use Clarity's Datagrid to display the data in a table and also have the capability to **Add**, **Edit**, and **Delete** products, as shown in the following screenshot:

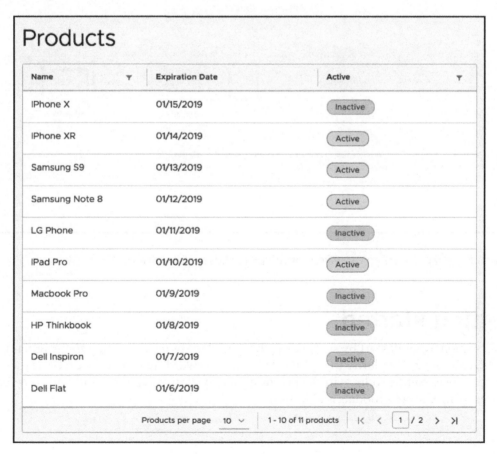

When we add or edit a product, a modal popup will open a multi-step form that we can use to create reactive forms in a step-by-step workflow using Clarity's wizard component. We will be using some built-in validations from Angular and creating a custom validator in this chapter:

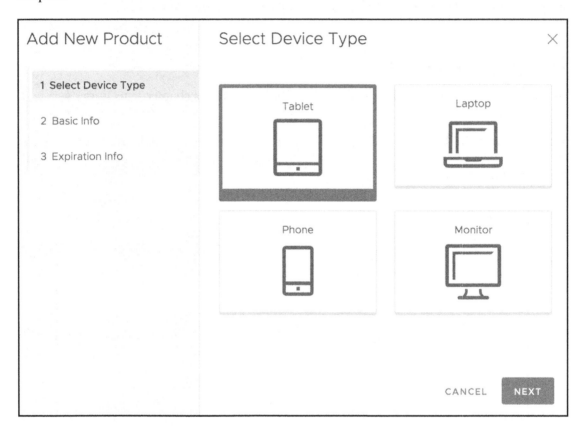

Now that we have seen an overview of the project, let's get started.

Getting started

In this section, we will start by scaffolding the Angular application using the Angular CLI, and then add Angular Clarity to our application. Afterward, we will create a basic data table to display some products in the inventory using Clarity Datagrid and add some basic features using Clarity's modals and buttons.

Let's create a simple Angular project using the Angular CLI, with `scss` as `styles` and `prefix` as `in`:

```
> ng new inventory-app --style scss --prefix in
```

In this chapter, we don't have to do any routing, so we will skip adding `SharedModule` and `CoreModule`. Please note, though, that most projects do require them.

Let's go into the `inventory-app` folder and add Clarity to the project using the `ng add` command:

```
> ng add @clr/angular
```

This should add all the relevant changes to the project so that we can add Clarity Angular. If you want to do this manually, then please refer to `https://clarity.design/documentation/get-started` and follow the instructions there.

Now, we need to serve the application using the `ng serve` command.

Let's replace the content of the `app.component.html` file with the following HTML. This should create a header and content area:

```html
<div class="main-container">
  <header class="header-6">
    <div class="branding">
      <h1>Inventory App</h1>
    </div>
  </header>
  <div class="content-container">
    <div class="content-area">
      <!-- TODO: DISPLAYING PRODUCTS -->
    </div>
  </div>
</div>
```

Then, we need to add some CSS in the `app.component.scss` file:

```scss
.branding h1 {
    color: white;
    font-size: 20px;
    margin-top: 10px;
}
```

Now, let's create a service to store all the products so that we can interact with them:

```
> ng g s product
```

Afterward, we will add a `products` array to it, and have a `products$` property as a `BehaviorSubject` so that the products can be consumed in any component:

```
import { Injectable } from '@angular/core';
import { BehaviorSubject } from 'rxjs';

export interface IProduct {
    id: number;
    name: string;
    active: boolean;
    expirationDate: string;
    description: string;
    type: string;
    features?: string[];
}

function generateId() {
    return Math.floor(Math.random() * 1000);
}

@Injectable({
  providedIn: 'root'
})
export class ProductsService {
    products: IProduct[] = [{
        id: generateId(),
        name: 'IPhone X',
        active: false,
        description: 'Like Brand New',
        expirationDate: '01/15/2019',
        type: 'mobile'
    },
    // Add 10 more random products using the same interface IProduct
    ...
    ];
    products$ = new BehaviorSubject<IProduct[]>(this.products);

}
```

Here, I have just added one product to the `products` list. Please add ten more items or use the source code from the GitHub repository for `Chapter04`.

Let's create a component for displaying `products`:

```
> ng g c products
```

Let's go ahead and add this component to our `app.component.html` file:

```html
<div class="main-container">
  <header class="header-6">
    <div class="branding">
      <h1>Inventory App</h1>
    </div>
  </header>
  <div class="content-container">
    <div class="content-area">
      <in-products></in-products>
    </div>
  </div>
</div>
```

Now, we need to get the `products` that we defined in `ProductsService` and display them on the product's component using the `datagrid` provided by Clarity components:

```typescript
import { Component, OnInit, ChangeDetectionStrategy } from '@angular/core';
import { ProductsService, IProduct } from './../product.service';
import { Observable } from 'rxjs';

@Component({
    selector: 'in-products',
    templateUrl: './products.component.html',
    styleUrls: ['./products.component.css'],
    changeDetection: ChangeDetectionStrategy.OnPush
})

export class ProductsComponent {
    products$: Observable<IProduct[]> = this.productsService.products$;

    constructor(private productsService: ProductsService) { }
    trackById(index, item) {
  return item.id;
 }
}
```

We have added `OnPush` as a `ChangeDetectionStrategy` here since we are using immutability to get all our products. This leads to better performance.

Let's use the datagrid documentation from Clarity's documentation (binding model properties to columns, https://clarity.design/documentation/datagrid/binding-properties, and pagination, https://clarity.design/documentation/datagrid/pagination) and also use the label from Clarity (https://clarity.design/documentation/labels) in order to show an active and inactive label with different colors:

```
<h1>Products</h1>
<clr-datagrid>
    <clr-dg-column clrDgField="name">Name</clr-dg-column>
    <clr-dg-column>Expiration Date</clr-dg-column>
    <clr-dg-column clrDgField="active">Active</clr-dg-column>
    <clr-dg-row *clrDgItems="let product of products$ | async; trackBy
     trackById"
        [clrDgItem]="product">
        <clr-dg-cell>{{product.name}}</clr-dg-cell>
        <clr-dg-cell>{{product.expirationDate}}</clr-dg-cell>
        <clr-dg-cell>
            <span class="label" [ngClass]="{'label-success':
              product.active, 'label-danger':
               !product.active}">{{product.active ?
                'Active': 'Inactive'}}</span>
        </clr-dg-cell>
    </clr-dg-row>
     <clr-dg-footer>
        <clr-dg-pagination #pagination [clrDgPageSize]="10">
            <clr-dg-page-size [clrPageSizeOptions]="[10,20,50]">Products
              per page</clr-dg-page-size>
            {{pagination.firstItem + 1}} - {{pagination.lastItem + 1}}
              of {{pagination.totalItems}} products
        </clr-dg-pagination>
    </clr-dg-footer>
</clr-datagrid>
```

Now, you should see a datagrid with the products, where you can filter by **Name** and **Active**. If you have more than **10** items, you will also see a paginator so that you can move from one page to another. This is available at the bottom of the form:

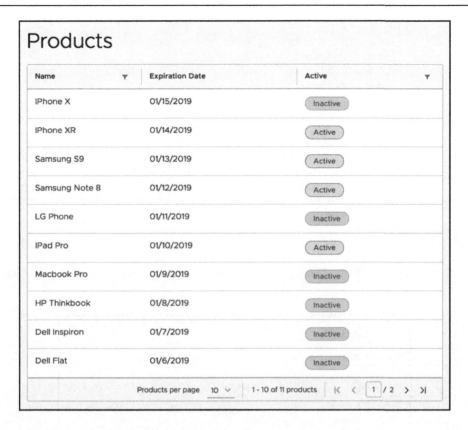

Let's add a button so that we can add a product. On each row in our grid, we will add action buttons for editing and deleting:

```
<h1>Products</h1>
<button class="btn btn-outline btn-sm" (click)="addProduct()">Add
Product</button>
<clr-datagrid>
    <clr-dg-column [clrDgField]="'name'">Name</clr-dg-column>
    <clr-dg-column>Expiration Date</clr-dg-column>
    <clr-dg-column [clrDgField]="'active'">Active</clr-dg-column>
    <clr-dg-row *clrDgItems="let product of products$ | async; trackBy id"
    [clrDgItem]="product">
        <clr-dg-action-overflow>
            <button class="action-item"
            (click)="onEdit(product)">Edit</button>
            <button class="action-item"
            (click)="onDelete(product)">Delete</button>
        </clr-dg-action-overflow>
        <clr-dg-cell>{{product.name}}</clr-dg-cell>
        <clr-dg-cell>{{product.expirationDate}}</clr-dg-cell>
```

```
        <clr-dg-cell>
            <span class="label" [ngClass]="{'label-success':
            product.active, 'label-danger':
            !product.active}">{{product.active ? 'Active':
            'Inactive'}}</span>
        </clr-dg-cell>
    </clr-dg-row>
     <clr-dg-footer>
        <clr-dg-pagination #pagination [clrDgPageSize]="10">
            <clr-dg-page-size [clrPageSizeOptions]="[10,20,50]">
             Products per page</clr-dg-page-size>
            {{pagination.firstItem + 1}} - {{pagination.lastItem + 1}}
            of {{pagination.totalItems}} products
        </clr-dg-pagination>
    </clr-dg-footer>
</clr-datagrid>
```

As you can see, we have three click handlers to write, that is, `onEdit`, `onDelete`, and `addProduct`:

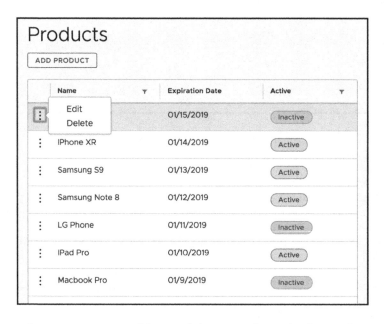

For deleting a product, we want to add a modal popup that asks for confirmation regarding whether the user is sure they want to delete the product. Let's create a component in which we will add Clarity's component:

```
> ng g c delete-product-modal
```

Let's add an input, `product` to our modal and two outputs, `cancel` and `confirm`, that we can use to dismiss or accept the deletion of the product:

```
import { Component, OnInit, Input, Output, EventEmitter } from
'@angular/core';

@Component({
    selector: 'in-delete-product-modal',
    templateUrl: './delete-product-modal.component.html',
    styleUrls: ['./delete-product-modal.component.css']
})
export class DeleteProductModalComponent implements OnInit {
    @Input() product;
    @Output() cancel = new EventEmitter();
    @Output() confirm = new EventEmitter();

    constructor() { }

    ngOnInit() {
    }

    cancelDelete() {
        this.cancel.emit();
    }

    confirmDelete() {
        this.confirm.emit();
    }
}
```

We also need to add the following template in `delete-product-modal.component.html`, which uses the `clr-modal` component:

```
<clr-modal [clrModalOpen]="true">
    <h3 class="modal-title">Delete Product</h3>
    <div class="modal-body">
        <p>Are you sure you want to delete?</p>
    </div>
    <div class="modal-footer">
        <button type="button" class="btn btn-outline"
          (click)="cancelDelete()">Cancel</button>
        <button type="button" class="btn btn-danger"
          (click)="confirmDelete()">Delete</button>
    </div>
</clr-modal>
```

Now, let's put this component into `products.component.html`:

```
<in-delete-product-modal
    (cancel)="handleCancel()"
    (confirm)="confirmDelete()"
>
</in-delete-product-modal>
```

By doing this, you should be able to see a modal pop up on your page automatically, without us having to trigger it:

Now, let's pass the product to the delete product modal component and use the `*ngIf` directive on our modal component to conditionally show it when the user clicks on **DELETE**:

```
<in-delete-product-modal
    *ngIf="delete"
    [product]="productToBeDeleted"
    (cancel)="handleCancel()"
    (confirm)="confirmDelete()"
>
</in-delete-product-modal>
```

In our `ProductsComponent` class, we need to add the logic for the `onDelete` method, which is where we assign the product to be deleted to the `productToBeDeleted` property. We also need to toggle the `delete` flag to `true`. Then, the `confirmDelete` method should toggle the `delete` flag to `false` and call the `removeProduct` method of `productsService`. The `handleCancel` method should simply toggle the `delete` flag to `false`, as follows:

```
...

@Component({
    ...
})
export class ProductsComponent {
```

```
    ...
    delete = false;
    productToBeDeleted;
    onDelete(product) {
        this.delete = true;
        this.productToBeDeleted = product;
    }

    handleCancel() {
        this.delete = false;
    }

    confirmDelete() {
        this.handleCancel();
        // We need to implement this method removeProduct in our
            ProductsService
        this.productsService.removeProduct(this.productToBeDeleted);
    }
}
```

Let's add the `removeProduct` method to our `ProductsService`:

```
    ...

@Injectable({
  providedIn: 'root'
})
export class ProductsService {
    ...

    removeProduct(product) {
        const index = this.products.indexOf(product);
        this.products = [
            ...this.products.slice(0, index),
            ...this.products.slice(index + 1),
        ];
        this.products$.next(this.products);
    }
}
```

Now, let's try and delete a product and see whether everything is wired up correctly. When you click on the action button, click on **Delete**, and then select **DELETE** in the delete modal, you should see that the item in the grid is removed.

Let's use an alert in the delete modal for when the product is active to warn the user about deleting an active product:

```html
<clr-modal [clrModalOpen]="true">
  <h3 class="modal-title">Delete Product</h3>
  <div class="modal-body">
    <clr-alert [clrAlertSizeSmall]="true" [clrAlertClosable]="false"
    [clrAlertType]="'warning'" *ngIf="product?.active">
    <clr-alert-item>
      <span class="alert-text">This is a active device!</span>
      </clr-alert-item>
   </clr-alert>
    <p>Are you sure you want to delete?</p>
  </div>
  <div class="modal-footer">
    <button type="button" class="btn btn-outline"
    (click)="cancelDelete()">Cancel</button>
    <button type="button" class="btn btn-danger"
    (click)="confirmDelete()">Delete</button>
  </div>
</clr-modal>
```

Now, if you click on **DELETE** for a product that's active, you should see the following in the delete modal:

Now that we can display existing products in the datagrid and are able to delete them, let's look at how we can use reactive forms to create a form. We will use this form to add a new product to the list of products in the inventory.

Using reactive forms

Now, we will use the Clarity components' wizard so that we can add/edit products. Wizards are used when we want to create a step-by-step workflow. You can find out more at `https://clarity.design/documentation/wizards`.

The following image shows the wizard's basic layout:

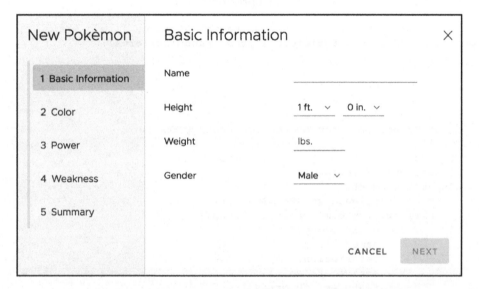

As you can see from the preceding screenshot, Clarity's wizard has steps described on the left, while the contents of the selected step are shown on the right. We will use this to enter product details. In step **1**, we will let the user select the device type; in step **2**, we will gather basic information; and in step **3**, we will get the expiration information.

First, let's add `ReactiveFormsModule` to our `AppModule` so that we can use reactive forms:

```
...
import { ReactiveFormsModule } from '@angular/forms';

@NgModule({
    ...
    imports: [
        BrowserModule,
        ClarityModule,
        BrowserAnimationsModule,
        ReactiveFormsModule,
    ],
```

```
        . . .
    })
    export class AppModule { }
```

Let's create a new component for this:

```
> ng g c product
```

Now, we can use `FormBuilder` to create a product form:

```
import { Component, OnInit, ChangeDetectionStrategy } from '@angular/core';
import { FormBuilder, FormGroup } from '@angular/forms';

@Component({
    selector: 'app-product',
    templateUrl: './product.component.html',
    styleUrls: ['./product.component.css'],
    changeDetection: ChangeDetectionStrategy.OnPush
})
export class ProductComponent implements OnInit {
    productForm: FormGroup;
    @Input() product;
    constructor(private fb: FormBuilder) {
        this.productForm = this.fb.group({
            basic: fb.group({
                name: '',
                description: '',
                active: false,
                features: fb.array([
                    fb.control('')
                ])
            }),
            expiration: fb.group({
                expirationDate: null,
            })
        });
    }

    ngOnInit() {
    }
}
```

We use `FormGroup` to group a set of `AbstractControl`. Here, we have two groups in our product form: one is `basic` and one is `expiration`. `basic` will be used in the second step of the wizard, while `expiration` will be used in the third step.

Now, let's use the wizard component in the HTML:

```html
<form [formGroup]="productForm">
    <clr-wizard #productWizard [clrWizardOpen]="true"
     clrWizardSize="lg" (clrWizardOnCancel)="handleClose()">
        <clr-wizard-title>{{product? 'Edit Product' : 'Add New
         Product'}}</clr-wizard-title>
        <clr-wizard-button [type]="'cancel'"
        (click)="handleClose()">Cancel</clr-wizard-button>
        <clr-wizard-button [type]="'previous'">Back</clr-wizard-button>
        <clr-wizard-button [type]="'next'">Next</clr-wizard-button>
        <clr-wizard-button [type]="'finish'"
        (click)="handleClose()">Finish</clr-wizard-button>
        <clr-wizard-page>
            <ng-template clrPageTitle>Select Device Type</ng-template>
            ...
        </clr-wizard-page>
        <clr-wizard-page>
            <ng-template clrPageTitle>Basic Info</ng-template>
            ...
        </clr-wizard-page>
        <clr-wizard-page>
            <ng-template clrPageTitle>Expiration Info</ng-template>
            ...
    </clr-wizard-page>
    </clr-wizard>
</form>
```

Here, we have wrapped the whole wizard component with a form and used the
formGroup directive on the form to assign productForm, which we created in the
component class as a form group. We used Clarity's clr-wizard component, which is a
top-level component. Inside it, we have used the clr-wizard-page, clr-wizard-
button, and clr-wizard-title wizard components, as well as the clrPageTitle
directive.

Now, when you add the product component to the products component, you should be
able to see the wizard in an open state:

```html
<in-product></in-product>
```

You should see the following three-step wizard open on your page:

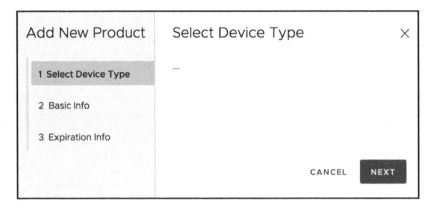

Let's set up the first step, **Select Device Type**, and add cards (https://clarity.design/ documentation/cards) so that we can select the device type:

```
...
export class ProductComponent implements OnInit {
    ...
    deviceType = 'tablet';

    deviceTypes = [{
        name: 'Tablet',
        icon: 'tablet',
    }, {
        name: 'Laptop',
        icon: 'computer'
    }, {
        name: 'Phone',
        icon: 'mobile'
    }, {
        name: 'Monitor',
        icon: 'display'
    }];
    selectDevice(device) {
        this.deviceType = device.icon;
    }
    ...
}
```

We created an array of deviceTypes, Tablet, Laptop, Phone, and Monitor, along with their respective icons. We have also set the default deviceType as tablet:

```
<clr-wizard-page>
    <ng-template clrPageTitle>Select Device Type</ng-template>
    <div class="clr-row devices">
        <div class="clr-col-md-6" *ngFor="let item of deviceTypes">
            <a href="javascript:void(0)" class="card clickable"
            (click)="selectDevice(item)" [ngClass]="{'active':
            item.icon === deviceType}">
                <div class="card-block">
                    <p class="card-text">
                        {{item.name}}
                        <clr-icon [attr.shape]="item.icon"></clr-icon>
                    </p>
                </div>
            </a>
        </div>
    </div>
</clr-wizard-page>
```

Now, we need to add some style for a card when it's selected, when it has a dynamic class of active, and for the icon and card-text:

```
.card.clickable.active {
    box-shadow: 0 .5rem 0 0 green;
    border: 5px solid green;
}

.devices clr-icon {
    width: 85px;
    height: 85px;
    display: block;
    margin: 0 auto;
}

.card-text {
    text-align: center
}
```

The first step in the wizard should look as follows:

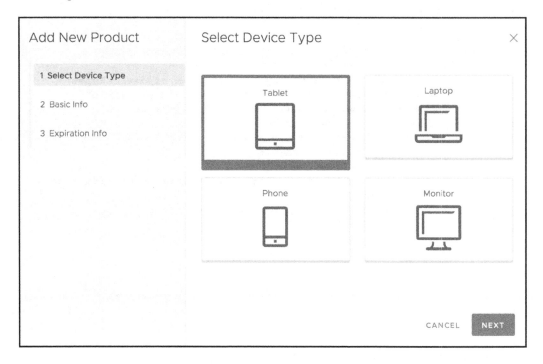

Now, let's add a form for **Basic Info** for step 2. Here, we will be using an `input` field
(`https://clarity.design/documentation/input`), `textarea` (`https://clarity.design/`
`documentation/textarea`), and `toggle-switch` (`https://clarity.design/`
`documentation/toggle-switches`):

```
<clr-wizard-page>
    <ng-template clrPageTitle>Basic Info</ng-template>
    <div formGroupName="basic">
        <!-- Input field for Product Name -->
        <clr-input-container>
            <label for="product-name">Product Name *</label>
            <input clrInput type="text" id="product-name"
            placeholder="IPhone X..." formControlName="name">
        </clr-input-container>
        <!-- Toggle Switch for active -->
        <div class="toggle-switch">
            <input type="checkbox" id="active"
            formControlName="active">
            <label for="active">Active</label>
        </div>
        <!-- Textarea for Product Description -->
```

```
        <clr-textarea-container>
            <label for="description">Product Description</label>
            <textarea clrTextarea id="description" placeholder="Enter
              description here..." formControlName="description"></textarea>
        </clr-textarea-container>
        <!-- Input FormArray for features -->
        <label class="clr-control-label">Features</label>
        <clr-input-container formArrayName="features" *ngFor="let control
         of basicFeatures.controls">
            <input clrInput type="text" [formControl]="control"
              placeholder="IPhone X...">
        </clr-input-container>
        <button class="btn btn-primary" (click)="addFeature()">Add
         Feature</button>
    </div>
</clr-wizard-page>
```

Let's add a few more styles in the product.component.scss file, as follows:

```
.clr-control-container,
textarea {
    width: 100%;
}

.toggle-switch {
    margin-top: 10px;
}

label.clr-control-label {
    padding-top: 14px;
}
```

For the form array, we used basicFeatures, which we can set in the component to get the features from the basic formGroup in our component class:

```
...
export class ProductComponent implements OnInit {
    ...
    get basicFeatures(): FormArray {
        return this.productForm.get('basic.features') as FormArray;
    }

    addFeature() {
        this.basicFeatures.push(this.fb.control(''));
    }
    ...
}
```

The form for step **2** should look as follows:

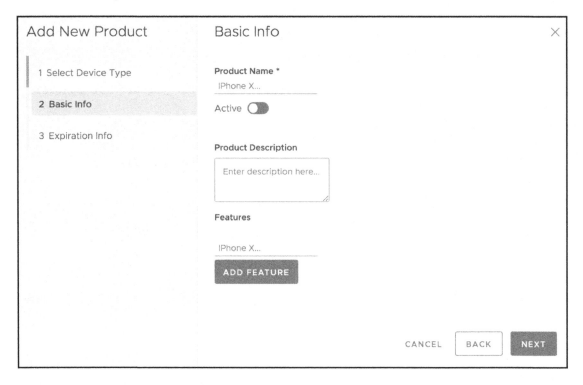

Let's wrap this section up by completing the last step. After, we will add some validations to the form and save the values that are entered in the wizard:

```
<clr-wizard-page>
    <ng-template clrPageTitle>Expiration Info</ng-template>
    <clr-input-container formGroupName="expiration">
        <input type="date" clrInput clrDate
          formControlName="expirationDate">
    </clr-input-container>
</clr-wizard-page>
```

The form in step **3** should look as follows:

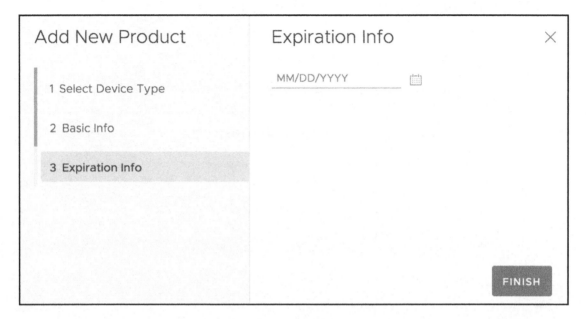

Now that we have our form in the template configured for the reactive form definition that's defined in the component class, we will add some validations to our `ProductComponent` using reactive forms.

Adding built-in and custom validations

Validations are an important part of forms, and reactive forms make it easier to manage them. Let's start by adding some validations to our basic information form.

First, we will add a required validation to our **Product Name** input field. In reactive forms, you will be adding the validations to the component class instead of the template:

```
import { FormBuilder, FormGroup, Validators } from '@angular/forms';
...
export class ProductComponent implements OnInit {
    ...
    constructor(private fb: FormBuilder) {
        this.productForm = fb.group({
            basic: fb.group({
                name: ['', Validators.required],
                description: '',
                active: false,
                features: fb.array([
                    fb.control('')
                ])
            }),
            expiration: fb.group({
                expirationDate: null,
            })
        });
    }
}
```

To display an error, we can use the `clr-control-error` component that's provided by Clarity:

```
<!-- Input field for Product Name -->
<clr-input-container>
    <label for="product-name">Product Name *</label>
    <input clrInput type="text" id="product-name" placeholder="IPhone X..."
     formControlName="name">
    <clr-control-error>This Field is Required!</clr-control-error>
</clr-input-container>
```

If we weren't using Clarity's `clr-control-error` component, we would have checked for any errors and whether the field was `pristine` using the form's status:

```
<div *ngIf="productForm.get('basic.name').invalid &&
productForm.get('basic.name').dirty">
This Field is Required!
</div>
```

Whenever such big logic is used in the templates, it is always recommended to create a `get` property in the class and use it in the template:

```
class ProductComponent {
    get basicFieldInvalid() {
        return this.productForm.get('basic.name').invalid &&
        this.productForm.get('basic.name').dirty;
    }
}
```

Then, we need to use the `basicFieldInvalid` property in the template. This way, we can keep the logic in the component class and also use the property in multiple places in the template or component class, if required.

Now, let's add some validations to our expiration date. We will be composing two validations for the expiry date: one is the required validation, while the other will state that the expiration should be after today's date, which would be a custom validation that's not built into the Angular framework, such as `minlength`, `maxlength`, and so on:

```
import { FormBuilder, FormGroup, Validators, ValidatorFn, AbstractControl }
from '@angular/forms';

function minDateValidation(date: Date): ValidatorFn {
    return (control: AbstractControl): {[key: string]: any} | null => {
        const forbidden = new Date(control.value) < date;
        return forbidden ? {minDateValidation: {value: control.value}}
        : null;
    };
}
...
export class ProductComponent implements OnInit {
    ...
    constructor(private fb: FormBuilder) {
        this.productForm = fb.group({
            basic: fb.group({
                name: ['', Validators.Required],
                description: '',
                active: false,
                features: fb.array([
                    fb.control('')
                ])
            }),
            expiration: fb.group({
                expirationDate: [null,
                Validators.compose([Validators.required,
                minDateValidation(new Date())]),
            })
```

```
            });
    }

    get expirationError() {
        if
(this.productForm.get('expiration.expirationDate').hasError('required')) {
    return 'This Field is Required!';
        }
        if
(this.productForm.get('expiration.expirationDate').hasError('minDateValidat
ion')) {
        return 'Expiration should be after today\'s date';
        }
    }
}
```

In our template, we'll show the respective error by using the following code:

```
<clr-input-container formGroupName="expiration">
    <input type="date" clrInput clrDate formControlName="expirationDate">
    <clr-control-error>{{expirationError}}</clr-control-error>
</clr-input-container>
```

Now, let's make sure that the user doesn't go to the next step if the current step is invalid. We can do that by overriding the buttons on the basic information and expiration steps. Let's begin with the basic information step:

```
<clr-wizard-page>
    <ng-template clrPageTitle>Basic Info</ng-template>
    ...
    <ng-template clrPageButtons>
        <clr-wizard-button [type]="'cancel'">Cancel</clr-wizard-button>
        <clr-wizard-button [type]="'previous'">Back</clr-wizard-button>
        <clr-wizard-button [clrWizardButtonDisabled]="isBasicInvalid"
          [type]="'next'">Next</clr-wizard-button>
    </ng-template>
</clr-wizard-page>
```

Let's create a get property, isBasicInvalid, in the component class:

```
get isBasicInvalid(): boolean {
    return this.productForm.get('basic').invalid;
}
```

This will make sure that if the basic information step is invalid, we cannot go to the next step.

Let's do the same thing for the expiration information step:

```
<clr-wizard-page>
    <ng-template clrPageTile>Expiration Info</ng-template>
    ...
    <ng-template clrPageButtons>
        <clr-wizard-button [clrWizardButtonDisabled]="isExpirationInvalid"
        (click)="handleFinish()" [type]="'finish'">Finish</clr-wizard-
        button>
    </ng-template>
</clr-wizard-page>
```

Now, let's create the isExpirationInvalid property, as well as the handleFinish and handleCancel methods:

```
import { ClrWizard } from '@clr/angular';
...
class ProductComponent {
    ...
    @Output() finish = new EventEmitter();
    @ViewChild('productWizard', { static: false }) productWizard:
    ClrWizard;

    ...

    get isExpirationInvalid(): boolean {
        return this.productForm.get('expiration').invalid;
    }

    handleClose() {
        this.finish.emit();
        this.close();
    }

    close() {
        this.productForm.reset();
        this.deviceType = 'tablet';
 this.productWizard.goTo(this.productWizard.pageCollection.pages.first.id);
        this.productWizard.reset();
    }

    handleFinish() {
        this.finish.emit({
            product: {
                type: this.deviceType,
                ...this.productForm.get('basic').value,
                ...this.productForm.get('expiration').value,
            }
```

```
        });
        this.close();
    }
}
```

Here, we use `EventEmitter` to send all the form values that we enter on the three steps as a product. Then, we call `close`, which resets the form and the wizard, and also takes us to the first step of the wizard on `close`. On `handleClose`, we emit nothing in `finish` and call `close`.

Now, in our products component, we will listen to the `finish` event and save the information:

```
<app-product
    *ngIf="productOpen"
    [product]="selectedProduct"
    (finish)="handleFinish($event)"
></app-product>
```

Now, we will implement the `handleFinish`, `addProduct`, and `onEdit` methods in our `ProductsComponent` class:

```
class ProductsComponent {
    productOpen;
    selectedProduct: IProduct;
    addProduct() {
        this.productOpen = true;
        this.selectedProduct = undefined;
    }

    onEdit(product) {
        this.productOpen = true;
        this.selectedProduct = product;
    }

    handleFinish(event) {
        if (event && event.product) {
            if (this.selectedProduct) {
                // Edit Flow
                this.productsService.editProduct(this.selectedProduct.id,
                  event.product);
            } else {
                // Save New
                this.productsService.addProduct(event.product);
            }
        }
        this.productOpen = false;
```

```
      }
   }
```

Now, we can add the `editProduct` and `addProduct` methods to our `ProductService`:

```
   ...

@Injectable({
  providedIn: 'root'
})
export class ProductsService {
    ...

    addProduct(product) {
        this.products = [
            {
                id: generateId(),
                ...product,
            },
            ...this.products,
        ];
        this.products$.next(this.products);
    }
    editProduct(id, product) {
        const index = this.products.findIndex(p => p.id === id);
        this.products = [
            ...this.products.slice(0, index),
            {
                id,
                ...product,
            },
            ...this.products.slice(index + 1),
        ];
        this.products$.next(this.products);
    }
}
```

Now that adding products works, we need to make sure that the wizard shows the values of the product that's being edited. We will have to set the values to the form in `ProductComponent`. We can do this by checking whether the product is available by making changes to the product component and setting the values.

We will be using the `pick` function from Lodash to do this, so let's install `lodash` and its types first using `npm`:

```
> npm install lodash @types/lodash --save
```

We will use this to pick values and put them in the proper `formGroup` in `productForm`:

```
import * as _ from 'lodash';
...
class ProductComponent implements OnInit, OnChanges {
    ngOnInit() {
        if (this.product) {
            this.productForm.setValue({
                basic: {
                    ..._.pick(this.product, ['name', 'description',
                    'active']),
                     features: this.product.features || [''],
                },
                expiration: {
                    ..._.pick(this.product, ['expirationDate']),
                }
            });
            this.deviceType = this.product.type;
        }
    }

    ngOnChanges() {
        this.ngOnInit();
    }
}
```

We are now able to add new products to the inventory, which completes our implementation of the project. In the next section, we will try to optimize the bundle of the application to improve its performance by using tools to calculate the size of the production bundles.

Optimizing the bundle

The performance of the application is a really important metric. One of the factors that we, as developers, can control is the bundle size of our application, as well as its optimization. Since we have used a couple of external libraries, namely Clarity components and Lodash, let's analyze our bundle and see whether we can reduce the bundle's size.

There are a couple of tools that we can use, such as `source-map-explorer` and `webpack-bundle-analyzer`. We will be using `source-map-explorer` here, but I will also show you how to use `webpack-bundle-analyzer` so that you can try it for yourself. You may prefer it over `source-map-explorer`.

Let's build our application using the `prod` setting and the flag for source maps. Source maps map the minified source code to the unminified version. `source-map-explorer` uses it to display what's being used in the bundle, and we, as developers, can analyze it to see whether we can make any improvements:

> **ng build --prod --source-map**

After this command has completed, we can use `npx` to run `source-map-explorer`:

> **npx source-map-explorer dist/inventory-app/main-es2015.*.js**

The hash code are unique characters that are created by Angular based on the content of the file. Each time you change the code in your application, you will have a new hash code. Check your `dist` directory for the code. Once you run this, a new tab will open in your browser, showing all the analysis:

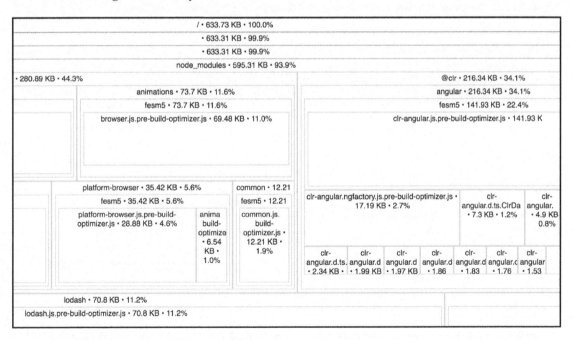

At the top, it tells us about the total size of the bundle, which in our case is **633.73 KB** (141 KB gzipped), and you can see where all of it is distributed.

We can see that the two external libraries that we have used, that is, Clarity and Lodash, are taking around **34.1%** and **11.2%** of space, respectively.

We know that we have used only one small method from Lodash, but it included **70.8 KB** of code. Lodash is not tree-shakable. Tree-shaking is a concept by which we can remove the unused code in our application from the bundle. Let's use the `lodash-es` package, which has all the functions of Lodash, but is also tree-shakable.

Let's install it using `npm`:

```
> npm install lodash-es
```

Now, we can change the import of `lodash` to `lodash-es` in `product.component.ts`, as follows:

```
// import * as _ from 'lodash'; Old
import pick from 'lodash-es/pick';

// _.pick old
pick()
```

Now, **build the project with** `source-map` **and run** `source-map-explorer`:

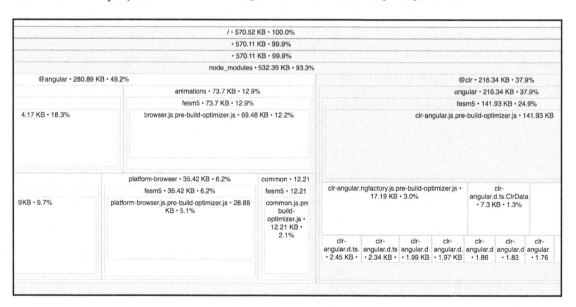

We can see that the whole bundle has reduced to **570.52 KB** (120 KB gzipped) from **633.73 KB** (141 KB gzipped). This is almost a 10-15% reduction in bundle size.

To run `webpack-bundle-analyzer`, we need `stats.json`, which we can get by building an application using the `stats-json` flag:

```
> ng build --prod --stats-json
```

After completion, you can run `webpack-bundle-analyzer` using `npx`, as follows:

```
> npx webpack-bundle-analyzer dist/inventory-app/stats-es2015.json
```

This should open analysis for `webpack-bundle-analyzer` in the browser.

Summary

In this chapter, we have created an inventory app, used one of the component libraries that we created using Angular, looked at Clarity components, and used reactive forms to create complex forms. We also added some built-in and custom validations. By doing this, we learned how to use Clarity components in our Angular application, as well as some of its more complex components, such as wizard and Datagrid. We also learned how reactive forms can be created.

You should now be able to create complex forms using `FormArray`, `FormGroup`, and `FormControl` and also be able to add custom validations to any web form. Learning how we can use bundle analyzers to optimize our bundles helped with this.

In the next chapter, we will create a simple e-commerce application that we will convert into a Progressive Web App. We will be able to use this as a standalone app on any device—even one that has a bad network connection or no network connection at all.

Questions

Test your knowledge of this chapter by answering the following questions:

- What are the three building blocks of reactive forms?
- What are the different methods and properties of `AbstractControl`?
- What is the difference between `pristine` and `touched`? What are the opposites of them?
- What are the two different methods we can use to set values? What are the differences between them?

- What does the `hasError` method do and how can we use it?
- What is `FormBuilder`? How can we use it?
- How do you add validations to reactive forms?
- How do you create a custom validator in Angular?
- How do you add synchronous and asynchronous validations?
- How can you optimize your JavaScript bundle?

Further reading

The following reading material will provide you with more information about Clarity components, reactive forms, and validations:

- Clarity Design documentation: `https://clarity.design/`.
- Angular documentation on reactive forms: `https://angular.io/guide/reactive-forms`.
- Angular documentation on form validations: `https://angular.io/guide/form-validation`.

5

Building a PWA E-Commerce Application Using Angular Service Worker

In this chapter, we will be creating an e-commerce application for an electronic store, and then we will convert it into a **Progressive Web App** (**PWA**), add support for offline usage, and also add the web app as an application on the home screen on both Android and iOS. We will also set up a Nest.js application so that we can get data from MongoDB.

The following topics will be covered in this chapter:

- We will create a Nest.js application for a backend service
- We will use Angular Material to create a simple e-commerce application
- We will use Lighthouse to measure and analyze our application for PWA
- We will convert our application so that it scores a perfect 100 on the Lighthouse for PWA
- We will make our application run offline
- We will deploy our application on Firebase Hosting

Technical requirements

This chapter's code can be found in this book's GitHub repository, `https://github.com/PacktPublishing/Angular-Projects`, in the `Chapter05` folder.

The code has been provided for you so that, whenever you are stuck, you can verify whether you've done something different and play with the working project in the repository.

We want you to follow the sections in this chapter in the order in which they appear and learn as much as you can about different aspects of Angular development.

Exploring Progressive Web Apps

Progressive Web Apps are just simple websites that can be reached using the web. However, they can also work as native apps on devices. They are fast, reliable, and engaging. You can add them to the home screen of your device (mobile/desktop), and can also work offline so that a user who has a weak network connection doesn't have to worry about network connectivity.

Let's look at what makes a website a Progressive Web App:

- **Service worker**: A service worker is a JavaScript worker that acts as a network proxy in your browser. Your application can communicate with the service worker using the `postMessage` interface.
- **manifest.json**: `manifest.json` is a JSON file that contains details about the application, as well as details about different assets that the application needs so that it can be saved on any device's home screen. The `manifest.json` file is linked in the HTML file of your website.

If you are writing a service worker from scratch, you need to be familiar with the service worker API and its life cycle. In this chapter, we will be utilizing the Angular service worker, which will make it easier to convert an existing Angular app into a service worker.

If an Angular service worker doesn't fulfill all your requirements, then you might want to look for Workbox. Alternatively, you can write your own service worker JavaScript file.

Now that we understand what PWAs are and what we need to do to create one, let's look at what project we want to create before adding PWA functionality to it.

Project overview

First, we will create a Nest.js application that will connect to MongoDB and gather product information. Then, we will create an Angular app to consume the API and use Angular Material to present the products. We will have some basic functionality, such as the ability to add and remove products, and also have a modal cart to show a list of products that were added to the cart.

The following screenshot shows the screen where we display our products. Each product can be added to the cart. At the top, we have the count that tells us how many products have been added to the cart:

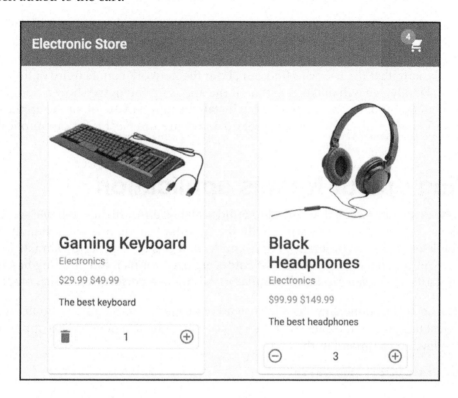

When you click on the cart in the top right-hand corner, a modal popup appears, as follows:

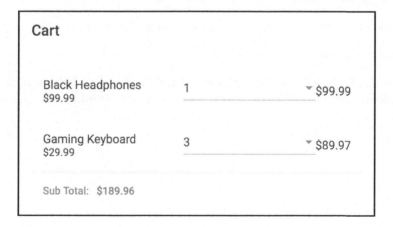

In the **Cart** menu, you can see the **Sub Total** and total for each product, as well as the total number of a certain product that has been added to the cart. We also have a drop-down that we can update which reflects whether the product list has been updated.

Once we are done with the application, we will check Lighthouse and measure how far we are away from being a full PWA app. We will add an Angular service worker to the application and make sure that we can add the app to the home screen of our device. Then, we will make sure that the user can find out about the network connectivity of the application. Finally, we will make sure that, if the app is updated, we show a notification to the user about the update, and then let them install the newest version of the application. In the next section, we will see how we can set up and configure Nest.js for our application.

Setting up our Nest.js application

Nest is a Node.js framework that's used to build scalable, efficient, and reliable server applications. It shares some similarities with the Angular framework, even though they solve completely different problems. For example, in terms of TypeScript, similar dependency injection techniques and decorators are used for its main building blocks. These similarities between Nest and Angular makes them a perfect fit for each other.

Let's create an application using Nest.js. Instead of installing `@nestjs/cli` globally using `npm`, let's just use `npx` to make use of `@nestjs/cli` and create a new Nest.js application. Run the following command in the CLI:

```
> npx @nestjs/cli new es-api
```

This should create a Nest.js app in the `es-api` folder. Let's add Mongoose to our application. Mongoose is used to connect to MongoDB.

Let's add the dependencies for `mongoose` in our root folder for `es-api`:

```
> yarn add mongoose @types/mongoose
```

Since this book does not focus on Nest.js, we will not go into detail about how to create modules, services, and controllers in Nest.js. The good part about Nest.js is how similar it is to Angular.

Let's add the `products` and `database` folders from the `Chapter 5/es-api/src` folder (`https://github.com/PacktPublishing/Angular-Projects/tree/master/Chapter05/es-api/src`) to our `src` folder and add `ProductsModule` to `AppModule`, as follows:

```
import { Module } from '@nestjs/common';
import { AppController } from './app.controller';

import { AppService } from './app.service';
import { ProductsModule } from './products/products.module';

@Module({
    imports: [ProductsModule],
    controllers: [AppController],
    providers: [AppService],
})
export class AppModule {}
```

We will also need to enable **Cross-Origin Request Sharing (CORS)** so that our Angular app will be able to access this API in the application. The CORS mechanism makes sure that the API's consumption by a client can only happen when the server allows it to.

We can enable CORS in `main.ts` in our Nest.js application as follows:

```
import { NestFactory } from '@nestjs/core';
import { AppModule } from './app.module';

async function bootstrap() {
    const app = await NestFactory.create(AppModule);
    app.enableCors({
        origin: '*',
    });
    await app.listen(3000);
}
bootstrap();
```

Now, when you want to run this app using the `npm start` command from inside the `es-api` folder, you should be able to use the API to get products. Use the following URL to check this: `http://localhost:3000/products`.

If you check `DatabaseModule`, you will find a MongoDB connection string starting with `mongodb://`. You can replace it with your local MongoDB or, if you don't have one, use `mlab.com` to create your own instance of MongoDB.

Now that we've got our API working by using the Nest.js framework, let's focus on building our client application using Angular.

Setting up our Angular application

In this section, we will scaffold the Angular application using the Angular CLI, add Angular Material to our application, and create a simple e-commerce application.

Let's create another application on the same level where you have the `es-api` folder. We will use the Angular CLI by using the following command:

```
> ng new electronic-store --prefix es
```

We will be using Angular Material for this application. Angular Material is a component library that follows the Material Design guidelines. It is maintained by the Angular Material team at Google. Angular Material follows the Material Design guidelines strictly and has very high-quality components with high standards for accessibility.

Let's go into the `electronic-store` folder and add Angular Material using the `ng add` command, as follows:

```
> ng add @angular/material
```

You will be prompted to answer a few questions; select the following options:

```
? Choose a prebuilt theme name, or "custom" for a custom theme: Indigo/Pink
[ Preview: https://material.angular.io?theme=indigo-pink ]
? Set up HammerJS for gesture recognition? Yes
? Set up browser animations for Angular Material? Yes
```

Once you've answered these questions, you will find that the following files have been updated:

```
UPDATE src/main.ts (391 bytes)
UPDATE src/app/app.module.ts (423 bytes)
UPDATE angular.json (4060 bytes)
UPDATE src/index.html (481 bytes)
UPDATE src/styles.css (181 bytes)
UPDATE package.json
```

This updates all the files and dependencies that we need so that we can add Material to our application. If you would like to manually add Angular Material to your application, follow the following steps: https://material.angular.io/guide/getting-started.

Angular Material provides additional schematics so that you can generate navigation, tables, dashboards, and tree and address forms. Let's use the nav generate command to create navigation for our application:

```
> ng g @angular/material:nav nav
```

Now, let's use the navigation in our application by replacing the content in app.component.html with just the nav component:

```
<es-nav></es-nav>
```

When we serve our application, we should see that our navigation with the header is generated by Angular Material, as follows:

Let's also go ahead and add all the Angular Material dependencies to our application that we will use in the rest of this chapter:

```
. . .

import { MatToolbarModule, MatButtonModule, MatSidenavModule,
MatIconModule, MatListModule, MatCardModule, MatSelectModule,
MatDialogModule, MatBadgeModule, MatSnackBarModule } from
'@angular/material';

const matDesignModules = [ MatToolbarModule, MatButtonModule,
MatSidenavModule, MatIconModule, MatListModule, MatCardModule,
MatSelectModule, MatDialogModule, MatBadgeModule, MatSnackBarModule ];

@NgModule({
```

```
    ...
    imports: [
        BrowserModule,
        BrowserAnimationsModule,
        LayoutModule,
        ...matDesignModules,
    ],
    ...
})
export class AppModule { }
```

I created a variable called matDesignModules so that I could keep all the Material
Component modules together.

We will make some modifications to the nav.component.html file since we don't need a
side menu in our application. We will also use ng-content to pass the main content. We
will pass this content via the right-hand side of the navigation bar:

```
<mat-sidenav-container class="sidenav-container">
    <mat-sidenav-content>
        <mat-toolbar color="primary">
            <span>Electronic Store</span>
            <span class="spacer"></span>
            <ng-content select="[right]"></ng-content>
        </mat-toolbar>
        <!-- Add Content Here -->
        <ng-content></ng-content>
    </mat-sidenav-content>
</mat-sidenav-container>
```

Let's add styles for the spacer class, which will make sure that the right slot is aligned on
the right-hand side, as follows:

```
.spacer {
    flex: 1 1 auto;
}
```

Let's pass the content for the right-hand side of the navigation and the main content:

```
<es-nav>
    <div right>
        <button aria-label="Cart" mat-icon-button>
            <mat-icon>shopping_cart</mat-icon>
        </button>
    </div>
    <div class="products">
        <h1>Products</h1>
```

```
    <!-- Products will come here -->
  </div>
</es-nav>
```

Add some styles to the `app.component.css` file, as follows:

```css
.product-card {
 max-width: 200px;
 margin-top: 20px;
}

.products {
 display: flex;
 flex-wrap: wrap;
 justify-content: space-around;
 margin-top: 30px;
}
```

Now, we will see a shopping cart icon on the header, as well as a heading in the content area of the page, as shown in the following screenshot:

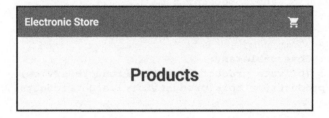

Now, let's create the `ProductsService` using the following command:

```
> ng g s products
```

From here, we will create a function so that we can call the `PRODUCTS_API` that we created using Nest.js:

```typescript
import { Injectable } from '@angular/core';
import { HttpClient } from '@angular/common/http';

const PRODUCTS_API = 'http://localhost:3000/products';

@Injectable({
    providedIn: 'root'
})
export class ProductsService {
    constructor(private http: HttpClient) { }
```

```
    getProducts() {
        return this.http.get(PRODUCTS_API);
    }
}
```

 Don't forget to add `HttpClientModule` to your `AppModule`.

Let's create a `products$` property in our `AppComponent` that will be used along with the `async` pipe in the template:

```
import { Component } from '@angular/core';
import { Observable } from 'rxjs';
import { ProductsService } from './products.service';

@Component({
    selector: 'es-root',
    templateUrl: './app.component.html',
    styleUrls: ['./app.component.scss']
})
export class AppComponent {
    products$: Observable<any>;
    constructor(private productsService: ProductsService) {
        this.products$ = this.productsService.getProducts();
    }
}
```

Now, we will display the products in a `mat-card`. You can find all the details about `mat-card` in the following: `https://material.angular.io/components/card/overview`:

```
<es-nav>
    ...
    <div class="products">
        <mat-card class="product-card" *ngFor="let product of
        products$ | async; let i = index">
            <img [attr.alt]="product.name" mat-card-image
              [src]="product.images[0]">
            <mat-card-content>
                <mat-card-title>{{product.name}}</mat-card-
                title>
                <mat-card-subtitle>{{product.category}}</mat-
                card-subtitle>
                <mat-card-subtitle class="sale-price">
                    {{product.salePrice | currency}}
```

```
                <span class="original-price">
                   {{product.price | currency}}</span>
             </mat-card-subtitle>
             <p>{{product.description}}</p>
          </mat-card-content>
       </mat-card>
    </div>
</es-nav>
```

Now, we can see the products in the Material cards, along with a description of each product, as shown in the following screenshot:

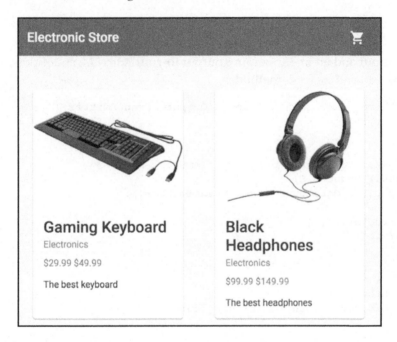

Now, let's create a button that can add/remove multiple items of each product to/from the cart. Let's call it the `add-to-cart` component, as follows:

```
> ng g c add-to-cart
```

Let's add a button. We will use a Material stroke button for this. When clicked, we will replace this with an element that will have two buttons for incrementing and decrementing the product count, and that also counts products that have been added to the cart:

```
<button class="buy-btn" (click)="add()" mat-stroked-button color="primary"
*ngIf="count === 0; else cartBtns">Buy Now</button>
<ng-template #cartBtns>
    <div class="btn-mimicry">
```

```html
        <button color="primary" mat-icon-button *ngIf="count === 1;
         else removeBtn" (click)="remove()"><mat-icon>delete</mat-
         icon></button>
        <ng-template #removeBtn>
            <button mat-icon-button color="primary"><mat-icon
            (click)="remove()">remove_circle_outline</mat-icon>
            </button>
        </ng-template>
        {{count}}
        <button mat-icon-button (click)="add()" color="primary">
            <mat-icon>add_circle_outline</mat-icon>
        </button>
    </div>
</ng-template>
```

Add a `count` input and an `updateCount` output to your `AddToCartComponent` and implement the `add` and `remove` methods:

```typescript
import { Component, OnInit, Input, Output, EventEmitter } from
'@angular/core';

...
export class AddToCartComponent implements OnInit {
    @Input() count = 0;
    @Output() updateCount = new EventEmitter();

    constructor() { }
    ngOnInit() {
    }

    add() {
        this.count++;
        this.updateCount.emit(this.count);
    }

    remove() {
        this.count--;
        this.updateCount.emit(this.count);
    }
}
```

Let's finish the `AddToCartComponent` with some styles to make the button fit the card better in `add-to-cart.component.css`:

```css
.buy-btn {
    width: 100%;
}

.btn-mimicry {
    border: 1px solid rgba(0,0,0,.12);
    border-radius: 5px;
    box-shadow: 0 0 0 0 rgba(0,0,0,.2), 0 0 0 0 rgba(0,0,0,.14), 0
    0 0 0 rgba(0,0,0,.12);
    display: flex;
    justify-content: space-between;
    align-items: center;
}

button[mat-icon-button] {
    width: 34px!important;
    height: 34px!important;
}

mat-icon {
    height: 32px;
    width: 25px;
}
```

Now, let's add our component to `app.component.html` within the `mat-card-actions` component:

```html
<es-nav>
    ...
    <div class="products">
        <mat-card class="product-card" *ngFor="let product of
        products$ | async; let i = index">
            ...
            <mat-card-actions>
                <es-add-to-cart></es-add-to-cart>
            </mat-card-actions>
        </mat-card>
    </div>
</es-nav>
```

Now, you should be able to see the add to cart button, which can be interacted with independently:

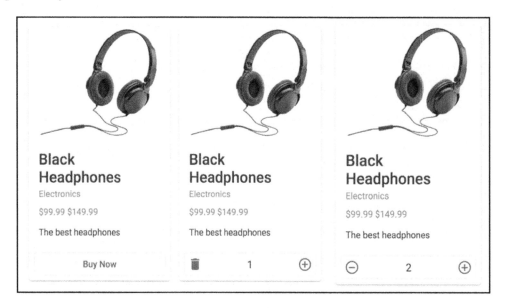

Let's create a `CartService` so that we can use this information in other components:

```
> ng g s cart
```

In our `CartService`, we will create a `cart` object with the product id as a key and product details with the count as the value. The `addToCart` method that will update the `cart` object is as follows:

```
import { Injectable } from '@angular/core';
import { BehaviorSubject } from 'rxjs';

@Injectable({
    providedIn: 'root'
})
export class CartService {
    cart: any = {};
    cart$;

    constructor() {
        this.cart.cartTotal = 0;
        this.cart$ = new BehaviorSubject(this.cart);
    }

    addToCart(count, product) {
```

```
            if (count === 0) {
                delete this.cart[product._id];
            } else {
                this.cart = {
                    ...this.cart,
                    [product._id]: {
                        ...product,
                        count,
                    }
                };
            }
            this.cart.cartTotal = 0;
            Object.values(this.cart)
                .filter(x => typeof x === 'object')
                .forEach((p: any) => this.cart.cartTotal = this.cart.cartTotal
                + p.count);
            this.cart$.next(this.cart);
    }
}
```

Let's add our CartService to our AppComponent:

```
import { Component } from '@angular/core';
import { Observable } from 'rxjs';
import { ProductsService } from './products.service';
import { CartService } from './cart.service';

@Component({
    selector: 'es-root',
    templateUrl: './app.component.html',
    styleUrls: ['./app.component.scss']
})
export class AppComponent {
    products$: Observable<any>;
    cart$: Observable<any>;
    cart;
    constructor(
        private productsService: ProductsService,
        private cartService: CartService
    ) {
        this.products$ = this.productsService.getProducts();
        this.cart$ = this.cartService.cart$.subscribe(cart => this.cart
        = cart);
    }
    onAddProduct(count, product) {
        this.cartService.addToCart(count, product);
    }
}
```

Let's display the `cartTotal` on the `shopping_cart` badge and display the product count from the cart. We will also pass the count to the `es-add-to-cart` component, as well as an event to `updateCount`, as follows:

```
<es-nav>
    <div right>
        <button aria-label="Cart" mat-icon-button>
            <mat-icon [matBadge]="cart.cartTotal"
            matBadgeColor="accent"
            matBadgePosition="before">shopping_cart</mat-icon>
        </button>
    </div>
    <div class="products">
        <mat-card class="product-card" *ngFor="let product of products$
        | async; let i = index">
            ...
            <mat-card-actions>
                <es-add-to-cart [count]="cart[product._id]?.count || 0"
                (updateCount)="onAddProduct($event, product)"></es-add-to-
                cart>
            </mat-card-actions>
        </mat-card>
    </div>
</es-nav>
```

Now, when you add a product, you should see the count of products in the cart in the header as the cart's badge, as shown in the following screenshot:

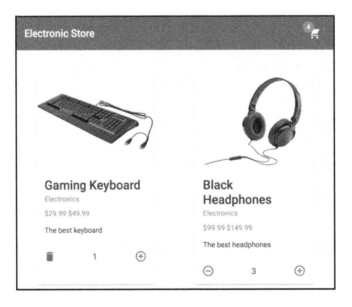

Let's end this application by showing the cart in a dialog box. Let's add a `cart` component via Angular CLI by using the following command:

```
> ng g c cart
```

We're adding the `CartComponent` to the `entryComponents` of the `AppModule` since it will be added dynamically by the `MatDialog` service provided by Angular Material:

```
...
import { CartComponent } from './cart/cart.component';
...
@NgModule({
    ...
    entryComponents: [CartComponent]
})
export class AppModule { }
```

Let's trigger a `click` event on the shopping cart button in our navigation:

```
<button aria-label="Cart" mat-icon-button (click)="openCart()">
    <mat-icon [matBadge]="cart.cartTotal" matBadgeColor="accent"
      matBadgePosition="before">shopping_cart</mat-icon>
</button>
```

Now, we'll use the `MatDialog` service to show the `Cart` component. This can be done with the following code:

```
...
import { MatDialog } from '@angular/material';
import { CartComponent } from './cart/cart.component';
...
export class AppComponent {
    ...
    constructor(
        ...
        private dialog: MatDialog
    ) {
        ...
    }
    openCart() {
        this.dialog.open(CartComponent, {
            width: '500px',
        });
    }
}
```

Now, when we click on the cart in the header, we should see the `CartComponent` displayed in the dialog:

Now, let's use `CartService` in our `CartComponent` to get all the items in the cart and also create the `getValues` method to convert the `cart` object into an array of objects. We will use the `onSelectionChange` method whenever the selected drop-down value changes (we will use `mat-select` to change the number of items in the cart for the product):

```
import { Component, OnInit } from '@angular/core';
import { CartService } from './../cart.service';

@Component({
    selector: 'es-cart',
    templateUrl: './cart.component.html',
    styleUrls: ['./cart.component.css']
})
export class CartComponent implements OnInit {
    cart$;
    constructor(private cartService: CartService) {
        this.cart$ = this.cartService.cart$;
    }

    ngOnInit() {
```

```
    }

    getValues(obj) {
        return Object.values(obj)
            .filter(x => typeof x === 'object');
    }

    onSelectionChange($event, product) {
        this.cartService.addToCart($event.value, product);
    }
}
```

Let's use the `async` pipe to display all the items in the card using `mat-list` and have `mat-select` change the number of items in the cart for the product:

```html
<ng-container *ngIf="(cart$ | async) as cart">
    <h1 mat-dialog-title>Cart</h1>
    <div mat-dialog-content>
        <mat-list>
            <mat-list-item *ngFor="let product of getValues(cart)">
                <h4 mat-line>{{ product.name }}</h4>
                <p mat-line>{{ product.salePrice | currency }}</p>
                <mat-form-field class="count">
                    <mat-select
                        [value]="product.count"
                        (selectionChange)="onSelectionChange($event,
                        product)"
                        >
                        <mat-option
                            *ngFor="let count of [1, 2, 3, 4, 5, 6, 7, 8,
                            9, 10]" [value]="count"
                            >
                            {{ count }}
                        </mat-option>
                    </mat-select>
                </mat-form-field>
                {{ product.count * product.salePrice | currency }}
            </mat-list-item>
            <mat-divider></mat-divider>
            <h3 mat-subheader>
                Sub Total:    <b><!-- Sub Total Placeholder-
                -></b>
            </h3>
        </mat-list>
    </div>
</ng-container>
```

Finally, to show the subtotal of all the products in the cart, we will create a pipe, to which we will pass the cart and get back the subtotal:

```
> ng g p sub-total
```

Let's add the transformation logic for the pipe in the `transform` method of the pipe:

```typescript
import { Pipe, PipeTransform, Injector } from '@angular/core';

@Pipe({
    name: 'subTotal'
})
export class SubTotalPipe implements PipeTransform {
    currencyPipe;

    constructor() {
    }

    transform(cart): any {
        let total = 0;
        Object.values(cart).forEach((product: any) => {
            if (product.count) {
                total += product.count * product.salePrice;
            }
        });
        return total;
    }
}
```

Now, let's use the pipe in the placeholder of our `cart.component.html` to get a subtotal:

```html
<h3 mat-subheader>
    Sub Total:    <b>{{ cart | subTotal | currency }}</b>
</h3>
```

Now, when you add the products and click on the cart in the navigation bar, you should see the following output:

```
Cart

Black Headphones          1                    ▾ $99.99
$99.99

Gaming Keyboard           3                    ▾ $89.97
$29.99

Sub Total:  $189.96
```

This is our simple e-commerce app, where we can view our products and add items to the cart. Before we go ahead and convert our application into a complete PWA with offline and home screen support, we will audit our application so that we can compare the beginning and end of our audit at each step.

Now, we'll learn how we can audit our application using Lighthouse and check whether it meets all our requirements so that it can become a PWA.

Auditing our application

Auditing an application is an important aspect when you develop your application. Whenever you want to improve performance, security, accessibility, or even the Progressive Web App itself, we need to audit our application and see how we can improve it.

To audit our application for PWA, we will be using Lighthouse, which is an open-source project that's used to improve the quality of the application. Lighthouse is built into the Chrome browser; to get to it, we need to open the developer tools. We can do this by right-clicking **Inspect** or using *command + option + I* on macOS and *Ctrl + Shift + I* on Windows. Afterward, we need to go to the **Audits** tab in developer tools, as follows:

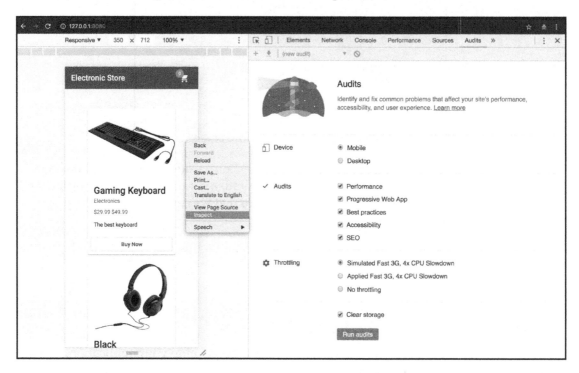

Before we run the Lighthouse audit, we need to build our application using a production setting, and also make sure that we run it in incognito mode (so that no browser extension makes our web page slower).

To build our application with the `prod` setting, run the following command:

```
> ng build --prod
```

Then, go to the `dist/electronic-store` folder and run your local server. We will be using `http-server`:

```
> http-server
```

Let's open the application in incognito mode and run the audits:

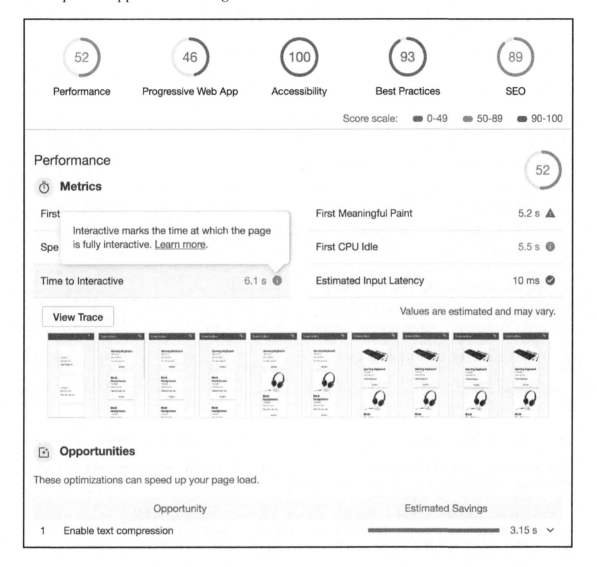

We will see that our application gets a score of **46** for **Progressive Web app**. To see how that score was calculated, just click on the **Progressive Web App** score; this will take you to the audit result for the PWA:

Progressive Web App   46

These checks validate the aspects of a Progressive Web App, as specified by the baseline PWA Checklist.

1   Does not respond with a 200 when offline   ⚠ ⌄

2   User will not be prompted to Install the Web App   ⚠ ⌄
     Failures: No manifest was fetched, Site does not register a service worker.

3   Does not redirect HTTP traffic to HTTPS   ⚠ ⌄

4   Does not register a service worker   ⚠ ⌄

5   Does not provide fallback content when JavaScript is not available   ⚠ ⌄
     The page body should render some content if its scripts are not available.

6   Is not configured for a custom splash screen   ⚠ ⌄
     Failures: No manifest was fetched.

7   Address bar does not match brand colors   ⚠ ⌄
     Failures: No manifest was fetched, No `<meta name="theme-color">` tag found.

🔍   **Additional items to manually check**   3 audits   ⌄

✓   **Passed audits**   4 audits   ⌄

⊖   **Not applicable**   1 audits   ⌄

The goal of this chapter is to get the score for the PWA to 100. We will address each of the checks in the following section and resolve them.

In this section, we have learned how to audit our application using Lighthouse and follow recommendations for best practices in various categories. In the next section, we will add an Angular service worker to our application using Angular schematics.

Adding PWA capability

We will be using an Angular service worker to add the service worker to our application. The Angular team has made it simpler to add PWA capability to our application. This is done by using the `ng add` command:

```
> ng add @angular/pwa
```

This command will add/update the following files:

```
CREATE ngsw-config.json (511 bytes)
CREATE src/manifest.json (1089 bytes)
CREATE src/assets/icons/icon-128x128.png (1253 bytes)
CREATE src/assets/icons/icon-144x144.png (1394 bytes)
CREATE src/assets/icons/icon-152x152.png (1427 bytes)
CREATE src/assets/icons/icon-192x192.png (1790 bytes)
CREATE src/assets/icons/icon-384x384.png (3557 bytes)
CREATE src/assets/icons/icon-512x512.png (5008 bytes)
CREATE src/assets/icons/icon-72x72.png (792 bytes)
CREATE src/assets/icons/icon-96x96.png (958 bytes)
UPDATE angular.json (4167 bytes)
UPDATE package.json (1475 bytes)
UPDATE src/app/app.module.ts (1496 bytes)
UPDATE src/index.html (656 bytes)
```

The `manifest.json` file is used by browsers to gather details about the application, such as its name, short name, assets, and so on. `ngsw-config.json` is the file that's used by the Angular service worker to get details about which files need to be cached and prefetched.

Let's look at what we see by default in our `ngsw-config.json` file:

```
{
    "index": "/index.html",
    "assetGroups": [
        {
            "name": "app",
            "installMode": "prefetch",
            "resources": {
                "files": [
                    "/favicon.ico",
                    "/index.html",
                    "/*.css",
                    "/*.js"
                ]
            }
        }, {
            "name": "assets",
```

```
            "installMode": "lazy",
            "updateMode": "prefetch",
            "resources": {
                "files": [
                    "/assets/**",
                    "/*.
            (eot|svg|cur|jpg|png|webp|gif|otf|ttf|woff|woff2|ani)"
                ]
            }
        }
    ]
}
```

The `assetGroups` property has different groups of assets. Here, we have two groups by default: app and assets. The app group has all the essential files for the application, while the asset group contains all the files that are in the assets folder.

The `manifest.json` file contains the following information. You will need to update the icons and other related information about your application here:

```
{
    "name": "electronic-store",
    "short_name": "electronic-store",
    "theme_color": "#1976d2",
    "background_color": "#fafafa",
    "display": "standalone",
    "scope": "/",
    "start_url": "/",
    "icons": [
        {
            "src": "assets/icons/icon-72x72.png",
            "sizes": "72x72",
            "type": "image/png"
        },
        ...
    ]
}
```

It also adds the `ServiceWorkerModule` to `AppModule`. We only enable it for production builds so that we don't cache the assets while we are developing:

```
import { ServiceWorkerModule } from '@angular/service-worker';
import { environment } from '../environments/environment';
@NgModule({
    ...
imports: [
...
```

```
            ServiceWorkerModule.register('ngsw-worker.js', { enabled:
            environment.production })
        ],
        ...
    })
    export class AppModule { }
```

`index.html` adds the link to `manifest.json` and adds a `meta` tag for theme-color, as well as a `noscript` element. The `noscript` element is shown to the user if JavaScript is disabled. Safari on iOS does not use `manifest.json`; instead, it uses `meta` tags so that we can modify how it needs to be added to the home screen on iOS. Let's add the following `meta` tags, all of which iOS understands:

```html
<!doctype html>
<html lang="en">
<head>
    <meta charset="utf-8">
    <title>Electronic Store</title>
    <base href="/">
    <meta name="viewport" content="width=device-width, initial-scale=1">
    <link rel="manifest" href="manifest.json">
    <meta name="theme-color" content="#1976d2">

    <!-- meta tags for iOS PWA -->
    <meta name="apple-mobile-web-app-capable" content="yes">
    <meta name="apple-mobile-web-app-title" content="ElectronicStore">
    <meta name="apple-mobile-web-app-status-bar-style" content="black-
      translucent">
    <meta name="apple-touch-icon" content="assets/icons/icon-144x144.png"
      sizes="180x180">
    <meta name="apple-touch-icon" content="assets/icons/icon-96x96.png"
      sizes="120x120"></head>

<body>
    <es-root></es-root>
    <noscript>Please enable JavaScript to continue using this
      application.</noscript>
</body>
</html>
```

Now, let's build our application using production mode and serve it using `http-server` before auditing our application again:

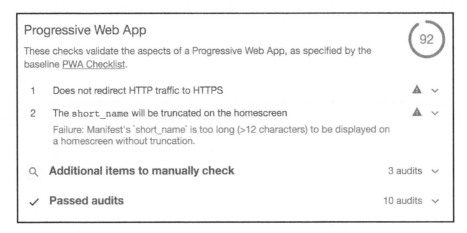

Now, the score has increased to **92**. We've increased from **46** to **92**, which is a great improvement. Now, the only two checks that remain are using **HTTPS** and reducing the characters in **short_name** in our `manifest.json` file. Let's go ahead and update the **short_name** to just `es` instead of electronic-store:

```
{
    ...
    "short_name": "es",
    ...
}
```

In this section, we have added an Angular service worker to our application and re-measured our PWA-ness using Lighthouse. The only checkpoint that's left to make our app score 100% in PWA is using HTTPS instead of HTTP. We can score this when we deploy our app on a server and use HTTPS, for which we will use Firebase. Now, let's dive into adding other capabilities to our PWA.

Offline support

Now, let's manually check our application by switching our network to offline mode and seeing if we can still access the application. We can switch to offline mode using our developer tools. In Chrome's DevTools, go to the **Network** tab and select **Offline** mode:

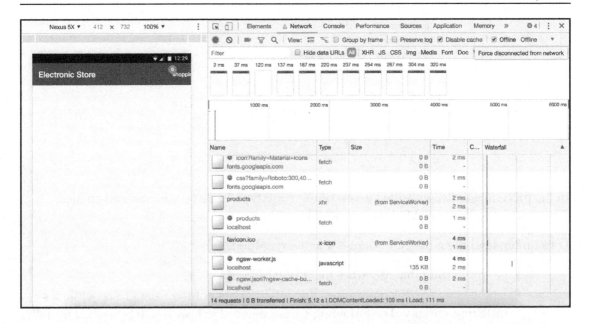

We can see that our application does not show the products and that the cart icon shows **shopping_cart** instead. This has happened because we did not add any caching mechanisms for those calls in our `ngsw-config.json` file. Let's go ahead with the code in `ngsw-config.json`, as follows:

```
{
    "index": "/index.html",
    "assetGroups": [
        ...
        }, {
            "name": "fonts",
            "installMode": "lazy",
            "updateMode": "prefetch",
            "resources": {
                "urls": [
                    "https://fonts.googleapis.com/**",
                    "https://fonts.gstatic.com/**"
                ]
            }
        }
    ],
    "dataGroups": [
        {
            "name": "api",
            "version": 1,
            "cacheConfig": {
```

```
                    "maxAge": "3d",
                    "maxSize": 50,
                    "strategy": "freshness",
                    "timeout": 1000
                },
                "urls": [
                    "http://localhost:3000/**"
                ]
            }
        ]
    }
```

In the preceding code, we added assets of the `font` type to `assetGroups` and created `dataGroups` so that our APIs can be cached.

Let's understand the new `assetGroup` that we've added:

- `name`: A string that identifies the group of assets.
- `installMode`: This determines the initial caching of the asset group while it's installing initially. The following values determine how it will be cached initially:
  - `prefetch`: Caches all the listed resources before they are requested by the browser
  - `lazy`: Caches when the service worker receives a request for the resource
- `updateMode`: Determines the caching behavior when a new version of the application is discovered. The following values determine how it will be cached while updating:
  - `prefetch`
  - `lazy`
- `resources`: Identifies the resources to be cached. It can be divided into two groups:
  - `files`: List of files in the distribution directory
  - `urls`: List of URLs or URL patterns that will be matched at runtime

We also need to understand the `dataGroup` that we added in the preceding code block:

- `name`: A string that identifies the group of assets.
- `version`: When the APIs change drastically and are not backward compatible, this version number determines whether the cached APIs should be discarded.

- `cacheConfig`: Defines the policy for caching requests:
  - `maxAge`: The maximum age the resources are to be cached that match the resources.
  - `maxSize`: The maximum number of resources to be cached that match the resources.
  - `strategy`: Can be either of the following two caching strategies.
    - `performance`: Uses the cached version first and, depending on `maxAge`, a new request is made for caching.
    - `freshness`: The network first strategy. It tries to get the fresh request from the server first; if it takes more than the timeout, then it gets the data from the cache.
  - `timeout`: Specifies the network timeout.
- `urls`: List of URLs or URL patterns that will be matched at runtime.

Now, let's build our application again and check what happens in offline mode. As in the following screenshot, we can now see the products and icons when our application is offline. Make sure that you refresh your browser twice so that our service worker is updated:

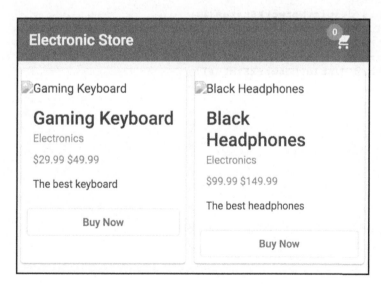

We can see that the products are loaded and that the icon font in the navigation bar is being displayed. The only thing that's missing is the product images.

Showing network changes

Whenever the network goes offline, we need to tell our users, and also tell them that some capabilities might not work when the network is offline. Let's add a listener for online and offline, and then update the body element's style by adding some `grayscale` to our application when it's offline:

```
import { Component, OnInit } from '@angular/core';
...
export class AppComponent implements OnInit {
    ...
    displayNetworkStatus() {
        if (navigator.onLine) {
            document.querySelector('body').style.filter = '';
        } else {
            document.querySelector('body').style.filter = 'grayscale(1)';
        }
    }

    ngOnInit() {
        this.displayNetworkStatus();
        window.addEventListener('online',
         this.displayNetworkStatus);
        window.addEventListener('offline',
         this.displayNetworkStatus);
    }
}
```

Now, if the network goes into offline mode, you should see the web page go into grayscale format:

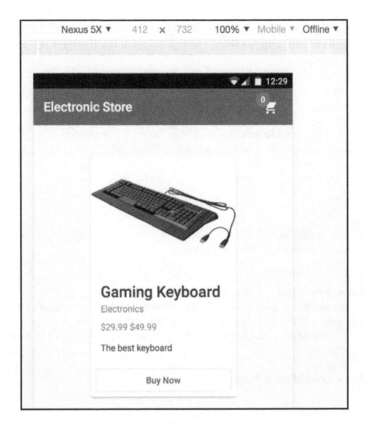

You can also create an `Observable` that updates the network status. This can be subscribed to in various places within the application in order to enable and disable various features based on the network status. This is done so that the user has a seamless experience of our application, irrespective of the network status. In the next section, we'll see how we can update the application when the application is cached by using a service worker on our user's machines.

Prompting for new updates

Now, let's show a notification by using Material Snackbar. This will happen whenever a new version of our service worker is worked. We want our users to be notified about any updates that are made to our app so they are not stuck with the cached version even after we push an update.

We will use `SwUpdate` and subscribe to the `update.available` observable. When we get an event for a new version, we will activate the update and reload it:

```
import { MatDialog, MatSnackBar } from '@angular/material';
import { SwUpdate } from '@angular/service-worker';
...
export class AppComponent implements OnInit {
    ...
    constructor(
        ...,
        update: SwUpdate,
        private snackBar: MatSnackBar,
    ) {
        ...
        update.available.subscribe(event => {
        this.snackBar.open('New Update available', 'Install Now', {
        duration: 4000 }).onAction().subscribe(() => {
                update.activateUpdate().then(() => location.reload());
            });
        });
        update.checkForUpdate();
    }

    ...
}
```

Now, when you update something in the application and refresh, you should see that a notification appears at the bottom so that the user is prompted to update the application:

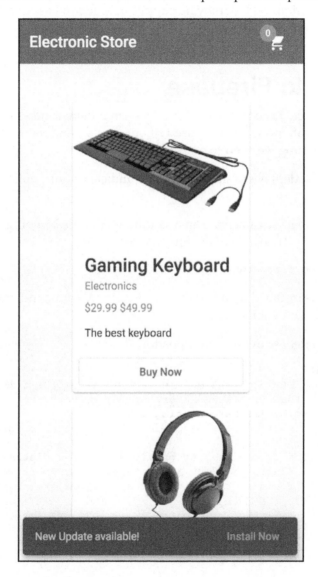

By showing an in-app notification, we can make sure that users always get an updated version of the application, even though our application was cached using the service worker. In the next section, we'll deploy our application to Firebase and audit our application using Lighthouse.

Deploying to Firebase

PWAs should always be protected using HTTPS, even if there is no sensitive communication. Up until now, we have used http-server and increased the Lighthouse score to 92. The only thing we need to do is move to HTTPS.

In this section, we will deploy our app to Firebase and check our application's score over HTTPS.

First, let's make sure that we can create an account on Firebase by going to https:// firebase.google.com/. Then, install the Firebase tools using npm:

```
> npm install -g firebase-tools
```

Verify that Firebase is installed by using the firebase -V command, which will return the version that's installed on your system.

Now, let's initialize Firebase in our root repository:

```
> firebase init
? Which Firebase CLI features do you want to setup for this folder? Press
Space to select features, then Enter to confirm your choices. Hosting:
Configure and deploy Firebase Hosting sites
? Select a default Firebase project for this directory: [create a new
project]
? What do you want to use as your public directory? dist/electronic-store
? Configure as a single-page app (rewrite all urls to /index.html)? No
? File dist/electronic-store/index.html already exists. Overwrite? No
```

Now, let's go to the Firebase console, `https://console.firebase.google.com/`, and add a new project, let's name it `electronic-store`, you will see a unique project ID, such as in the image below `electronic-store-41e9f`, click **Continue**, and select **Not at the moment** for Google Analytics and then click **Create Project**:

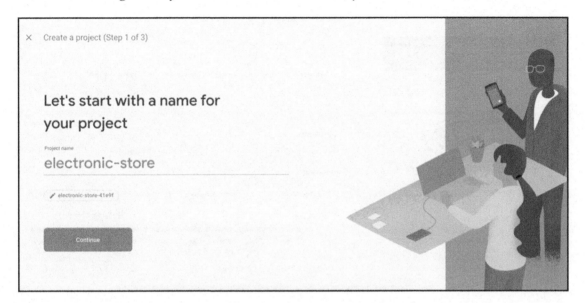

We will be using the project ID while deploying our application.

Now, let's log in to Firebase in our Terminal by using the `firebase login` command. Then, we will deploy our application using the following command:

```
> firebase deploy --project electronic-store-41e9f
```

Once the command completes, you should see the hosting URL where you can access the website. Now, let's open the website in incognito mode and run our Lighthouse audit again:

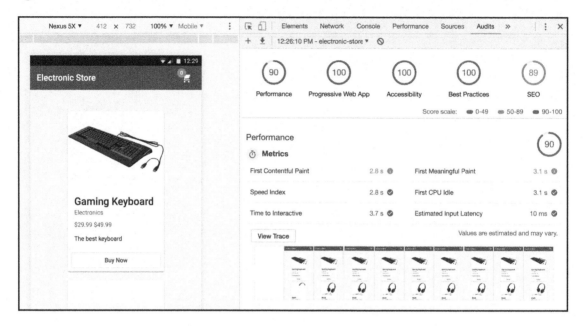

We can see that we have a perfect score of **100** for **Progressive Web App**. We can also observe that the score for performance has increased from our last run.

Summary

In this chapter, we created a simple e-commerce Angular app that used Nest.js to get products from MongoDB. Then, we added a service worker to make the app work offline. This also allows us to add the app to our home screen so that we can use it as a standalone application. In the end, we found ways to update our application whenever a new version of the service worker is available and able to install a new version.

Now, you should be able to convert any Angular web application into a Progressive Web Application and understand various configurations to make it work offline. You will have also learned how to improve app experience by using different strategies, such as showing the network's status, updating to a new version of apps using in-app notifications, and so on.

In the next chapter, we will create a native mobile app for iOS and Android by using the Ionic Framework alongside Angular. We will create an application to audit apartments and use the Firebase Realtime Database to save the updates to the audit in real time. Finally, we will use `ngx-formly` to create dynamic forms without the need to write a template to do so.

Questions

Test your knowledge of this chapter by answering the following questions:

- What are the benefits of a Progressive Web App?
- What is a service worker?
- How do you add PWA support to an existing Angular CLI application?
- What tools do you use to analyze PWAs?
- How do you listen to a network status change in a browser?
- Why is HTTPS important for PWAs?
- What is the importance of the `manifest.json` file?
- What is in the `ngsw-config.json` file?

Further reading

The following reading material will provide you with more information about Nest.js, Angular Material, Angular service workers, and PWAs:

- Nest.js docs: `https://nestjs.com/`.
- Angular Material docs: `https://material.angular.io/`.
- Introduction to Angular service workers: `https://angular.io/guide/service-worker-intro`.
- Get started with Angular service workers: `https://angular.io/guide/service-worker-getting-started`.
- Service worker configuration: `https://angular.io/guide/service-worker-config`.

6
Building an Auditing Application Using Angular and Ionic

In this chapter, we will be using the Firebase Realtime Database to create a Native application that runs on iOS and Android. This will use the Ionic 4 framework. We will also be using `ngx-formly` in order to create a dynamic form without having to write an HTML code for the whole form.

The following topics will be covered in this chapter:

- Exploring the Ionic framework
- Getting started with the Ionic CLI
- Theming an Ionic application
- Setting up Firebase
- Getting data from the Firebase Realtime Database
- Creating dynamic forms using `ngx-formly`
- Using Ionic Native so that we can use a camera

Technical requirements

This chapter's code can be found in this book's GitHub repository, `https://github.com/PacktPublishing/Angular-Projects`, in the `Chapter06` folder.

The code has been provided for you so that whenever you are stuck, you can verify whether you've done something different and play with the working project in the repository.

We want you to follow the sections in this chapter in the order in which they appear and learn as much as you can about different aspects of Angular development.

Exploring the Ionic framework

The Ionic framework is an open source mobile UI toolkit that's used to develop high-quality applications that can be used across different platforms using just one code base. It's primarily used to create Native mobile apps for iOS and Android, but it can also be used on the web as a **Progressive Web App (PWA)**.

In this chapter, we will be using Ionic 4, which is a complete rewrite of the framework. Instead of using Angular to build components, we are going to use a library called Stencil, which converts Stencil components into web components.

Some of the unique features of the Ionic framework are as follows:

- It allows for the easy installation and creation of Ionic apps.
- It uses a web platform, so you don't have to worry about maintaining multiple applications for different platforms.
- Ionic 4 components are built using web components. This means that Ionic 4 is framework-agnostic, that is, it can be used with any UI framework/library, such as Angular, React, Vue, and so on.
- Applications look and feel Native to the specific platform. The components, the navigation system, and other essential items for the platform adapt to different platforms.
- It comes with PWA capability out of the box.
- It has good theming support, which it does by using CSS variables.
- It uses a set of Native APIs that use Cordova plugins to get different device capabilities, such as camera functionality, Bluetooth, and so on.

The following is an example of what an Ionic alert looks like on iOS and Android. It adapts the components to the platform it runs in:

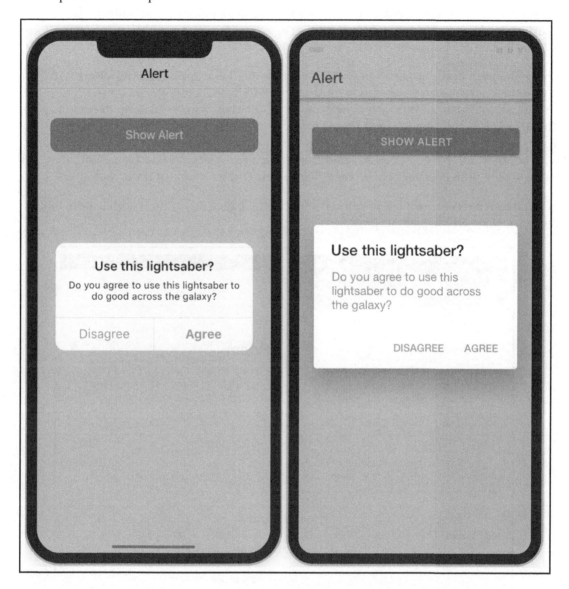

All of these features are what make the Ionic framework one of the widely used frameworks for developing mobile applications. Now that we have seen what Ionic is capable of, we'll look at what we are going to build in this chapter using the Ionic application.

Project overview

In this chapter, we will be creating a Native application so that we can audit/inspect apartments. The people who will be auditing apartments will get real-time updates about the audits that are happening in the apartments.

The home page of the application will have all the available appointments, along with information about each appointment and whether they are complete, incomplete, or if the auditing hasn't started. If the user clicks on the audit, they will be taken to the details page. The details page will contain a dynamic form based on the rooms in that particular apartment. For each room, the auditor will have items to check so that the user can specify whether they are in a good or bad condition. If the user selects **In Bad Condition**, they will be presented with another field so that they can enter the reason for their choice.

In the following screenshot, you can see a few of the pages of our final application, that is, the home page and the details page:

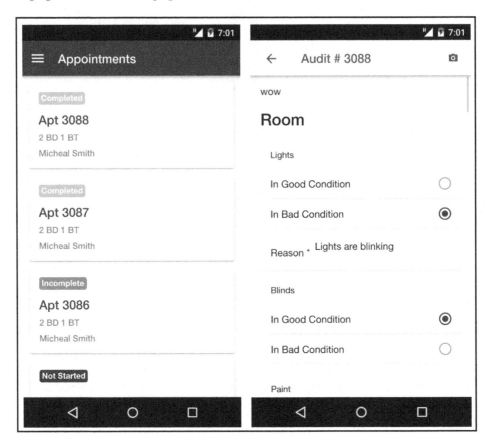

Now that we understand what we are going to develop, we will install the Ionic CLI and scaffold an application with it.

Getting started with the Ionic CLI

The Ionic framework uses the Ionic CLI as its preferred way of creating Ionic applications. This provides a lot of different tools for creating great Ionic applications. Use the following command to install the Ionic CLI globally:

```
> npm install -g ionic
```

The Ionic CLI provides the three most common starters: blank, menu, and side menu. We will be using the sidebar starter for this project as it provides a side menu navigation for us.

Use the `ionic start` command and name our application `apartment-auditing`. Then, choose `sidemenu` as our starter template, like so:

```
> ionic start apartment-auditing sidemenu
? Install the free Ionic Appflow SDK and connect your app? No
```

Now, enter a name for the folder, `apartment-auditing`, and serve the application using the following command, which will open the application in your browser using Ionic Lab:

```
> cd apartment-auditing
> ionic serve --lab
? Install @ionic/lab? Yes
```

This will open Ionic Lab in your browser after the build is complete:

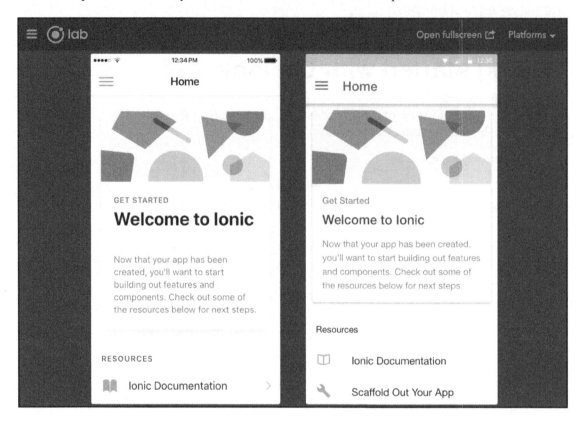

The Ionic framework provides an application called Ionic DevApp, which is available on both iOS and Android. When your phone and the system where you served the Ionic app are on the same Wi-Fi, you will see it as available in the Ionic DevApp, which you can access and run the application on.

Now that we have successfully served the Ionic application, we will start customizing the theme of the Ionic application.

Theming the Ionic application

Being able to easily customize the theme of a component library is one of the important factors when it comes to the adoption of a component library. Ionic not only makes it easy to customize—it also provides tools to make the process much simpler.

Ionic uses CSS variables to theme the application. It also provides a Color Generator tool (`https://ionicframework.com/docs/theming/color-generator`), which can be used to customize the application.

Let's change the **Primary** color to #002544 in the **Color Generator** tool, as shown in the following screenshot:

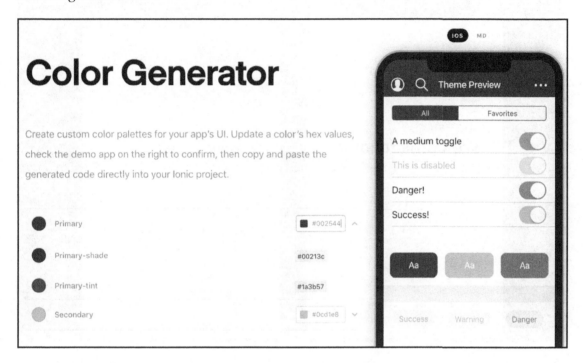

Now, scroll down and copy the CSS variables that were produced by this application and paste them into the `src/theme/variables.scss` file.

Let's go ahead and use the `primary` color for the toolbar on our home page, in the `home.component.html` file:

```
<ion-header>
    <ion-toolbar color="primary">
        ...
    </ion-toolbar>
</ion-header>
```

The toolbar will be updated with the color we selected in the Color Generator tool:

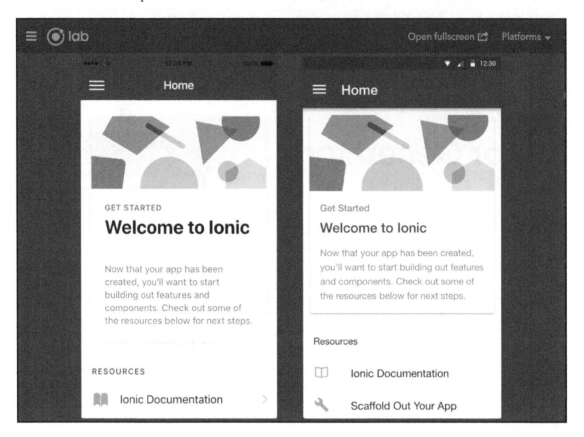

Using simple CSS variables, the Ionic theme can be customized, with or without the Color Generator tool that's provided by Ionic. Now that we have set up our theme, let's set up Firebase. We will use this as part of the Realtime Database for our Ionic application.

Setting up Firebase

Firebase is a mobile and web application development platform that was acquired by Google in 2014. It's well-known for its **Backend as a Service (BaaS)** feature, sometimes known as **Database as a Service (DBaaS)**, due to its Realtime Database, an API that synchronizes data across the web, iOS, and Android devices. In this section, we will add a new project to the Firebase console and connect the Realtime Database to our application using AngularFire.

To set up Firebase, follow these steps:

1. First, go to the Firebase console (`https://console.firebase.google.com`) and click on **Add project**.
2. Give the project a **Project name**, click **Continue**, and select **Not at the moment** for Google Analytics, and click on **Continue**:

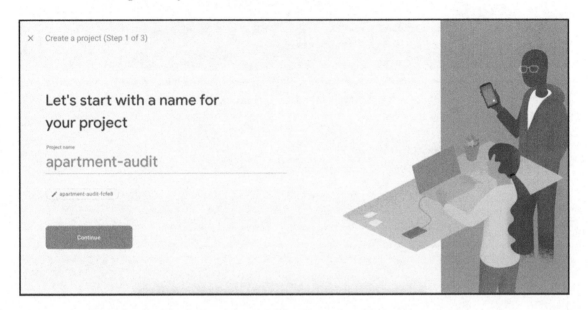

3. Next, we'll create a Realtime Database and import some data that we will use for our application.

4. Click on **Database** from the navigation bar and click on **Create database**. Make sure you select **Start in test mode** which will give anyone read-write access. Click **Next**, and select any location, then click **Done**:

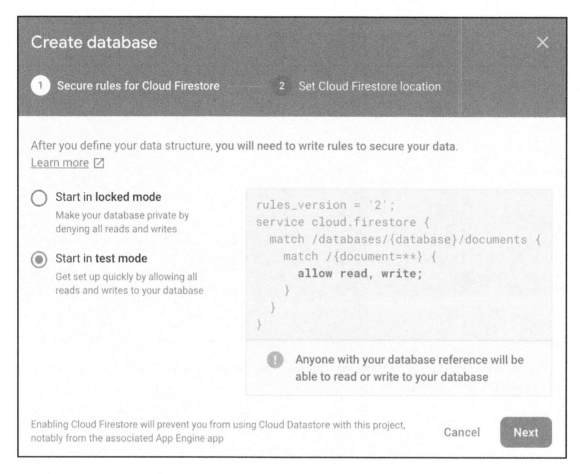

5. For a production app, you should add some authentication and security rules.

6. Next, go to **Realtime Database** instead of **Cloud Firestore**:

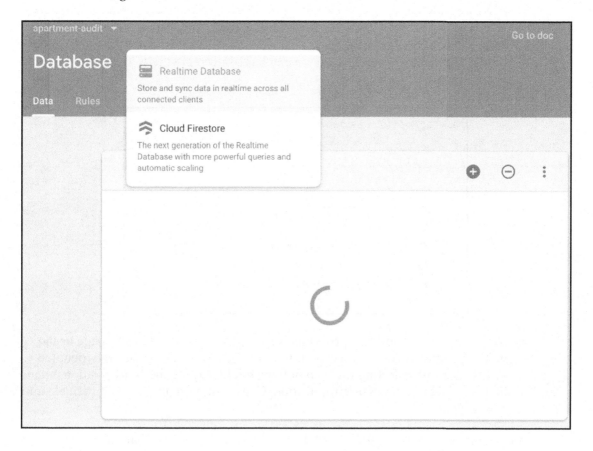

7. Use the three dots on the right-hand side and click on **Import JSON**. Use the JSON provided in `Chapter06` of the project documentation, which can be found at `https://github.com/PacktPublishing/Angular-Projects/blob/master/Chapter06/apartment-auditing/auditing.json`. Once you've uploaded it, you should see that an `appointments` array has been created with five different appointments:

8. Next, you need to add an app, which you can do from the project's page or the project's settings. You will see an option for iOS, Android, or the web (denoted by the </> icon). Selecting the web option should display the configuration details that we will be using in our application. Copy and paste the `config` variable into our `AppModule`.

In our application, we need to install `@angular/fire` and `firebase` from `npm`:

```
> npm install -save firebase @angular/fire
```

Let's configure `AngularFireModule` with the `config` details in `AppModule`:

```
...
import { AngularFireModule } from '@angular/fire';
import { AngularFireDatabaseModule } from '@angular/fire/database';

const config = {
    apiKey: '---YOUR--CONFIG---',
    authDomain: '---YOUR--CONFIG---',
    databaseURL: '---YOUR--CONFIG---',
    projectId: '---YOUR--CONFIG---',
    storageBucket: '---YOUR--CONFIG---',
    messagingSenderId: '---YOUR--CONFIG---'
```

```
};

@NgModule({
    ...
    imports: [
        ...
        AngularFireModule.initializeApp(config),
        AngularFireDatabaseModule,
    ],
    ...
})
export class AppModule {}
```

Make sure that you set the `config` variable with the configurations that you got from the Firebase console.

We've successfully configured the application with the Firebase project. Now, we should be able to communicate with Firebase, which we will look at in the next section.

Getting data from the Firebase Realtime Database

Before we get data from the Firebase Realtime Database that we set up, let's do some refactoring. Here, we will remove the list route from our application. For that, we need to delete the `list` folder, remove the route from `AppRoutingModule`, and remove the list route from the `appPages` of `AppComponent`, as well as change the home routes title to `Appointments`.

Now, use the `AngularFireDatabase` list method to gather appointments and use `snapshotChanges` as an observable to gather data. We will use a `map` pipe to format the data that we get from Firebase in order to set the label, color, and a string to display the total number of rooms and bathrooms. We are using `snapshotChanges` here because we need the keys for our appointments. If we had used `valueChanges`, we wouldn't have received the keys for the objects.

First, let's add a helper function so that we can get the label and color based on the status, as well as a reducer function so that we can calculate the number of beds and baths in the `HomePage` component, as follows:

```
...
function statusLabel(status) {
    return status === 'incomplete' ? 'Incomplete' : status === 'complete' ?
     'Complete' : 'Not Started';
}

function statusColor(status) {
    return status ==='incomplete' ? 'danger' : status === 'complete' ?
      'success' : 'primary';
}

function bedsAndBathsCalc(acc, curr) {
    if (curr.type === 'room') {
        acc.beds += 1;
    }

    if (curr.type === 'bath') {
        acc.baths += 1;
    }
    return acc;
}
...
```

Let's get the collection of items and transform the response. Afterward, we will calculate the number of bedrooms and bathrooms to display, as shown in the following code:

```
import { Component } from '@angular/core';
import { AngularFireDatabase, AngularFireList } from
'@angular/fire/database';
import { map } from 'rxjs/operators';
import { IAppointment } from '../appointment.model';
import { Observable } from 'rxjs';

...
export class HomePage {
    itemRef: AngularFireList<IAppointment>;
    appointments$: Observable<IAppointment[]>;

    constructor(private database: AngularFireDatabase) {
        this.itemRef = this.database.list('/appointments');
        this.appointments$ = this.itemRef.snapshotChanges().pipe(
            map((res) => {
                return res.map(value => {
                    const appointment: IAppointment = value.payload.val();
```

```
              const count = appointment.units.reduce(bedsAndBathCalc,
                { beds: 0, baths: 0 });
              const label = statusLabel(appointment.status);
              const color = statusColor(appointment.status);
              const roomsAndBaths = `${count.beds} BD ${count.baths}
                BT`;

              return {
                  ...appointment,
                  key: value.key,
                  label,
                  color,
                  roomsAndBaths,
              };
          });
        }),
      );
    }
}
```

Let's use the Ionic card component and Ionic badge component to display the appointment details on our home page. We will use the `async` pipe on the appointments observable that we got by using `snapshotChanges`:

```html
<ion-header>
    <ion-toolbar color="primary">
        ...
        <ion-title>
            Appointments
        </ion-title>
    </ion-toolbar>
</ion-header>
<ion-content>
    <ion-card class="welcome-card" *ngFor="let appointment of appointments$
      | async">
        <ion-card-header>
            <ion-badge class="card-end" [attr.color]="appointment.color">
                {{appointment.label}}</ion-badge>
            <ion-card-title>Apt {{appointment.number}}</ion-card-title>
            <ion-card-subtitle>{{appointment.roomsAndBaths}}</ion-card-
                subtitle>
            <ion-card-subtitle>{{appointment.assignedTo}}</ion-card-
                subtitle>
        </ion-card-header>
    </ion-card>
</ion-content>
```

You should see that the cards have been populated with all of this information, as shown in the following screenshot:

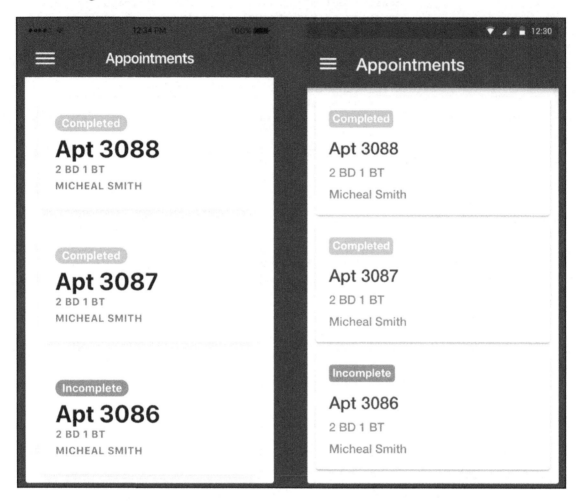

Now that we have our **Appointments** page set up, let's go ahead and create the page for when we wish to view a single appointment. We will call this page `audit`:

```
> ionic generate page audit
```

Let's modify the path that was created to also include the key that we will pass from our Appointments page:

```
{ path: 'audit/:key', loadChildren: './audit/audit.module#AuditPageModule'
}
```

Let's use `routerLink` to go to our audit page:

```
<ion-content>
    <ion-card class="welcome-card" [routerLink]="['/audit',
      appointment.key]" *ngFor="let appointment of appointments$ | async">
        ...
    </ion-card>
</ion-content>
```

Now, when you click on the appointment, you should see that it goes to a new page with the **audit** as the title of the header. Let's add a back button to our `start` slot in the toolbar:

```
<ion-header>
    <ion-toolbar>
        <ion-buttons slot="start">
            <ion-back-button></ion-back-button>
        </ion-buttons>
        <ion-title>audit</ion-title>
    </ion-toolbar>
</ion-header>
...
```

Now, let's use the `object` method of `AngularFireDatabase` to get a particular appointment and use `valueChanges` to view the `appointment` object in the console:

```
import { Component, OnInit } from '@angular/core';
import { AngularFireDatabase, AngularFireObject } from
'@angular/fire/database';
import { ActivatedRoute } from '@angular/router';
import { IAppointment } from '../appointment.model';

...
export class AuditPage implements OnInit {
    itemRef: AngularFireObject<IAppointment>;

    constructor(private db: AngularFireDatabase, private route:
      ActivatedRoute) {
        const params = this.route.snapshot.params;
        this.itemRef = this.db.object<IAppointment>
            (`/appointments/${params.key}`);

        this.itemRef.valueChanges().subscribe(appointment => {
```

```
            console.log(appointment);
        });
    }
    ...
}
```

Now that we are on the `AuditPage` with the data for the appointment, we need to create our dynamic form by installing and using `ngx-formly`.

Creating dynamic forms using ngx-formly

Now that we can get to the audit page and get the appointment data, let's set up the form so that we can audit the appointment. Since our appointments can have different units, and we need to inspect different things in each unit type, it would be best to use some type of dynamic form. `ngx-formly` makes dynamic forms simpler and takes away all the setup with a simple API. By using `ngx-formly`, you can set up different field types and reuse the template in your dynamic forms throughout the whole application.

`ngx-formly` supports different UI libraries, such as Bootstrap, Angular Material, Ionic, NativeScript, Kendo UI, PrimeNG, and others. The configuration for the `ngx-formly` field can do a lot of different things. You can find various examples at `https://ngx-formly.github.io/ngx-formly/examples`.

Let's use the schematics for `ng add` to add `ngx-formly` to our project. We'll be using `ionic` as the `ui-theme`:

```
> ng add @ngx-formly/schematics --ui-theme=ionic
```

Since we are using lazy loaded routes, we need to make sure that the reusable modules that are included by the `ng add` command are added to `SharedModule`. Let's create a `shared` module using the following Angular CLI command:

```
> ng g m shared
```

Now, we need to remove `FormlyModule`, `Formly IonicModule`, and `ReactiveFormsModule` from `AppModule` and add them to `SharedModule`:

```
import { NgModule } from '@angular/core';
import { CommonModule } from '@angular/common';
import { FormlyModule } from '@ngx-formly/core';
import { FormlyIonicModule } from '@ngx-formly/ionic';
import { ReactiveFormsModule } from '@angular/forms';

@NgModule({
    declarations: [],
    imports: [
        CommonModule,
        ReactiveFormsModule,
        FormlyModule.forRoot(),
        FormlyIonicModule
    ],
    exports: [
        ReactiveFormsModule,
        FormlyModule,
        FormlyIonicModule
    ]
})
export class SharedModule { }
```

By doing this, we can add `SharedModule` to our page modules, `AuditModule` and `HomeModule`.

Now, let's use the `formly-form` component and pass `model`, `fields`, `options`, and `form` to it:

```
<ion-content padding>
    <form [formGroup]="form">
        <formly-form [model]="model" [fields]="fields" [options]="options"
          [form]="form">
        </formly-form>
        <ion-button shape="round" (click)="submit()" expand="full"
          color="primary">
            Save
        </ion-button>
    </form>
</ion-content>
```

Let's initialize `form` as a `FormGroup` object, `model` and `options` as empty objects, and `fields` as an array with one object. The object type defines what type of field is going to be used. In this case, we want the field to be an input field. The key in the object defines where the value of the field is in the model. The label can be passed to the `templateOptions` of the field:

```
...
import { FormGroup } from '@angular/forms';
import { FormlyFieldConfig, FormlyFormOptions } from '@ngx-formly/core';
...

export class AuditPage implements OnInit {
    ...
    form = new FormGroup({});
    options: FormlyFormOptions = {};
    model = {};
    fields: FormlyFieldConfig[] = [{
        type: 'input',
        key: 'name',
        templateOptions: {
            label: 'Name'
        }
    }];
    ...
}
```

Now, you should be able to see one field on the **audit** page:

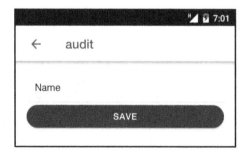

Let's replace the console in our `valueChanges` subscription and dynamically create the fields before assigning them to the `fields` array and assigning the appointment to the model.

Let's add a function that returns a `FormlyFieldConfig` array of two items: one that has radio options for the good and bad condition of an item, and another so that the user can state why the item is bad. We will add this to our `AuditPage` component class, at the top:

```
const getFields = (id: number, key: string): FormlyFieldConfig[] => {
    const label = startCase(key);
    return [{
        key: `units.${id}.${key}`,
        type: 'radio',
        templateOptions: {
            label,
            options: [{
                value: 'good', label: 'In Good Condition'
            }, {
                value: 'bad', label: 'In Bad Condition'
            }]
        }
    }, {
        key: `units.${id}.${key}Reason`,
        type: 'textarea',
        templateOptions: {
            label: 'Reason',
            placeholder: `Reason for bad condition of ${label}`
        }
    }];
};
```

Now, we'll use the `getFields` function to get all the formly fields configurations. We can do this by using `UNIT_KEYS`:

```
...
import startCase from 'lodash-es/startCase';

const UNIT_KEYS = {
    'room': ['lights', 'blinds', 'paint', 'carpet', 'door', 'alarm'],
    'kitchen': ['sink', 'stove', 'microwave', 'fridge'],
    'bath': ['lights', 'paint', 'floor', 'door', 'knobs'],
    'hall': ['lights', 'paint', 'carpet', 'door'],
    'patio': ['clean']
};

const getUnitFields = (type: string, id: number): FormlyFieldConfig[] => {
    return [
```

```
        {
            template: `<h1>${startCase(type)}</h1>`,
        },
        ...UNIT_KEYS[type].flatMap(unitKey => {
            return getFields(id, unitKey);
        })
    ];
};


...
class AuditPage implements OnInit {
    constructor(
        ...
    ) {
        ...

        this.itemRef.valueChanges().subscribe(appointment => {
            const fields = appointment.units.map((unit, index) => {
                return getUnitFields(unit.type, index);
            });
            // Flattening the fields array using reduce
            this.fields = fields.reduce((acc, e) => acc.concat(e), []);
            this.model = appointment;
        });
    }
}
```

We used `UNIT_KEYS` to get various items, all of which will be checked in each unit type. The `getFields` method returns two fields for each item to be checked. The first field is a `radio` field with two options, `In Good Condition` and `In Bad Condition`, while the second field is a `textarea` field so that the user can state their reason for choosing `In Bad Condition`. Let's also use the number key from the model to show this in the title of the page:

```
<ion-header>
    <ion-toolbar>
        <ion-buttons slot="start">
            <ion-back-button></ion-back-button>
        </ion-buttons>
        <ion-title>Audit # {{model.number}}</ion-title>
    </ion-toolbar>
</ion-header>
...
```

Now, we can see that the **Reason** field for the bad condition shows up, even if we have **In Good Condition** selected:

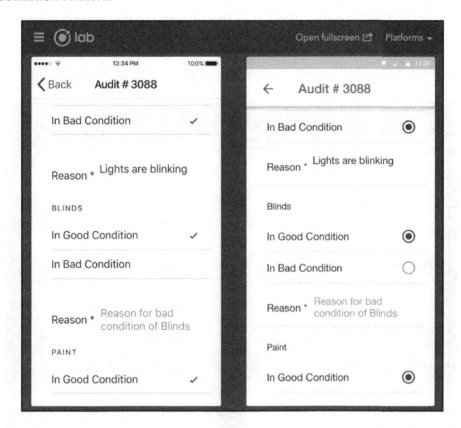

Let's make both fields `required` and use `hideExpression` to show the **Reason** field only if the `radio` field that corresponds to it has a value of `bad`:

```
const getFields = (id: number, key: string): FormlyFieldConfig[] => {
    ...
    return [{
        key: `units.${id}.${key}`,
        type: 'radio',
        templateOptions: {
            required: true,
            ...
        }
    }, {
        key: `units.${id}.${key}Reason`,
        type: 'textarea',
        hideExpression: `model.units[${id}].${key} !== 'bad'`
```

```
        templateOptions: {
            required: true,
            ...
        }
    }];
};
```

Now, when the value of the `radio` field is `good`, you won't see the **Reason** field:

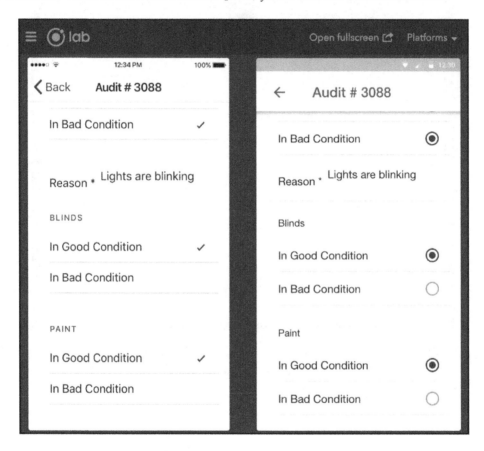

Before we submit the form, we need to update our item with the changes that we made to the model, as well as update its status based on the form's valid status. Then, we will route it to our home page:

```
import { Router } from '@angular/router';

class AuditPage implements OnInit {

    constructor(
        ...
        private router: Router
    ) {
        ...
    }

    ...

    submit() {
        this.itemRef.update({
            ...this.model,
            status: this.form.invalid ? 'incomplete' : 'complete',
        });
        this.router.navigateByUrl('/home');
    }
}
```

We have created and completed our first dynamic form using ngx-formly. Now, let's add some Native app functionality to our application so that we can use a camera to capture a photo.

Using Ionic Native so that we can use a camera

Now that our audit page is all set up, we can add some Native capability to our application. Let's add the Cordova plugin for the camera and install the Ionic Native camera service:

```
> ionic cordova plugin add cordova-plugin-camera
> npm install @ionic-native/camera
```

Let's provide the Camera service in our AuditPageModule first:

```
import { Camera } from '@ionic-native/camera/ngx';
@NgModule({
    ...
```

```
    providers: [Camera],
    ...
})
export class AuditPageModule {}
```

Afterward, add a button so that you can open the camera to the right of the header:

```
<ion-header>
    <ion-toolbar>
        <ion-buttons slot="start">
            <ion-back-button></ion-back-button>
        </ion-buttons>
        <ion-title>Audit # {{model.number}}</ion-title>
        <ion-buttons slot="end">
            <ion-icon padding name="camera" (click)="openCamera()"></ion-
            icon>
        </ion-buttons>
    </ion-toolbar>
</ion-header>
```

Finally, call the camera service in our openCamera method and save the image to the base64Images property:

```
import { Camera } from '@ionic-native/camera/ngx';

class AuditPage implements OnInit {
    ...
    base64Images: string[];
    constructor(
        ...
        private camera: Camera
    ) {
        ...
    }

    ...

    submit() {
        this.itemRef.update({
            ...this.model,
            photos: this.base64Images,
            status: this.form.invalid ? 'incomplete' : 'complete',
        });
        this.router.navigateByUrl('/home');
    }

    openCamera() {
        const options: CameraOptions = {
```

```
            quality: 100,
            cameraDirection: this.camera.Direction.BACK,
            destinationType: this.camera.DestinationType.DATA_URL,
            encodingType: this.camera.EncodingType.JPEG,
            mediaType: this.camera.MediaType.PICTURE
        };

        this.camera.getPicture(options).then((imageData) => {
            this.base64Images.push(`data:image/jpeg;base64,${imageData}`);
        });
    }
}
```

Now, we can show the photos that we took on the camera on our audit page:

```
<ion-content padding>
    <div class="image-container" *ngFor="let photo of base64Images">
        <img width="30" height="30" [src]="photo" />
    </div>
    . . .
</ion-content>
```

Let's finish this by adding some style to the `image-container` class:

```
.image-container {
    display: inline-block;
    margin-right: 5px;
}
```

Now, when you click on the camera icon on the audit page, you should see the camera open to take a photo. When you take a photo, it should be displayed in the `image-container` we created.

That completes our Ionic project, where we used `ngx-formly` to create a dynamic form and also added Native functionality using Ionic Native.

Summary

In this chapter, we introduced you to the Ionic framework, and also installed and created an application using the Ionic CLI. Then, we modified the theme using the Color Generator tool provided by Ionic, configured a new Firebase application for our auditing application, and integrated it into our Ionic app. We also used `ngx-formly` to create a dynamic form, without having to write a template for the form, which was one of our objectives. Finally, we used the Native app so that we could use a camera in our application.

Now, we can get started with other Ionic applications and use different Angular modules.

In the next chapter, we will take our blog and improve the performance and SEO of the application by rendering our Single-Page Application on the server. We will use Express as a server on Node.js and make sure that our posts are visible, not only on different search engines but also on social media services such as Twitter, Facebook, and LinkedIn.

Questions

Test your knowledge of this chapter by answering the following questions:

- What is the Ionic framework?
- What benefits does the Ionic framework provide us with?
- What is Ionic Lab?
- How do you theme your Ionic app?
- What is the Firebase Realtime Database?
- How do you configure Firebase in your Angular application?
- When and why should you use `ngx-formly` in your application?
- What is Ionic Native?

Further reading

The following reading material will provide you with more information about Ionic, Firebase, `ngx-formly`, and Ionic Native:

- Ionic Framework documentation: `https://ionicframework.com/docs`.
- AngularFire: `https://github.com/angular/angularfire2`.
- ngx-formly documentation: `https://ngx-formly.github.io/ngx-formly/`.
- Ionic Native documentation: `https://ionicframework.com/docs/native`.

7
Building a Server-Side Rendering Application Using Angular

In this chapter, we will continue to work on our personal blog from Chapter 3, *Building a Personal Blog Using Angular Router and WordPress*, where we created a **Single-Page Application (SPA)** using Angular Router. We will render the application on the server so that the performance and the search engine's optimization can be optimized. We will use TransferState to make sure that the APIs are cached when rendered in the server so that the APIs are not called redundantly on the client. We will use different forms of **Search Engine Optimization (SEO)** to make it discoverable on search engines and so that it can be shared properly on social media platforms such as Twitter, Facebook, and LinkedIn.

The following topics will be covered in this chapter:

- Understanding Angular Universal
- Deployment and performance analysis
- Adding Universal support
- Transferring state from the server to the client
- Deployment and performance analysis of **Server-Side Rendering (SSR)**
- Understanding SEO optimizations
- Social media scraping

Technical requirements

This chapter's code can be found in this book's GitHub repository, `https://github.com/PacktPublishing/Angular-Projects`, in the `Chapter07` folder.

The code has been provided for you so that whenever you are stuck, you can verify whether you've done something different and play with the working project in the repository.

We want you to follow the sections in this chapter in the order in which they appear and learn as much as you can about different aspects of Angular development.

Understanding Angular Universal

Angular Universal is a project that's used for rendering Angular applications on the server side. This is a great way to improve the performance of our application and also add additional features to our application to make it more scrapable and sharable on search engines and social media.

Before we understand how this is done, let's go back and see how our application is viewed by rendering it. Our application, when requested, will return an HTML file with links to CSS and JavaScript, and if we look into our body, we will see only the root element.

To see this, open your application in a web browser, right-click anywhere, and click on **View page source**, which will open a new tab with the content that the server sends for our page.

You will see a body with a single element, `app-root`, without any content rendered in it, like so:

```
<body>
    <app-root></app-root>
</body>
```

When the browser parses the HTML, it will download the CSS and JavaScript that was requested in the HTML file. After the JavaScript has been downloaded and parsed, it will run all the JavaScript code and render our `app-root` component.

Here, the end user has to wait for the JavaScript code to be loaded, parsed, and run before they see anything on the browser. Similarly, search engines scrape your HTML file and get content from it. Only a few search engines, such as Google and Bing, can run JavaScript and scrape the content of your application. If you were building an application that you wanted to be scraped by search engines, then you probably want the entirety of its content in the HTML file, even before the JavaScript runs.

Angular is built in such a way that it does not have to run only on the browser. Angular is not tied to the **Document Object Model (DOM)**, and it can run on any other platform that is supported—even a native mobile application. Angular provides a package called `platform-browser-dynamic` so that you can run the application on a browser. To run an Angular application heedlessly on a server, Angular provides a module called `platform-server` to render our application on the server. In this chapter, we will use Express, which is a Node.js framework for servers. Once we have rendered our application on our browser, search engines will be able to scrape the content of the web page, thereby allowing us to optimize our application for search engines.

Now that we understand why we need Angular Universal, let's deploy our application on ZEIT Now and do some performance analysis using Lighthouse.

Deployment and performance analysis

Before we add any server-side capabilities to our personal blog application, we need to deploy our application to a server. In this section, we will upload our application to ZEIT Now, which is a multi-cloud platform that makes it easy to deploy applications onto their server and makes them cloud fast. You will need to go to `https://zeit.co/now` and create an account on their platform.

Now, install ZEIT Now's CLI on your machine using npm. This is done by using the following command:

```
> npm install -g now
```

After installation, you will need to log in to now in your Terminal. You can do this by running the following command, which will ask you to enter an email address and verify it:

```
> now login
```

Let's deploy our application as a static website. Since we are using Angular Router, we will use a hash mechanism for our routing. Hash routing adds the hash to different routes, such as `http://localhost:4200/#about` instead of `http://localhost:4200/about`. This can be done in the `AppRoutingModule` as follows:

```
@NgModule({
    imports: [RouterModule.forRoot(routes, {
            ...
            useHash: true
        }),
    ...
],
    ...
})
export class AppRoutingModule { }
```

Now, let's build our personal blog application using the `prod` flag:

```
> ng build --prod
```

To deploy our application on Now, we need to run the following `now` command:

```
#change your-domain with a random string
> now --public && now alias <your-domain>.now.sh
```

If, for example, you used `static-personal-blog.now.sh` as your alias, then you'll need to open `https://static-personal-blog.now.sh` in your browser, which should load your application. Your deployment will be successful if the application loads completely without errors.

Now, let's measure its performance by using the **Audit** tool in the developer tools. From here, we can run audits. The following report will be generated:

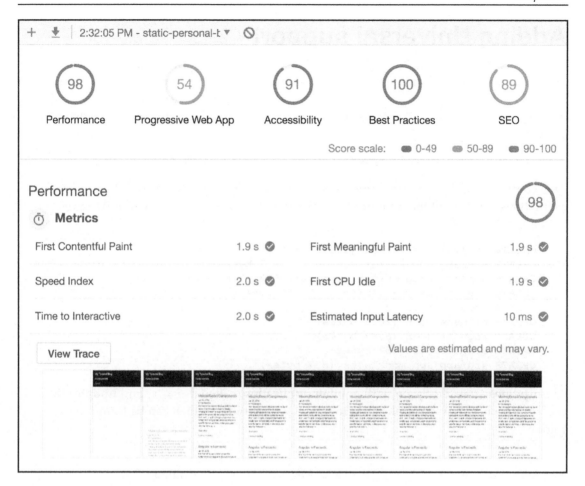

Here, we can see the important metrics for performance in terms of duration. For us, **First Contentful Paint**, which is **1.9** seconds long, is the most important metric as it measures the time it took to load the content that could be viewed by the user. The other important metric is **Time to Interactive**, which measures the time duration when the user can interact with the application; that is, when all the JavaScript is loaded, parsed, and run in the browser.

You can also use online tools such as `https://www.webpagetest.org/` to test the performance of your application, which, instead of simulating a network like Lighthouse, uses actual devices in various locations to determine different metrics for performance.

Adding Universal support

There are various ways we can add Universal support to our application. But one of the best ways is mentioned in the Angular documentation, in the Angular Universal guide (https://angular.io/guide/universal): we can use the `ng add` command, along with `@nguniversal/express-engine` and `clientProject`, to add Universal support to our project:

```
> ng add @nguniversal/express-engine --clientProject personal-blog
```

This command adds all the required dependencies to the `package.json` file and installs them. It also creates all the different files, along with code changes. The following files are created and updated:

```
CREATE src/main.server.ts (220 bytes)
CREATE src/app/app.server.module.ts (427 bytes)
CREATE src/tsconfig.server.json (219 bytes)
CREATE webpack.server.config.js (1360 bytes)
CREATE server.ts (1472 bytes)
UPDATE package.json (2013 bytes)
UPDATE angular.json (5282 bytes)
UPDATE src/main.ts (432 bytes)
UPDATE src/app/app.module.ts (837 bytes)
```

This updates `angular.json` with another application, called `server`, and updates the path of the output of the application to the `browser` folder, which can be found in the `dist` folder.

`main.server.ts` exports `AppServerModule`, which uses `ServerModule` from `@angular/platform-browser`, and also imports `AppModule`, along with `ModuleMapLoaderModule` from `@nguniversal`, which helps the lazy-loaded routes run in the application. The command also creates `webpack.server.config.js`, which is a webpack configuration that compiles the `server.ts` file. The `server.ts` file sets up the server using Express, which allows it to compile the application using `ngExpressEngine`, as follows:

```
app.engine('html', ngExpressEngine({
    bootstrap: AppServerModuleNgFactory,
    providers: [
        provideModuleMap(LAZY_MODULE_MAP)
    ]
}));
```

Here, `AppServerModuleNgFactory` and `LAZY_MODULE_MAP` are loaded from the compiled server's main file.

The command also adds some `npm` build commands, more specifically `build:ssr` and `server:ssr`. The `build:ssr` command compiles our application for browsers and servers using production configuration. It creates a couple of folders in the `dist` folder, that is, `browser` and `server`, and also compiles the `server.ts` file with `server.js` in the `dist` folder. The `serve:ssr` command runs `server.js` using Node.js.

Let's build and serve our application using the `npm` scripts:

```
> npm run build:ssr && npm run serve:ssr
```

These scripts should run the application in `http//localhost:8080`. The application should work without any errors.

Now, let's view the page source using **View page source** again. We will see that all the content has been loaded into `pb-root`:

```
<body>
    <pb-root _nghost-sc0="" class="ng-tns-c0-0" ng-version="7.2.4"><pb-header _ngcontent-sc0="" class="ng-tns-c0-0" _nghost-sc1=""><nav _ngcontent-sc1="" class="navbar navbar-
expand-lg navbar-dark bg-dark"><a _ngcontent-sc1="" class="navbar-brand" href="/home">My Personal Blog</a><button _ngcontent-sc1="" aria-controls="navbarSupportedContent" aria-
expanded="false" aria-label="Toggle navigation" class="navbar-toggler" data-target="#navbarSupportedContent" data-toggle="collapse" type="button"><span _ngcontent-sc1=""
class="navbar-toggler-icon"></span></button><!----></nav></pb-header><div _ngcontent-sc0="" class="route-container ng-trigger ng-trigger-routerTransition" style=""><router-outlet
_ngcontent-sc0=""></router-outlet><pb-home _nghost-sc2="" class="ng-tns-c2-1 ng-star-inserted" style=""><div _ngcontent-sc2="" class="row"><!----><div
_ngcontent-sc2="" class="col-md-6 ng-tns-c2-1 ng-trigger ng-trigger-postsAnimation ng-star-inserted" style=""><div _ngcontent-sc2="" class="card flex-md-row mb-4 shadow-sm h-md-
250"><div _ngcontent-sc2="" class="card-body d-flex flex-column align-items-start"><h3 _ngcontent-sc2="" class="mb-0"><a _ngcontent-sc2="" class="text-dark" href="/post/19/master-
detail-components">Master/Detail Components</a></h3><div _ngcontent-sc2="" class="mb-1 text-muted">Jan 25, 2019</div><p _ngcontent-sc2="" class="card-text mb-auto"><p>At the
moment, the HeroesComponent displays both the list of heroes and the selected hero's details. Keeping all features in one component as the application grows will not be
maintainable. You'll want to split up large components into smaller sub-components, each focused on a specific task or workflow. In this page, you'll take the first step in</p>
<div><a class="btn-filled btn" href="https://testing-ng-proj.000webhostapp.com/2019/01/master-detail-components" title="Master/Detail Components">Read More</a></div>
</p><a _ngcontent-sc2="" class="ng-tns-c2-1" href="/post/19/master-detail-components">Continue reading</a></div></div></div><div _ngcontent-sc2="" class="col-md-6 ng-tns-c2-1 ng-
trigger ng-trigger-postsAnimation ng-star-inserted" style=""><div _ngcontent-sc2="" class="card flex-md-row mb-4 shadow-sm h-md-250"><div _ngcontent-sc2="" class="card-body d-flex
flex-column align-items-start"><h3 _ngcontent-sc2="" class="mb-0"><a _ngcontent-sc2="" class="text-dark" href="/post/17/angular-is-fantastic">Angular is Fantastic</a></h3><div
_ngcontent-sc2="" class="mb-1 text-muted">Jan 25, 2019</div><p _ngcontent-sc2="" class="card-text mb-auto"><p>The Tour of Heroes tutorial covers the fundamentals of
Angular.In this tutorial you will build an app that helps a staffing agency manage its stable of heroes. This basic app has many of the features you'd expect to find in a data-
driven application. It acquires and displays a selected hero's detail, and</p>
<div><a class="btn-filled btn" href="https://testing-ng-proj.000webhostapp.com/2019/01/angular-is-fantastic" title="Angular is Fantastic">Read More</a></div>
</p><a _ngcontent-sc2="" class="ng-tns-c2-1" href="/post/17/angular-is-fantastic">Continue reading</a></div></div></div><div _ngcontent-sc2="" class="col-md-6 ng-tns-c2-1 ng-
trigger ng-trigger-postsAnimation ng-star-inserted" style=""><div _ngcontent-sc2="" class="card flex-md-row mb-4 shadow-sm h-md-250"><div _ngcontent-sc2="" class="card-body d-flex
flex-column align-items-start"><h3 _ngcontent-sc2="" class="mb-0"><a _ngcontent-sc2="" class="text-dark" href="/post/1/hello-world">Hello World!</a></h3><div _ngcontent-sc2=""
class="mb-1 text-muted">Dec 20, 2018</div><p _ngcontent-sc2="" class="card-text mb-auto"><p>Welcome to WordPress. This is your first post. Edit or delete it, then start writing!
The more and more I love WordPress.</p>
</p><a _ngcontent-sc2="" class="ng-tns-c2-1" href="/post/1/hello-world">Continue reading</a></div></div></div></pb-home></div></pb-root>
<script type="text/javascript" src="runtime.js"></script><script type="text/javascript" src="es2015-polyfills.js" nomodule=""></script><script type="text/javascript"
src="polyfills.js"></script><script type="text/javascript" src="styles.js"></script><script type="text/javascript" src="vendor.js"></script><script type="text/javascript"
src="main.js"></script>
```

Again, the power of the `ng add` command makes it so much easier to add new functionality to our application. With just one command, we can get our application running on the Express server. Next, we will create one small problem in our application, solve it using `TransferStateModule`, and then deploy our application on Now.

 If you want to use Nest.js instead of Express server for Angular Universal, you can use `ng add @nestjs/ng-universal`.

We now have a simple Angular Universal application. In the next section, we'll understand how the state of the application is being transferred from the server to the client and optimize the transition of the state using `TransferState`.

Transferring state from the server to the client

Since we are using `HttpClient` to get posts from the server, one potential problem that could occur in server-rendered, client-side applications is that the API is called twice, once on the server and once in the client. You can check that in the **Network** tab of the developer tools. Observe the screenshots in the **Network** tab; you will see that, at **630 ms** and **747 ms**, the content was available on the page, and then all of a sudden at **1.21 s** and **2.03 s**, the content was removed and comes back at **2.35 s** onward. This happens because, at **630 s**, we got data in HTML format from the server, and at **1.21 s**, Angular became bootstrapped and called the `/posts` API:

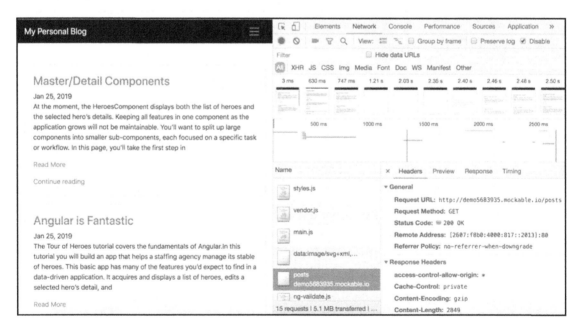

To overcome this issue, we use `TransferStateModule`, which allows us to cache any data when the code runs on the server and use that cached data instead of calling the API. First, let's configure `TransferStateModule`. To configure `TransferStateModule`, we need to include two different modules, one in `AppServerModule` and one in `AppModule`:

1. Let's add `BrowserTransferStateModule` to our `AppModule`, as follows:

```
import { BrowserModule, BrowserTransferStateModule } from
'@angular/platform-browser';
...
@NgModule({
    ...
    imports: [
    BrowserModule.withServerTransition({ appId: 'serverApp' }),
        BrowserTransferStateModule,
        ...
    ],
    ...
})
export class AppModule { }
```

2. In `AppServerModule`, include `ServerTransferStateModule`, as follows:

```
import { ServerModule, ServerTransferStateModule } from
'@angular/platform-server';
...
@NgModule({
    imports: [
        AppModule,
        ServerModule,
        ServerTransferStateModule,
        ModuleMapLoaderModule,
    ],
    bootstrap: [AppComponent],
})
export class AppServerModule {}
```

Now that the appropriate modules for `TransferState` have been included in `AppModule` and `AppServerModule`, we can create an interceptor that intercepts our API call and use the `TransferState` service to cache data when the application runs on the server.

3. Manually create the `transfer-state.interceptor.ts` file in the `app` folder and use the snippet provided by Angular snippets, `a-http-interceptor`, which should create the following snippet:

```
import { Injectable } from '@angular/core';
import { HttpInterceptor, HttpEvent, HttpHandler, HttpRequest } from
'@angular/common/http';
import { Observable } from 'rxjs';
@Injectable({providedIn: 'root'})
export class HeaderInterceptor implements HttpInterceptor {
    intercept(req: HttpRequest<any>, next: HttpHandler):
    Observable<HttpEvent<any>> {
        return next.handle(req);
    }
}
```

4. Update the name of the class from `HeaderInterceptor` to `TransferStateInterceptor` and add this service to our `AppModule`:

```
...
import { HTTP_INTERCEPTORS } from '@angular/common/http';
import { TransferStateInterceptor } from './transfer-
state.interceptor';
@NgModule({
    ...
    providers: [{
        provide: HTTP_INTERCEPTORS,
        useClass: TransferStateInterceptor,
        multi: true,
    }],
    ...
})
export class AppModule { }
```

5. Now, we need to identify the platform where our Angular application is running. We can check whether it is running in our server by using `isPlatformServer`. This needs `PLATFORM_ID` to work, which can be injected. When the request returns the response, we'll use `transferState` to set the `StateKey`, which we can create using `makeStateKey`, to get the response of the API:

```
import { Injectable, Inject, PLATFORM_ID } from '@angular/core';
...
import { makeStateKey, TransferState } from '@angular/platform-
browser';
```

```
import { isPlatformServer } from '@angular/common';
import { tap } from 'rxjs/operators';
export class TransferStateInterceptor implements HttpInterceptor {
    constructor(
        private transferState: TransferState,
        @Inject(PLATFORM_ID) private platformId,
    ) {}

    intercept(req: HttpRequest<any>, next: HttpHandler):
    Observable<HttpEvent<any>> {
        const key = makeStateKey(req.url);
        return next.handle(req).pipe(
            tap((res) => {
                if (isPlatformServer(this.platformId)) {
                    this.transferState.set(key, res);
                }
            }),
        );
    }
}
```

6. Now that our state will be cached when the code runs in the server, let's make sure that, if the cached data exists, we can read it and then remove it so that when we are in the client application, the API can be called again on route change:

```
import { HttpInterceptor, HttpEvent, HttpHandler, HttpRequest,
HttpResponse, HttpHeaders } from '@angular/common/http';
export class HeaderInterceptor implements HttpInterceptor {
    ...
    intercept(req: HttpRequest<any>, next: HttpHandler):
    Observable<HttpEvent<any>> {
        const key = makeStateKey(req.url);
        if (this.transferState.hasKey(key)) {
            const response: any = this.transferState.get(key, {} as
            any);
            this.transferState.remove(key);
            return of(new HttpResponse({
                ...response,
                headers: new HttpHeaders(response.headers),
            }));
        }
        ...
    }
}
```

Here, we are checking whether the cached data exists by using the `hasKey` method, and then we get the data by using the `X` method on the `transferState` service. Then, we remove it using the `remove` method and respond with the observable of the `HttpResponse`.

Now, let's run the build and serve our application again using `npm run build:ssr && npm run serve:ssr` before verifying that the API is not called after the page loads. You can also view the cached API response in the page view of the source, at the bottom.

In this section, we successfully transferred the state of the application from the server to the client using `TransferState`. Next, we will deploy our Node.js application to ZEIT Now and check the performance of our application.

Deployment and performance analysis of SSR

In terms of our server-side application, we can no longer deploy it as a static website. We need to run it using Node.js on the server. Let's create a `local.js` file in the `root` directory, which will serve our application using `server.js` in the `dist` directory:

```
const port = process.env.PORT || 8080;

const server = require('./dist/server');

server.app.listen(port, () => {
    console.log("Listening on: http://localhost:"+port);
});
```

Next, we need to export the `app` variable in our `server.ts` file and comment out our `app.listen` call since we are listening to it in the `local.js` file:

```
...
export const app = express();


...
// app.listen(PORT, () => {
// console.log(`Node Express server listening on
   http://localhost:${PORT}`);
// });
```

Since we are exporting `server.ts`, we need to update the output in our
`webpack.server.config.js` file in order to output the bundle as the `commonjs2`
`libraryTarget`:

```
...
module.exports = {
    ...
    output: {
        libraryTarget: 'commonjs2',
        ...
    }
    ...
}
```

Now, let's add the Now configuration to our `package.json` file so that the
Node.js application can run on it:

```
{
    ...
    "scripts": {
        "start": "node local.js",
        ...
        "now-build": "true",
        "now": "now deploy --public && now alias"
    },
    "now": {
        "name": "<your-app-name>",
        "alias": [ "<your-app-name>.now.sh" ],
        "files": [
            "dist",
            "package.json",
            "local.js"
        ]
    },
    ...
}
```

Now, we can build our application and deploy it on ZEIT Now using the following
command:

```
> npm run build:ssr && npm run now
```

After the preceding command completes, open the alias that you configured in the browser.

Now, we can run the audit of our application and compare it with our benchmark:

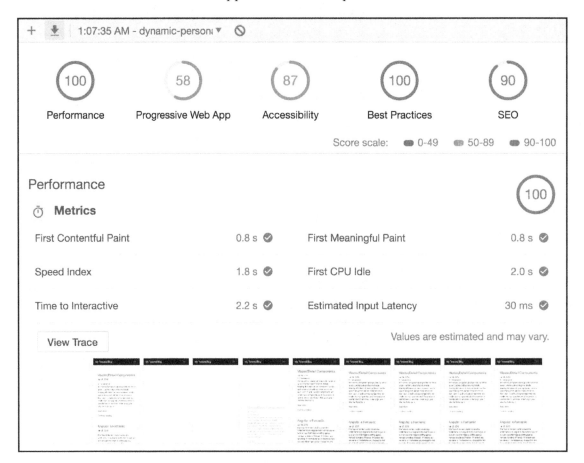

We can see that our **First Contentful Paint** metric has considerably improved from **1.9** seconds to just **0.8** seconds. However, we can also see that **Time to Interactive** has increased from **2** seconds to **2.2** seconds, which can be explained because of the increase of JavaScript in our bundle. Here, the user can see that the page loaded in **0.8** seconds, but cannot interact with the web page until after **2.2** seconds. The Angular team provides a `PrebootModule`, which, if included, can track all the events on the page until the page becomes interactive and then replay all the events after the page becomes interactive. This way, you can trick users into thinking the application is interactive when, in reality, it's not.

If you have a client-side Angular application and want to deploy your application on Now, you can use the Angular schematics provided by ZEIT Now, which let you deploy the Angular application through the use of the `ng add @zeit/ng-deploy` command. Such schematics are also provided by other deployment platforms, such as Firebase, Azure, Netlify, and GitHub with the `ng add [provider]` command, where `[provider]` could be `@angular/fire`, `@azure/ng-deploy`, `@netlify-builder/deploy`, or `ngx-gh`, respectively.

Now that we've got a 100% performance score in Lighthouse, we need to figure out how we can optimize our application for search engines.

Understanding SEO optimizations

Search engines such as Google, Bing, Yandex, and so on scrape the web using web crawlers. They search for content on your application and try to determine the keywords that are important on the web page and then try to determine the uniqueness and importance of the page in terms of its words, all of which are related to billions of web pages on the internet. They use a very complicated algorithm to determine which words are the keywords on the website.

Now, we will look at various tips to improve SEO and try to incorporate them in our application. Some of the ones we will cover in this chapter are as follows:

- Content is king
- Accessibility
- Using anchor tags for links
- Using `sitemap.xml`
- Using `robots.txt`
- Title and description

Let's look at them one by one.

Content is king

The most important thing that a web page should consist of is good content. Search engines such as Google scrape the website and determine the importance of the topic and legitimacy of the web page. Your page should consist of information that's relevant to the topic at hand, and not just consist of a whole lot of content that has no relevance to what's going on. Scrapers can easily determine whether the content is related to the topic at hand using different algorithms, which includes artificial intelligence and machine learning algorithms.

Accessibility

When a website is coded properly, it can be used by all, including disabled users such as blind users. Accessibility and search engines have one thing in common, that is, both of them use machine scraping and read the content that was scraped. Blind users use screen readers to access the application. You can try using NVDA if you use Windows, which can be downloaded from `https://www.nvaccess.org/download/`. If you are a macOS user, then you can use VoiceOver, which comes built into macOS. A lot of similar principles and rules apply on the website to make it accessible and SEO optimized, such as the following:

- **Use markup to convey the meaning of the content**: Use proper elements to convey the meaning of the content; for example, the title of the page should use heading tags. Heading tags should be in order; the `h1` tag should be followed by `h2`, which should be followed by `h3`, and so on. It is important that the `h3` tag doesn't appear before `h1` and `h2`, as that will make the context of the website confusing to the user.
- **Alternative text for image, audio, and video**: Images should have alternative text so that a blind user can understand what the image is about. By doing this, even the search engine can understand what the image is about.

Now that we understand why accessibility is important, let's continue with other important things to consider for SEO.

Using anchor tags for links

Make sure that you use `anchor` tags to go between pages. Don't just add `href` or `routerLink` to elements other than `anchor` elements. Search engines see `anchor` tags in the page, and then index those pages and use them to crawl all of the web pages of your application. Don't use `onclick` or JavaScript to go from one page to another.

Using sitemap.xml

A sitemap is an XML file that many search engines use to view all the web pages that need to be scraped. Our personal blog has a couple of static pages but also has dynamic pages based on the blog posts that are on it. We need to generate `sitemap.xml` dynamically every time a new post is added or deleted:

```xml
<urlset xmlns="http://www.sitemaps.org/schemas/sitemap/0.9">
    <url>
        <loc>https://dynamic-personal-blog.now.sh/home</loc>
    </url>
    <url>
        <loc>https://dynamic-personal-blog.now.sh/about</loc>
    </url>
    <url>
        <loc>https://dynamic-personal-blog.now.sh/post/1/hello-world</loc>
    </url>
    <url>
        <loc>https://dynamic-personal-blog.now.sh/post/19/master-detail-
            components</loc>
    </url>
    <url>
        <loc>https://dynamic-personal-blog.now.sh/post/17/angular-is-
            fantastic</loc>
    </url>
</urlset>
```

Generate a `sitemap.xml` file and place it somewhere in your application. Then, create a folder called `generated` in the `src` folder and create the `sitemap.xml` file with the preceding content. You will need to make sure that you add the `generated` folder as `assets` to the `angular.json` folder:

```json
{
    ...
    "projects": {
        "personal-blog": {
            ...
```

```
"architect": {
    "build": {
        ...
        "assets": [
            "src/favicon.ico",
            "src/assets",
            "src/generated"
        ],
        ...
```

You can now optionally submit your `sitemap.xml` file to different search engines, which you can find after building and serving it at `<your-application-site-domain>/generated/sitemap.xml`.

Using robots.txt

Search engines use a `robots.txt` file to determine whether any web pages need to be indexed by them. They also provide information about where the `sitemap.xml` file resides.

Before a search engine crawls your website, it tries to see whether the `robots.txt` file exists at `<your-application-site>/robots.txt`, and if it does, it uses it to check which pages are excluded from indexing. This can be used if you do not want certain pages to be indexed.

Let's include the `robots.txt` file in our application in the `src` folder and update the assets of `angular.json` once more. Your `robots.txt` file should look as follows if all the pages are allowed:

```
# Allow all URLs (see http://www.robotstxt.org/robotstxt.html) User-agent:
* Disallow: Sitemap:
https://dynamic-personal-blog.now.sh/generated/sitemap.xml
```

`robot.txt` file is very important when you want to disallow search engines from scraping some URLs in the application. Next, let's see how the title and description are important.

The title and description

The title and description are also important for search engines as they are displayed to users when they search on different search engines.

In the following screenshot, you can see the results of searching for `what is angular?`. The search engine displays the title, URL, and the description for the pages:

Let's set the title and description statically in the `index.html` file for our application:

```
<head>
    <meta charset="utf-8">
    <title>My Personal Blog</title>
    <meta name="description" content="My Personal Blog where I write about
        my life and hobbies">
    <base href="/">
    <meta name="viewport" content="width=device-width, initial-scale=1">
    <link rel="icon" type="image/x-icon" href="favicon.ico">
</head>
```

All our routes in the application will use this updated static title and description. We also need to update the title and meta description dynamically using meta and title services that are provided by `platform-browser`, which we will cover in the next section when we optimize our application for social media websites.

Social media scraping

Social media websites also scrape the website so that shared links can be shown properly on the web page. If you are creating a marketing website, you need to make sure that they are shared properly on social media platforms such as Twitter, Facebook, and LinkedIn. These social media platforms also provide tools for developers so that they can test their websites and check whether they are being shared properly on their platforms.

Let's take one of our posts and test it with these tools.

The Facebook tool for debugging shareability can be found at `https://developers.facebook.com/tools/debug/sharing/`. Let's enter the URL and check out the preview:

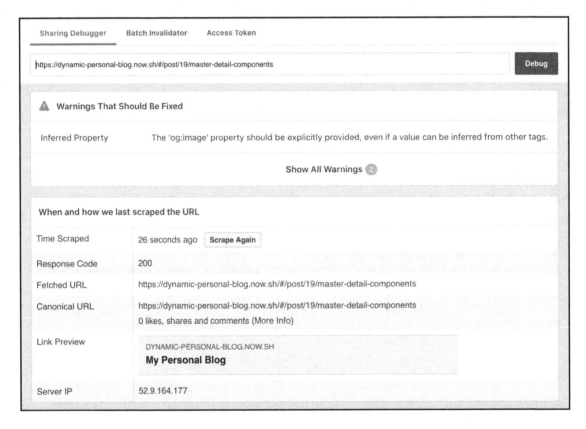

Here, we can see that instead of the blog post's name, it shows **My Personal Blog**, which is the title that was set in `index.html`.

Let's also check out what our post looks like in the Twitter validator, which can be found at `https://cards-dev.twitter.com/validator`. Let's enter the URL of our site and check out the preview:

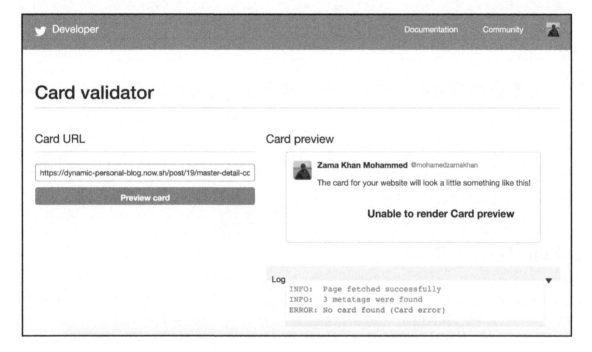

We can see that it shows **Unable to render Card preview**. Once again, this page has not been optimized so that it can be shared on Twitter.

Lastly, let's see what our post looks like in LinkedIn's Post Inspector, which can be found at `https://www.linkedin.com/post-inspector/`. When we enter our website's URL in the inspector, we will see the following:

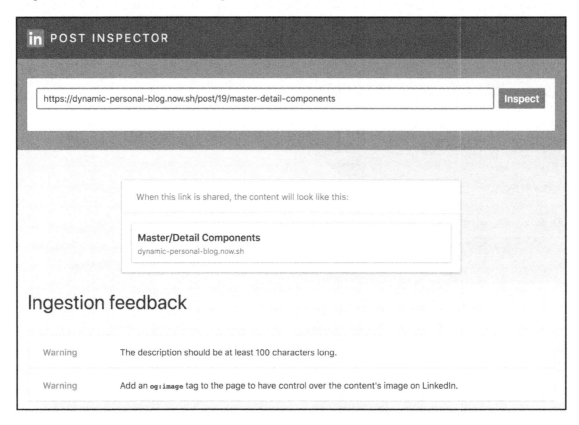

We can see that LinkedIn shows the correct title but still throws up a few warnings.

Angular provides a couple of services that you can use to set the title of the page, as well as meta tags. Let's try to use them in our `PostComponent`, as follows:

```
...
import { Meta, Title } from '@angular/platform-browser';

...
export class PostComponent implements OnInit {
    ...
    constructor(
        ...
        private titleService: Title,
        private metaService: Meta,
```

```
    ) { }

    ngOnInit() {
        this.wordpressService.post$.subscribe(data => {
            this.post = data;
            this.titleService.setTitle(data.title.rendered);
            this.metaService.removeTag('name="description"');
            this.metaService.addTag({
                name: 'description',
                content: data.excerpt.rendered
            });
        });
        ...
    }
}
```

Many other meta tags need to be added to our website so that our content can be scraped on social media platforms. Facebook and LinkedIn use Open Graph meta tags, while Twitter has its own meta tags. Instead of us manually adding all of these meta tags, we will use the ngx-seo library, which adds all the required meta tags for us:

```
> npm install ngx-seo --save
```

Let's remove the title and meta service from our post component and use the ngx-seo package to set the title and the other required meta tags on the page:

```
...
import { SeoSocialShareService } from 'ngx-seo';

...
export class PostComponent implements OnInit {
    ...
    constructor(
        ...
        private seoService: SeoSocialShareService,
    ) { }

    ngOnInit() {
        this.wordpressService.post$.subscribe(data => {
            this.post = data;
            this.seoService.setData({
                title: data.title.rendered,
                author: 'My Name',
                description: data.excerpt.rendered,
                published: data.date,
                type: 'post',
            });
        });
```

```
        . . .
    }
  }
```

The preceding code adds the SEO meta tags for the individual post pages. Let's also try to add the meta tags for the home page and about page. We can do this by adding SEO data to the route configuration in `AppRoutingModule` in the `app-routing.module.ts` folder, as follows:

```
const routes: Routes = [
    { path: '', pathMatch: 'full', redirectTo: 'home' },
    { path: 'home', component: HomeComponent, data: {
        routeState: 1,
        seo: {
            title: 'My Personal Blog - Home Page',
            description: 'My Personal Blog where I write about my life and
                hobbies'
        }
    } },
    { path: 'about', component: AboutComponent, data: {
        routeState: 2,
        seo: {
            title: 'My Personal Blog - About Page',
            description: 'I\'m Software Architect...'
        }
    } },
    { path: 'post/:id/:slug', loadChildren:
        './post/post.module#PostModule', data: {routeState: 3} },
    { path: '**', component: HomeComponent }
];
```

To use the preceding SEO data that was added to routes, we need to create a server called `route-helper` using the following command:

```
> ng g s route-helper
```

In RouteHelperService, we need to listen to the router events and use our SeoSocialShareService to add the SEO metadata using setData, as follows:

```
import { Injectable } from '@angular/core';
import { SeoSocialShareService } from 'ngx-seo';
import { Router, Route, NavigationEnd, ActivatedRoute } from
'@angular/router';
import { filter, map } from 'rxjs/operators';

@Injectable({
    providedIn: 'root'
})
export class RouteHelperService {
    constructor(
        private router: Router,
        private activatedRoute: ActivatedRoute,
        private seoService: SeoSocialShareService,
    ) {
        this.router.events.pipe(
            filter(event => event instanceof NavigationEnd),
            map(() => this.activatedRoute),
            filter(r => r.outlet === 'primary'),
        )
        .subscribe((activeRoute: ActivatedRoute) => {
            const seo: any = activeRoute.snapshot.data.seo;
            if (seo) {
                this.seoService.setData({
                    title: seo.title,
                    description: seo.description,
                    image: seo.shareImg,
                    author: 'My Name',
                    type: 'website',
                });
            }
        });
    }
}
```

For this service to run, we need to inject this service into AppComponent.

By doing this, we can build and deploy our application and run it using the npm run build:ssr && npm start command.

Now, when you load the application in your browser and use view source on the post page, you should see all the meta tags and titles in their updated forms, as shown in the following screenshot:

```html
<html lang="en" class="gr__dynamic-personal-blog_now_sh fa-events-icons-ready" preflight-installed="true">
▼<head>
    <meta charset="utf-8">
    <title>Angular is Fantastic</title>
    <meta name="description" content="<p>The Tour of Heroes tutorial covers the fundamentals of Angular.In this tutorial you will
    build an app that helps a staffing agency manage its stable of heroes. This basic app has many of the features you&#8217;d expect to find in
    a data-driven application. It acquires and displays a list of heroes, edits a selected hero&#8217;s detail, and</p>
    <div><a class="btn-filled btn" href="https://testing-ng-proj.000webhostapp.com/2019/01/angular-is-fantastic" title="Angular is
    Fantastic">Read More</a></div>
    ">
    <base href="/">
    <meta name="viewport" content="width=device-width, initial-scale=1">
    <link rel="icon" type="image/x-icon" href="favicon.ico">
  ▶<script class="preboot-inline-script">...</script>
    <meta name="twitter:title" content="Angular is Fantastic">
    <meta name="twitter:image:alt" content="Angular is Fantastic">
    <meta property="og:image:alt" content="Angular is Fantastic">
    <meta property="og:title" content="Angular is Fantastic">
    <meta name="title" content="Angular is Fantastic">
    <meta name="twitter:description" content="<p>The Tour of Heroes tutorial covers the fundamentals of Angular.In this tutorial you
    will build an app that helps a staffing agency manage its stable of heroes. This basic app has many of the features you&#8217;d expect to
    find in a data-driven application. It acquires and displays a list of heroes, edits a selected hero&#8217;s detail, and</p>
    <div><a class="btn-filled btn" href="https://testing-ng-proj.000webhostapp.com/2019/01/angular-is-fantastic" title="Angular is
    Fantastic">Read More</a></div>
    ">
    <meta property="og:description" content="<p>The Tour of Heroes tutorial covers the fundamentals of Angular.In this tutorial you
    will build an app that helps a staffing agency manage its stable of heroes. This basic app has many of the features you&#8217;d expect to
    find in a data-driven application. It acquires and displays a list of heroes, edits a selected hero&#8217;s detail, and</p>
    <div><a class="btn-filled btn" href="https://testing-ng-proj.000webhostapp.com/2019/01/angular-is-fantastic" title="Angular is
    Fantastic">Read More</a></div>
    ">
    <meta name="article:published_time" content="2019-01-25T09:20:05.000Z">
    <meta name="published_date" content="2019-01-25T09:20:05.000Z">
    <meta name="article:author" content="My Name">
    <meta name="author" content="My Name">
    <meta property="og:type" content="post">
```

Now, let's use the social media tools again and check whether the page is shareable on their platforms. Here's what our page will look like on Twitter:

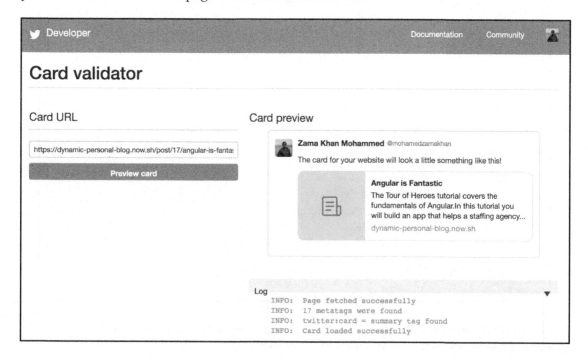

This is what it will look like on Facebook:

When and how we last scraped the URL	
Time Scraped	2 seconds ago Scrape Again
Response Code	200
Fetched URL	https://dynamic-personal-blog.now.sh/post/17/angular-is-fantastic
Canonical URL	https://dynamic-personal-blog.now.sh/post/17/angular-is-fantastic 0 likes, shares and comments (More Info)
Link Preview	DYNAMIC-PERSONAL-BLOG.NOW.SH **Angular is Fantastic** The Tour of Heroes tutorial covers the fundamentals of Angular.In this tutorial you will build an app that helps a staffing agency manage its stable of heroes. This basic app has many of the features you'd expect to find in a data-driven application. It acquires and displays a list o...
Server IP	13.57.131.79

Now, our application is not only optimized for search engines but also optimized so that it can be shared on social media accounts that can increase our traffic.

Summary

In this chapter, we added Angular Universal to our personal blog and improved the performance of our application by rendering content on the server and transferring state from the server to the client. Then, we made a few changes in order to improve our website so that it can be crawlable by search engines and scrapable by social media platforms.

Now, other than being able to build client-side Angular applications, we can also render them on a server to optimize our applications for performance and SEO. We have learned how to audit our application for performance and also validate them for social scraping using various social media tools.

In the next chapter, we will convert our e-commerce application into a monorepo application, and add a new application for admins so that they can add new products and edit information about them. We will also add authentication using OAuth so that only authorized users can log in and modify information about different products.

Questions

Test your knowledge of this chapter by answering the following questions:

- How do you measure the performance of your application?
- How do you add Angular Universal to a Angular CLI application?
- Why do we need to use `TransferStateModule` in Angular Universal projects?
- What are the different methods that you can use in `TransferState` services to cache data?
- How do you check whether the code is running on a server or browser?
- What are the different things you need to consider for SEO?
- How do different social media platforms scrape websites?
- What is a preboot? How can it help your Angular Universal application?
- What services do you use to set the title and meta tags?

Further reading

The following reading material will provide you with more information about Angular Universal, SEO, performance, and ZEIT Now:

- Angular Universal guide: `https://angular.io/guide/universal`.
- *Better sharing on social media platforms*, by Sam Vloeberghs: `https://samvloeberghs.be/posts/better-sharing-on-social-media-platforms-with-angular-universal`.
- Lighthouse: `https://developers.google.com/web/tools/lighthouse/`.
- ZEIT Now documentation: `https://zeit.co/docs`.

8

Building an Enterprise Portal Using Nx, NgRx, and Redux

In this chapter, we will be creating an enterprise application for admins so that they can log in and check the sales of the e-commerce application we've developed. We will be using OAuth, along with Auth0, to authenticate users of our application and check the sales of each product using D3 visualizations. We will be using the Nx workspace to create our monorepo application, which will include not only our e-commerce application and admin application, but also libraries that can be shared by them.

The following topics will be covered in this chapter:

- Exploring the monorepo application
- Redux using NgRx
- Understanding token-based authentication
- Adding an authentication library
- Using `ngx-charts` for D3 visualizations

Technical requirements

This chapter's code can be found in this book's GitHub repository, `https://github.com/PacktPublishing/Angular-Projects`, under the `Chapter08` folder.

The code has been provided for you so that whenever you are stuck, you can verify whether you've done something differently and play with the working project in the repository.

We want you to follow the sections in this chapter in the order in which they appear and learn as much as you can about different aspects of Angular development.

Exploring the monorepo application

In our organizations, we typically have multiple applications, from backend applications to multiple frontend applications, and all of them have their own repository where the code resides. Each team that develops a particular application deals with multiple repositories related to that project. In such projects, it's really difficult to share common code between multiple applications and manage their dependencies.

One way to solve this is by using just one repository for all the applications. However, this kind of setup will be complicated to manage. Building anything in such an environment is difficult, as any changes we make mean that we have to build all the applications again, which increases the build time significantly. To solve this, we just need to build the applications that are affected by the changes, rather than building all the applications from scratch.

To solve this, we can use Nx, developed by the experts at Nrwl, which is a monorepo solution. Huge enterprises such as Google, Facebook, Uber, Twitter, and so on use monorepos to manage all of their applications.

The Nx `workspace` structure is structured as follows:

```
<workspace name>/
├──── apps/
├──── libs/
├──── nx.json
├──── package.json
├──── tools/
├──── tsconfig.json
└──── tslint.json
```

Nx creates one `workspace`, can have multiple applications, and can also have multiple libraries that can be shared between the multiple applications. Applications can be of two types: web applications such as Angular or React (probably more in the future) and Node applications that use Nest.js or Express. Likewise, libraries can be generated using Angular, React, or none at all (without any framework set up). It uses Prettier for code formatting.

Nx also provides good support for Nx, along with helpers for Data Persistence. It also gives you the option to use Jest for testing and Cypress for **end-to-end (e2e)** testing. Along with all of these goodies, it adds a bunch of new `npm` scripts so that you can run linting, testing, e2e testing, and so on on the affected applications.

 For more information about Nx's capabilities, go to `https://nx.dev/`.

Now that we have understood what Nx workspaces are, let's look at NgRx, which we can use to maintain our application's state through the use of Redux.

Redux using NgRx

Redux is one of the ways we can manage the state of the application. In Angular, we normally use services to keep the data of our application intact. Sometimes, if we don't use observables to manage the data in the services and instead update the Object and Array references directly, we won't see the data from our services update the components due to the change in the references. To solve this problem, we normally use observables (`Subjects`, `BehaviorSubject`, and so on) to constantly update our components with new data. For a huge enterprise application, we might want to have a store that can maintain the state of the entire application.

Typically, when we use Redux, we have one single store that manages the state of the application. To update the store on user interaction or any other event, we dispatch actions. An action is a simple object with a type and a payload. To create actions, we normally create action creators, which are simple classes with a `type` property, as well as a constructor for accepting a payload. Once an action has been dispatched using the action creator, the reducers receive the action and update the state synchronously. A reducer is a simple function that takes the initial state and action and returns a new state. Reducers use a `switch` statement to check the type of the action. In the end, we observe the changes to some parts of the store and then update the UI whenever state updates.

This entire process is a synchronous one. When we talk about the asynchronous nature of events, such as API calls, or asynchronous events such as setTimeout, then reducers are not enough to update the state. We need middleware to handle such events. NgRx provides us with a way to handle asynchronous events by using effects. Effects listen to the **action** and **dispatch** actions when the asynchronous event completes:

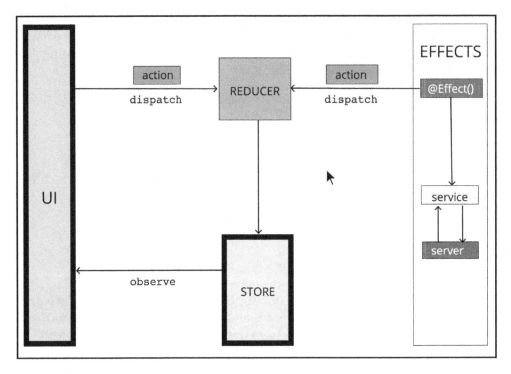

The architecture of Redux using NgRx

Understanding the NgRx data flow is essential for us to maintain the state in an Angular application. Next, we will look at token-based authentication and how it works.

Understanding token-based authentication

Authentication is the process of giving access to the resources of your application to select individuals. You can authenticate users in two different ways: by using cookies or by using tokens, which we can store in either the `localStorage` or `sessionStore` of the browser. In this chapter, we will be using OAuth (pronounced as, oh Auth) using a third-party service called Auth0 (Auth zero). Using OAuth, the application is not exposed to passwords since the authentication happens in a different application altogether.

Let's look at how authentication occurs using OAuth. This is explained in the following diagram:

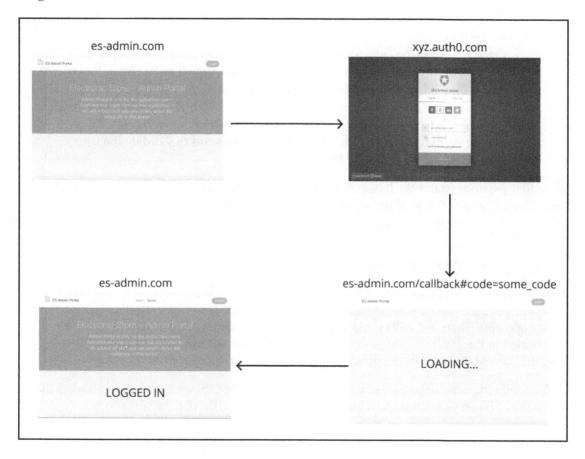

You need to follow these steps to authenticate the user:

1. In our web app, we will have a **Log In/Sign In** button in our application. The routes will be hidden and guarded based on whether the browser has the Auth token included or not.
2. We will integrate `auth0-js`, the JavaScript provided by Auth0, into our web application. Here, we pass the `clientId` and the domain, which we get from Auth0 when we create a new project.
3. When we click on the **Log In** button, we will be redirecting users to Auth0's domain, where the user will either use email login or social login to log in to our application.
4. Once authenticated, Auth0 will redirect the users to the callback URL provided to Auth0's project, along with some codes.
5. Once we get to the callback page, we will let Auth0 process the URL parameters so that we can get details about the authorization, such as the Auth token.
6. We will save that token alongside the expiration details of the Auth token. Once we have the Auth token, we will use `JWTModule`, which includes the Angular interceptor, to add the authorization header to all the whitelisted URL requests via the Auth token. This will be used by the backend to validate the user's request and then authorize them.

Now that we understand the basics of what we will be implementing in this chapter, let's take a look at an overview of the project we will be building.

Project overview

In this chapter, we will be using the application that we built in `Chapter 5`, *Building a PWA E-Commerce Application Using Angular Service Worker*, and convert the application into an Nx monorepo app. Then, we will create a new app so that admin users can log in, as we mentioned in the *Understanding token-based authentication* section, and check the visualization of the sales of the products on the public-facing e-commerce website.

In the following screenshot, we can see that the **Sales** page shows the visualization of the sales. We will use `ngx-charts`, which uses D3, to build different visualizations:

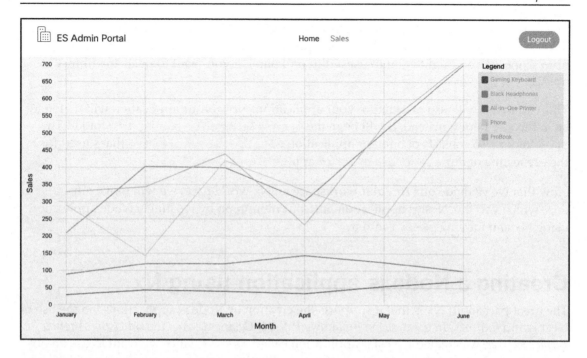

We will be using NgRx to maintain the state of the application using Redux. We will also be adding authentication to the application using Auth0 so that only authorized users can log in and view the application.

Now that we have looked at an overview of the project, we can get started.

Getting started

In Chapter 5, *Building a PWA E-Commerce Application Using Angular Service Worker*, we created two applications: one called electronic-store, which was a **Progressive Web App (PWA)**, and another called es-api, which was a Nest.js application that exposed an API using MongoDB.

Let's go into our electronic-store folder, which was an application we created using the Angular CLI, and convert it into an Nx workspace using the following commands:

```
> ng add @nrwl/workspace --npmScope ngprojects
> ng add @nrwl/angular
```

The `npmScope` is used when you publish any library to `npmjs` and also while using the libraries from our monorepo in the monorepo application. I have already used `ngprojects` npm scope, so you might want to use a different name if you want to push any library to npmjs.

This command will also restructure your application. Now, your application will no longer be in the `src` folder; instead, it will be in the `apps/electronic-store/src` folder. The `apps` folder also consists of another application `electronic-store-e2e` that's used for the e2e testing of our `electronic-store` app.

Now that we've made our Angular workspace an Nx workspace, we will move our `es-api`, which was our Nest.js application, into our monorepo by creating a Node application using Nx and moving `es-api` into it.

Creating a Node.js application using Nx

The great part about Nx is that it supports the creation of Node.js applications via the use of Nest.js and Express. In Chapter 5, *Building a PWA E-Commerce Application Using Angular Service Worker*, we created a Nest.js application called `es-api`. Since we want to use an Nx workspace, which requires us to have all our applications in one repository, we will try to retrieve the `es-api` application without using our new Nx workspace, `electronic-store`.

Let's first add nest application capability to our application using the following command:

```
> ng add @nrwl/nest
```

Let's create a new `node` application using the Nx command, as follows:

```
> ng g @nrwl/nest:app es-api --frontendProject electronic-store
? In which directory should the node application be generated?
```

The `fronendProject` flag will add a proxy to the `electronic-store` app. We can use the API directly from our application.

Let's update the API URL in `products.service.ts` in the `electronic-store` app:

```
const PRODUCTS_API = '/api/products';
```

Now, let's copy and paste our `es-api` folder from the `books` repository, `https://github.com/PacktPublishing/Angular-Projects/tree/master/Chapter08/electronic-store/apps/es-api`.

```
> npm i express-jwt jwks-rsa @nestjs/common@5.5.0 @nestjs/core5.5.0
```

Now, we can serve both applications using the Angular CLI command in two different Terminals:

```
> ng serve es-api
```

In a different Terminal, run the following command:

```
> ng serve electronic-store
```

Now, when you open `http://localhost:4200` in a browser, you should see that our application works fine and that all the products are displayed.

Now that we have successfully created a monorepo with two existing applications, that is, `electronic-store` and `es-api`, we will create a new client application that will be used by admins to check the sales data.

Creating a client application using Nx

Now, let's create another client application for admin users using the Angular CLI command:

```
> ng g application es-admin --prefix es --routing
? In which directory should the application be generated?
? Which stylesheet format would you like to use? SCSS [
 http://sass-lang.com ]
? Which Unit Test Runner would you like to use for the application? Jest
[https://jestjs.io ]
? Which E2E Test Runner would you like to use for the application? Cypress
[https://www.cypress.io ]
```

You should see that a new Angular app was created in the `apps` folder, along with the e2e app for it. Let's use the same proxy that we used for `electronic-store` for this application too in `angular.json` file:

```
{
    ...
    "projects": {
        ...
        "es-admin": {
```

```
...
"architect": {
    ...
    "serve": {
        "builder": "@angular-devkit/build-angular:dev-server",
        "options": {
            "browserTarget": "es-admin:build",
            "proxyConfig": "apps/electronic-
            store/proxy.conf.json"
        },
        ...
}
```

Now that our proxy is set up, let's install some dependencies in our application using npm:

```
> npm install @angular/cdk lodash-es @auth0/angular-jwt auth0-js --save
```

Now that we have all the dependencies installed and the new client application has been configured, let's create a new library using Nx for SharedModule.

Creating a library using Nx

Nx allows us to add a library in the monorepo, which can be used by multiple applications and also published as a reusable library to the package manager. We will look at the latter in Chapter 10, *Building a Component Library Using Angular CDK and Elements*.

Let's create a library for SharedModule that can be used by multiple applications if required:

```
> ng g library shared --prefix es
? In which directory should the application be generated?
? Which stylesheet format would you like to use? SASS [
 http://sass-lang.com ]
? Which Unit Test Runner would you like to use for the application? Jest
 [https://jestjs.io ]
? Which E2E Test Runner would you like to use for the application? Cypress
 [https://www.cypress.io ]
```

Now that we have created a SharedModule, let's go ahead and add Momentum Design components to it so that this SharedModule can be shared between multiple projects that want to use the same components.

Adding Momentum Design to an Angular CLI application

Momentum Design is a collection of design guidelines and a software toolkit for designers and developers. It provides various components that are required for building a cohesive experience for web applications. You can find out more information about the various components provided by Momentum Design at `https://momentum.design/components`. They provide components for React, Angular, and Vue.

Now, let's add Momentum Design for Angular to our application using the following `ng add` command:

```
> ng add @momentum-ui/angular --project es-admin --module apps/es-admin/src/app/app.module.ts
```

Let's also add a `nav` component from Momentum Design using Momentum Design's schematics:

```
> ng generate @momentum-ui/angular:nav nav --project es-admin --style scss
```

Let's remove the Momentum Design's modules declaration from the `AppModule` of the `es-admin` project and add it to the `SharedModule`:

```
import { NgModule } from '@angular/core';
import { CommonModule } from '@angular/common';
import { TopbarModule, ButtonModule, ListItemModule } from '@momentum-ui/angular';

const SHARED_MODULES = [
    TopbarModule,
    ButtonModule,
    ListItemModule
];

@NgModule({
    imports: [CommonModule, ...SHARED_MODULES],
    exports: [...SHARED_MODULES]
})
export class SharedModule {}
```

Now, let's use the `nav` in our `app.component.html` file by replacing all the content with the following:

```
<div class="md md--sites">
    <es-nav></es-nav>

    <router-outlet></router-outlet>
</div>
```

In the Terminal, we need to stop our `electronic-store` application so that the ports do not conflict when we run `ng serve` in a new Terminal:

```
> ng serve es-admin --port 4201
```

This should serve our application on `http://localhost:4201`.

You should be able to see a navigation bar in the browser. Now, we need to set up NgRx so that we can manage our application's state.

Setting up NgRx in our application using Nx

Nx provides schematics that we can use to generate the NgRx setup and state of the application using simple commands. Let's generate a new `ngrx` state as the root state of the application:

```
> ng g ngrx --module apps/es-admin/src/app/app.module.ts
 ? What name would you like to use for the ngrx state? app
 ? What is the path to the module where this ngrx state should be added to?
  apps/es-admin/src/app/app.module.ts
 ? Is this the root state of the application? Yes
 ? Would you like to add a Facade to your ngrx state No
```

You should see that a new folder called `+state` has been generated in the `es-admin` project, as well as some updates to `AppModule` so that we can include the necessary modules. This folder also includes a module that we can use to set up the Redux store for DevTools. First, let's install the browser extension, Redux DevTools. Once installed, we need to open up our browser's developer tools, navigate to the **Redux** tab, and refresh our `es-admin` application. You should see that it shows the actions on the left-hand side and some more details on the right-hand side. This will be helpful when we wish to perform debugging and use the time-traveling feature of Redux to replay certain actions:

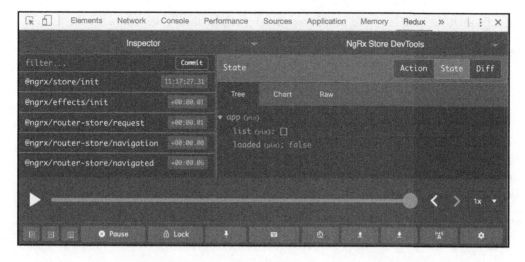

Now, we have a setup for NgRx up and running in our application. Next, using NgRx, we will create an authentication library that can be reused by applications in our Nx monorepo.

Adding an authentication library

We will be adding a library that will use NgRx to maintain the authentication of any app. It will handle all the login and logout behavior of the application.

Now that our application has the necessary setup for NgRx and Momentum Design, let's add authentication to our application using Auth0.

Adding a library using Nx

First, we need to create a library for authentication so that if a new application wants to reuse it, it can just use our `auth` library and update it if required:

```
> ng g library auth
? In which directory should the library be generated?
? What framework should this library use? Angular [
  https://angular.io/ ]
? Which stylesheet format would you like to use? SCSS [
  http://sass-lang.com ]
? Which tags would you like to add to the library? (used for linting)
? Which Unit Test Runner would you like to use for the library? Jest
  [https://jestjs.io/]
```

Now, let's include `AuthModule` in our `es-admin` application's `AppModule`:

```
import { AuthModule } from '@ngprojects/auth';

@NgModule({
    ...
    imports: [
        ...
        AuthModule,
    ],
    ...
})
export class AppModule {}
```

Now that our `AuthModule` has been scaffolded and added to the `es-admin` application, let's add the `ngrx` state to it for authentication.

Generating an NgRx state for the library

Now, let's create an `ngrx` state for authentication in our library:

```
> ng g ngrx --module libs/auth/src/lib/auth.module.ts
? What name would you like to use for the ngrx state? auth
? Is this the root state of the application? No
? Would you like to add a Facade to your ngrx state No
```

This time, we said No regarding its root state of the application. We will only have a root state once for the application, and since we already created an app state in the `es-admin` application, we don't need another root state.

Updating NgRx auth actions

Now, let's update `auth.actions.ts` by replacing the old actions with the new actions related to authentication:

```
import { Action } from '@ngrx/store';
import { Entity } from './auth.reducer';

interface AppSecrets {
    clientId: string;
    callbackUrl: string;
    domain: string;
}
```

```
export enum AuthActionTypes {
    RegisterApp= '[Auth] Register App',
    Login = '[Auth] Login',
    LoginSuccess = '[Auth] Login Success',
    LoginFailure = '[Auth] Auth Login Failure',
    LoginInProgress = '[Auth] Login In Progress',
    HandleLoginCallback = '[Auth] Handle Login Callback',
    Logout = '[Auth] Logout',
}

export class RegisterApp implements Action {
    readonly type = AuthActionTypes.RegisterApp;
    constructor(public payload: AppSecrets) { }
}

export class Login implements Action {
    readonly type = AuthActionTypes.Login;
}

export class LoginInProgress implements Action {
    readonly type = AuthActionTypes.LoginInProgress;
}

export class HandleLoginCallback implements Action {
    readonly type = AuthActionTypes.HandleLoginCallback;
}

export class LoginSuccess implements Action {
    readonly type = AuthActionTypes.LoginSuccess;
}

export class LoginFailure implements Action {
    readonly type = AuthActionTypes.LoginFailure;
}

export class Logout implements Action {
    readonly type = AuthActionTypes.Logout;
}

export type AuthAction = Login | HandleLoginCallback | LoginInProgress |
LoginSuccess | LoginFailure | RegisterApp | Logout;

export const fromAuthActions = {
    Login,
    LoginInProgress,
    LoginSuccess,
    LoginFailure,
    RegisterApp,
```

```
        HandleLoginCallback,
        Logout
};
```

We have successfully defined all the actions for authentication. Now, we will update the state of Redux using reducers and actions.

Updating the NgRx Auth reducer

Now, let's update the reducer. Our `initialState` will have the `auth` object, which we will create when the `RegisterApp` action is dispatched. We will also have an `authenticated` property, which will be `boolean`, for whether the user is authenticated or not, and properties for whether the login is in progress or it failed. We will update the state based on the authentication actions.

Let's react to different actions of authentication here in our reducer:

```
import { AuthAction, AuthActionTypes } from './auth.actions';
import * as auth0 from 'auth0-js';

...

export interface AuthState {
    authenticated: boolean;
    auth?: any;
    loginInProgress: boolean;
    loginFailed: boolean;
}

...

let authenticated = false;
if (localStorage.getItem('access_token')) {
    authenticated = true;
}

export const initialState: AuthState = {
    auth: undefined,
    authenticated,
    loginInProgress: false,
    loginFailed: false,
};

export function authReducer(
    state: AuthState = initialState,
```

```
        action: AuthAction
): AuthState {
    switch (action.type) {
        case AuthActionTypes.Login: {
            state = {
                ...state,
                loginInProgress: true,
            };
            break;
        }
        case AuthActionTypes.LoginFailure: {
            return {
                ...state,
                loginInProgress: false,
                loginFailed: true,
            };
            break;
        }

        case AuthActionTypes.LoginSuccess: {
            return {
                ...state,
                loginInProgress: false,
                authenticated: true,
            };
            break;
        }

        case AuthActionTypes.RegisterApp: {
            const { clientId, callbackUrl, domain } = action.payload;
            const auth = new auth0.WebAuth({
                clientID: clientId,
                domain,
                responseType: 'token id_token',
                redirectUri: callbackUrl,
                scope: 'openid'
            });

            state = {
                ...state,
                auth,
            };
            return state;
        }

        case AuthActionTypes.Logout: {
            return {
                ...state,
```

```
                authenticated: false,
            };
            break;
        }
    }
    return state;
}
```

Let's also remove the existing selectors from `auth.selectors.ts` file, as our state structure is updated.

Now, we have our reducer's setup completed. Next, we need to add some effects that are going to call asynchronous calls when authentication is being processed.

Updating NgRx Auth effects

Now, let's handle all the asynchronous actions that need to be done while authenticating. First, we need a login effect that will call the `authenticate` method on Auth0's `auth` object. Next, when our callback page has been loaded with the parameters, we need to handle the login callback. We've already created a login observable that wraps the logic of parsing the hash parameters and getting the Auth results, which it then uses to store an Auth token and expiry in `localStorage`. Lastly, we will have a logout effect, which just removes the Auth token and expiry from `localStorage` and redirects us to the **Home** page.

Let's add our first effect for login, `login$`, which listens for the `Login` action and then calls Auth0's `authorize` method, which will open a new tab with an Auth0 sign-in page where the users will log in, as follows:

```
...
import { map, catchError, } from 'rxjs/operators';
import { AuthPartialState, AUTH_FEATURE_KEY, AuthState } from
'./auth.reducer';

import {
    Login,
    AuthActionTypes
} from './auth.actions';
import { State, Store } from '@ngrx/store';

@Injectable()
export class AuthEffects {

    @Effect() login$ =
```

```
    this.dataPersistence.fetch(AuthActionTypes.Login, {
        run: (action: Login, state: AuthPartialState) => {
            state[AUTH_FEATURE_KEY].auth.authorize();
        },
        onError: (err) => {
            console.error(err);
        }
    });

    ...
}
```

Next, let's add another effect for logout. This effect will basically remove access tokens and expiration from `localStorage` and use the router to go to the default route of the application:

```
import { Router } from '@angular/router';
...


export class AuthEffects {
    ...
    @Effect() logout$ = this.dataPersistence.fetch(AuthActionTypes.Logout,
    {
        run: () => {
            localStorage.removeItem('access_token');
            localStorage.removeItem('exp');
            this.router.navigate(['']);
        },
        onError: () => {}
    });

    constructor(
        ...
        private router: Router
    ) {}


}
```

The last effect we will add is for `handleLoginCallback$`, which will be called by the callback component we will be creating in the next section. We will get the hash code on this callback URL, which we will parse and get the Auth token for, and persist it in `localStorage`. Based on the success or failure of the authentication, we will route the user to `successUrl` or `failureUrl`, respectively, as follows:

```
...
import { bindNodeCallback, of, Observable } from 'rxjs';
```

```
import {
    ...
    LoginSuccess,
    LoginFailure,
    HandleLoginCallback
} from './auth.actions';
import { Router } from '@angular/router';


...
export class AuthEffects {
    onAuthSuccessUrl = '/';
    onAuthFailureUrl = '/';
    ...

    @Effect() handleLoginCallback$ =
     this.dataPersistence.fetch(AuthActionTypes.HandleLoginCallback, {
        run: (action: HandleLoginCallback, state: AuthPartialState) => {
            return this.loginObservable$(state).pipe(
                map(token => {
                    this.router.navigate([this.onAuthSuccessUrl]);
                    return new LoginSuccess();
                }),
                catchError(() => {
                    this.router.navigate([this.onAuthFailureUrl]);
                    return of(new LoginFailure());
                })
            );
        },
        onError: () => {}
    });

    parseHash$ = (state: any) =>
bindNodeCallback(state[AUTH_FEATURE_KEY].auth.parseHash.bind(state[AUTH_FEA
TURE_KEY].auth));

    loginObservable$ = (state) => Observable.create((observer) => {
        if (window.location.hash && !state[AUTH_FEATURE_KEY].authenticated)
{
            this.parseHash$(state)().subscribe({
                next: (authResult: any) => {
                    localStorage.setItem('access_token',
                    authResult.idToken);
                    localStorage.setItem('exp',
                    authResult.idTokenPayload.exp);
                    observer.next();
                },

                error: err => {
```

```
                console.error('Error', err);
                observer.error(err);
            }
        });
    }
  })
}
```

Now that we have our NgRx actions, reducers, and action creators ready, let's go ahead and add the callback route to our Auth application to complete the authentication implementation.

Adding a callback route

Now, let's create a `callback` route in our `auth` library:

```
> ng g c callback --project auth
```

Update the `callback.component.html` file to show `Loading...`:

```
<p>
    Loading...
</p>
```

Next, let's create the route using `RouterModule.forChild`:

```
import { RouterModule } from '@angular/router';

@NgModule({
    declarations: [CallbackComponent],
    imports: [
        ...
    RouterModule.forChild([
            { path: 'callback', component: CallbackComponent },
        ]),
    ]
})
export class AuthModule {}
```

When the callback page loads, we need to dispatch the `HandleLoginCallback` action:

```
import { Component, OnInit } from '@angular/core';
import { Store } from '@ngrx/store';
import { AuthState } from '../+state/auth.reducer';
import { HandleLoginCallback } from '../+state/auth.actions';
```

```
...
export class CallbackComponent implements OnInit {
    constructor(private store: Store<AuthState>) { }

    ngOnInit() {
        this.store.dispatch(new HandleLoginCallback());
    }
}
```

Now that we have our authentication set up, ready for our es-admin application, let's add some routes and guard them if the user isn't authenticated.

Routes in our application

Let's create a couple of routes for our application: one home route and another to show the sales data. Let's make two lazy loaded routes, similar to what we did in Chapter 3, *Building a Personal Blog Using Angular Router and WordPress*:

```
@NgModule({
    imports: [
    BrowserModule,
    RouterModule.forRoot(
        [
            { path: '', pathMatch: 'full', redirectTo: 'home' },
            {
                path: 'home',
                loadChildren: () => import('./home/home.module').then(mod
                => mod.HomeModule);
            },
            {
                path: 'sales',
                loadChildren: () => import('./sales/sales.module').then(mod
                => mod.SalesModule);
            }
        ],
        { initialNavigation: 'enabled' }
    ),
    ...
    ],
    ...
})
export class AppModule {}
```

Let's update the navigation routes:

```
<ng-template #list>
    <a md-list-item routerLink="/home" routerLinkActive="active"
     label="Home"></a>
    <a md-list-item routerLink="/sales" routerLinkActive="active"
     label="Sales"></a>
</ng-template>
```

Let's also update our `home.component.html` file with the following code:

```
<div class="hero hero--fluid hero--dark" style="background-color: rgb(0,
 179, 135);">
    <div class="page-header__container ">
        <h1 class="hero__title">Electronic Store - Admin Portal</h1>
        <h3 class="hero__lead">
            Admin Portal is only for the authorized users.
            Administrator users can use this application to do advanced
            stuff and get details about the sales and so on in this portal.
        </h3>
    </div>
</div>
```

Now, when we check our browser, we should see the **Home** page with the navigation updated:

Now that we have a couple of routes, let's register for Auth0 and initiate authentication from our application.

Registering for Auth0 and signing in

Let's get the `clientId` and domain from Auth0's project. For that, we need to sign in to our Auth0 account. Let's create a new application in Auth0 from its dashboard. Once created, go to the **Applications** settings to get the **Client ID** and **Domain**. Also, update the **Allowed Callback URL** to `http://localhost:4201/callback`:

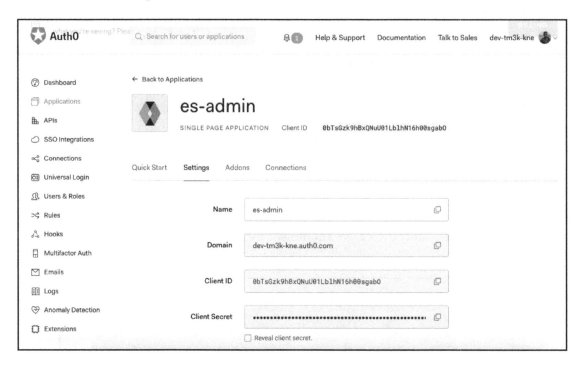

Let's store our **Client ID** and **Domain** in the `environment` files:

```
export const environment = {
    production: false,
    auth: {
        domain: '--- YOUR OWN DOMAIN ---',
        clientId: '--- YOUR OWN CLIENT ID ---',
        logoutUrl: 'http://localhost:4201/home',
        callbackUrl: 'http://localhost:4201/callback'
    }
};
```

We also need to update the `domain` and `clientId` in our Nest.js application. Go to `apps/es-api/src/app/shared/auth.middleware.ts` and update the `domain` and `clientId`.

Now, let's connect everything by dispatching the action for `RegisterApp` in our Auth state:

```
import { Component } from '@angular/core';
import { Store } from '@ngrx/store';
import { RegisterApp } from '@ngprojects/auth';
import { environment } from '../environments/environment';


...
export class AppComponent {
    constructor(
        private store: Store<any>,
    ) {
        this.store.dispatch(new RegisterApp({
            clientId: environment.auth.clientId,
            domain: environment.auth.domain,
            callbackUrl: environment.auth.callbackUrl,
        }));
    }
}
```

Now that our app is registered with Auth0, let's dispatch our login action on the click of the **Sign In** button in our navigation.

First, let's update the `NavComponent` class:

```
import { Component, OnInit } from '@angular/core';
import { AUTH_FEATURE_KEY, Logout, Login } from '@ngprojects/auth';
import { Store } from '@ngrx/store';


...
export class NavComponent implements OnInit {
    title = 'ES Admin Portal';
    authenticated: any;

    constructor(private store: Store<any>) {
        this.store.select(state => state[AUTH_FEATURE_KEY].authenticated)
        .subscribe(auth => {
            this.authenticated = auth;
        });
    }
    ...

    loginOrLogout() {
```

```
            if (this.authenticated) {
                this.store.dispatch(new Logout());
            } else {
                this.store.dispatch(new Login());
            }
        }
    }
```

Now that we have our `NavComponent` class observing the authentication from the NgRx store and updating our `authentication` property, and a function to dispatch a login or logout action based on the current authentication of the app, let's use them to update the navigation template:

```
...
<md-top-bar-nav>
    <ng-container *ngIf="authenticated">
        <ng-container *ngTemplateOutlet="list"></ng-container>
    </ng-container>
</md-top-bar-nav>
<md-top-bar-right>
    <div class="md-top-bar__user"></div>
    <div class="md-top-bar__logged-out">
        <button md-button color="blue" (click)="loginOrLogout()">
            {{authenticated ? 'Sign Out': 'Sign In'}}
        </button>
    </div>
</md-top-bar-right>
<md-top-bar-mobile [shouldCloseOnClick]="false">
    <ng-container *ngTemplateOutlet="brand" ngProjectAs="brand"></ng-
      container>
    <ng-container *ngIf="authenticated">
        <ng-container *ngTemplateOutlet="list"></ng-container>
    </ng-container>
    <button md-button color="blue" (click)="loginOrLogout()">
        {{authenticated ? 'Sign Out': 'Sign In'}}
    </button>
</md-top-bar-mobile>
...
```

Now, when you click on the **Sign In** button, you should see that the Auth0 authentication page loads up. After logging in by using any of the sign-in processes, you should be redirected to our callback page, which should then dispatch the `HandleLoginCallback` action, and sign the user in. After signing in, you should see that the button gets updated to **Sign Out**. When you refresh the page, since we already have the Auth token in `localStorage`, you should still see the user logged in.

Securing routes using route guards

When you sign out of the application and manually go to the sales URL in the browser, you will still see that the user is able to navigate to the **Sales** page without being authenticated. This is a potential security issue since the unauthenticated user is able to navigate to a page that they aren't authorized to view.

Guarding routes is very important for the security of our applications. We want to make sure that only the users who are allowed to view the page are able to access the page. In our case, we want our **Sales** page to only be viewed by authenticated users. Angular provides a way to guard the routes using Angular guards. For that, we need to create a service and implement CanActivate from Angular router and implement the canActivate method, which returns a Boolean or an observable of a Boolean. If the return value results in true, then a user can see the page, otherwise, they won't be able to view it. Let's use store.select to know if the user is authenticated or not from the store. If the user is authenticated, return true; otherwise, navigate to the **Home** page and return false.

Let's create AuthGuard using the following Angular CLI command:

```
> ng g guard auth --project es-admin
```

Let's update the guard to use our store, using the following code:

```
import { Injectable } from '@angular/core';
import { ActivatedRouteSnapshot, CanActivate, RouterStateSnapshot, Router }
from '@angular/router';
import { Store } from '@ngrx/store';
import { AUTH_FEATURE_KEY } from '@ngprojects/auth/src';
import { map } from 'rxjs/operators';

@Injectable({providedIn: 'root'})
export class AuthGuard implements CanActivate {

    constructor(private store: Store<any>, private router: Router) { }

    canActivate(route: ActivatedRouteSnapshot, state: RouterStateSnapshot)
{
        return this.store.select(state =>
state[AUTH_FEATURE_KEY].authenticated).pipe(
            map(authenticated => {
                if (authenticated) {
                    return true;
                } else {
                    this.router.navigate(['home']);
                    return false;
                }
```

```
            }),
        );
    }
}
```

Now, let's use our `AuthGuard` to guard our sales route, using `canActivate` for the route, as follows:

```
import { AuthGuard } from './auth.guard';

@NgModule({
    imports: [
    BrowserModule,
    RouterModule.forRoot(
        [
            ...
            {
                path: 'sales',
                loadChildren: () => import('./sales/sales.module').then(mod
                => mod.SalesModule),
                canActivate: [AuthGuard]
            }
        ],
        { initialNavigation: 'enabled' }
    ),
    ...
    ],
    ...
})
export class AppModule {}
```

Now, when you click on the **Sales** link in the navigation, you should see that it does not navigate to the **Sales** page, instead remaining on the **Home** page because of our Auth guard.

Using an interceptor to add an authorization token to headers

We can use an HTTP interceptor to do stuff while the API calls are being made. Instead of creating an HTTP interceptor, we are going to use a third-party module from Auth0 that does the same thing.

Let's wire up the `JWTModule` that's provided by Auth0 by passing the config details, which includes the `tokenGetter` method to get the Auth token and whitelisted domains so that the interceptor can add the tokens:

```
. . .
import { JwtModule } from '@auth0/angular-jwt';

export function tokenGetter() {
    return localStorage.getItem('access_token');
}

@NgModule({
    . . .
    imports: [
        . . .
        JwtModule.forRoot({
            config: {
                tokenGetter,
                whitelistedDomains: ['localhost:4200'],
            }
        }),
    ]
})
export class AuthModule {}
```

Now, our authentication process should work properly, and we should be able to log in to our application. Next, let's work on the **Sales** page, which we can only go to once we've logged in. We will be displaying visualizations on this page using `ngx-charts`.

Using ngx-charts for D3 visualizations

Visualizations help simplify complex data via the use of graphs, charts, images, diagrams, and so on. In this section, we will get the sales data from the past six months and display it using line charts for all five products in our e-commerce application. This will not only give us a representation of how a product has been doing for the past months but will also show you the comparison between different products, which can help us understand and improve the future sales of our products.

D3 visualizations are widely used by the data science community, especially when it comes to displaying visualizations on the web. D3 uses **Scalable Vector Graphics** (**SVG**) to create beautiful visualizations. You can find more information about D3 and its library at https:/ /d3js.org/.

`ngx-charts` is an Angular module that uses D3 and has a lot of predefined visualizations, from line charts, bar charts, pie charts, and so on, to bubble charts, heat maps, tree charts, and others. It can also be extended if you need to create any custom visualization using a simple API.

Let's install the Angular module using `npm`:

```
> npm install @swimlane/ngx-charts --save
```

Let's import `BrowserAnimationModule` in `AppModule` as follows:

```
...
import { BrowserAnimationsModule } from '@angular/platform-
browser/animations';

@NgModule({
    ...
    imports: [
        ...
        BrowserAnimationsModule
    ],
  ...
})
export class AppModule {}
```

Next, we need to include the module in the shared module. We will be using `LineChartModule` from the line chart component to display our data:

```
...
import { LineChartModule } from '@swimlane/ngx-charts';

const SHARED_MODULES = [
    ...
    LineChartModule
];
...
```

Before we use the line chart component, let's fetch the product sales data using NgRx. Let's create a new state called `products`:

```
> ng g ngrx --module apps/es-admin/src/app/app.module.ts
  ? What name would you like to use for the ngrx state? products
  ? Is this the root state of the application? No
  ? Would you like to add a Facade to your ngrx state No
```

Let's update the `loadProducts` effect in `products.effect.ts` and call the `secure` endpoint to get the sales data of the products:

```
...
import { HttpClient } from '@angular/common/http';
import { map } from 'rxjs/operators';

@Injectable()
export class ProductsEffects {
    @Effect() loadProducts$ = this.dataPersistence.fetch(
        ProductsActionTypes.LoadProducts,
        {
            run: (action: LoadProducts, state: ProductsPartialState) => {
                return this.http.get('/api/products/secure').pipe(
                    map((res: any) => {
                        return new ProductsLoaded(res);
                    })
                );
            },
            onError: (action: LoadProducts, error) => {
                console.error('Error', error);
                return new ProductsLoadError(error);
            }
        }
    );
    ...

    constructor(
        ...
        private http: HttpClient,
}
```

Since we are using `HttpClient`, include the `HttpClientModule` in the `AppModule`.

Now, in our `SalesComponent`, let's dispatch the event so that it loads the products, and then subscribe to the store to get the products. Afterward, we need to format the data according to what is required for the line chart component:

```
...
import { Store } from '@ngrx/store';
import { ProductsState } from '../+state/products.reducer';
import { productsQuery } from '../+state/products.selectors';
import { LoadProducts } from '../+state/products.actions';

export class SalesComponent implements OnInit {
    products;
    view;
```

```
constructor(private store: Store<ProductsState>) {
    this.store.dispatch(new LoadProducts());

    this.store.select(productsQuery.getAllProducts).subscribe(products
    => {
        this.products = products.map((item: any) => ({
            name: item.name,
            series: item.sales.map(sale => ({
                name: sale.month,
                value: sale.sold,
            })),
        }));
    });
}
...
}
```

Now, let's use the line chart component from `ngx-charts` and pass the data to it, along with other configuration to make the line chart have the axis, legend, and a label for the axes:

```
<div style="width: 100vw; height: calc(100vh - 150px);">
    <ngx-charts-line-chart
        *ngIf="products"
        [results]="products"
        [view]="view"
        [xAxis]="true"
        [yAxis]="true"
        [legend]="true"
        [showXAxisLabel]="true"
        [showYAxisLabel]="true"
        [xAxisLabel]="'Month'"
        [yAxisLabel]="'Sales'"
    ></ngx-charts-line-chart>
</div>
```

Now, when we go to our `Sales` route, we should see the `SalesComponent` displayed, along with a beautiful line chart:

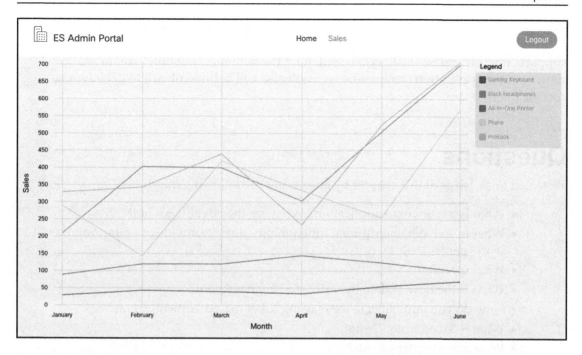

Now that we have our sales visualizations on the **Sales** page, which can only be accessed by authenticated users, we have come to the end of this chapter.

Summary

In this chapter, we used monorepo to manage multiple applications. We created an admin portal for our existing e-commerce application, where we authorized users using Auth0. We made sure that only authorized users can call APIs by sending an Auth token to the backend, where it validates the token. We also made sure that only authenticated users are allowed to view certain pages using Angular guards. To display our sales data, we used D3 visualization via `ngx-charts`.

In this chapter, we have learned how to use Nx workspaces to manage multiple applications in one monorepo. We have also learned how we can use Auth0 for authentication, wire the state management of the application using NgRx, and use D3 visualization using `ngx-charts`.

In the next chapter, we will create a Native mobile application that runs on iOS and Android using NativeScript. We will be creating a multilingual news application that supports English and Spanish. When switching the language, not only will the static content of the application change—but we will also call a different API to get language-specific data.

Questions

Test your knowledge of this chapter by answering the following questions:

- What is a monorepo application? What are the advantages of it?
- What is Nx? What additional functionality does it provide over the Angular CLI workspace?
- What is NgRx?
- What is the flow of data in NgRx state management?
- How do you authenticate users using token-based authentication?
- What is Momentum Design?
- What are Angular guards?
- What are Angular HTTP interceptors?
- Why and when do we need to use visualizations in our application?

Further reading

The following reading material will provide you with more information about Nx, Auth0, Momentum Design, and ngx-charts:

- Nx: `https://nx.dev/`.
- Auth0 quickstart for Angular applications: `https://auth0.com/docs/quickstart/spa/angular2`.
- Momentum Design: `https://momentum.design/`.
- ngx-charts documentation: `https://swimlane.github.io/ngx-charts/`.

Building a Multi-Language NativeScript Application with Angular

9

In this chapter, we are going to develop a NativeScript application with the use of Angular to display news posts. We will allow the user to select from a range of different languages and display the news in the selected language. We will be mocking the API to fetch news posts in different languages. We will use two languages—English and Spanish—and use `ngx-translate` to add internationalization to our application. We will do this by using a NativeScript plugin for use as a Native Snackbar.

The following topics will be covered in this chapter:

- Introducing NativeScript Playground
- Creating your first NativeScript with an Angular application
- Exploring UI layout containers
- Implementing internationalization using `ngx-translate`
- Adding a NativeScript plugin to our application

Technical requirements

This chapter's code can be found in this book's GitHub repository, `https://github.com/PacktPublishing/Angular-Projects`, in the `Chapter09` folder.

The code has been provided for you so that whenever you are stuck, you can verify whether you've done something different and play with the working project in the repository.

We want you to follow the sections in this chapter in the order in which they appear and learn as much as you can about different aspects of Angular development.

Introducing NativeScript Playground

NativeScript Playground is a solution that allows you to write your NativeScript code in a web client and deploy it to your device with the help of the NativeScript Playground app. No setup is required so you can start writing your code straightaway. All you need is a modern web browser.

When you navigate to `https://play.nativescript.org/`, you will be presented with a choice of four different templates (**Angular**, **Vue.js**, **Plain TypeScript**, and Plain JavaScript). Once you've chosen your desired template, you will be asked to scan the QR code with the NativeScript Playground app, which will open the NativeScript preview app.

The links where you can download the NativeScript Playground app in terms of iOS and Android are as follows:

- App Store (iOS): `https://itunes.apple.com/us/app/nativescript-playground/id1263543946?mt=8ls=1`.
- Google Play (Android): `https://play.google.com/store/apps/details?id=org.nativescript.play`.

Creating your first NativeScript with an Angular application

NativeScript Angular projects can be created using different commands, but the best way to create one is by using Angular CLI's NativeScript schematics. You can create a NativeScript application by following these steps:

1. Open your Terminal or Command Prompt and run the following command to create a new NativeScript application:

   ```
   > npm i -g @nativescript/schematics
   ```

2. This installs the `schematics` module we need to create basic NativeScript applications. This looks as follows:

   ```
   > ng new --collection=@nativescript/schematics HelloWorld
   ```

3. Now, change the directory to the newly created directory, `HelloWorld`, and run the following command to preview the application:

```
> npx -p nativescript tns preview
```

This will generate a barcode for the application that you can preview with the Playground app:

Keep the Playground app running as it listens to all the changes that you make and updates automatically.

Before we start building different components for our application, let's go ahead and look at some NativeScript layouts.

Exploring UI layout containers

NativeScript provides a recursive layout system that sizes and positions views on the screen. The layout system starts by measuring and positioning the layout containers and their child views. Layout is an intensive process whose speed and performance depend on the count of children and the complexity of the layout container. For example, a simple layout container, such as an absolute layout, might perform better than a more complex layout container, such as `GridLayout`.

Layout completes in two passes—a measure pass and a layout pass. To this end, each view provides a measure and layout methods. Additionally, each layout container provides its own `onMeasure` and `onLayout` to achieve its own specific layout.

NativeScript provides us with the following six different layout containers so that we can develop applications:

- Absolute layout
- Dock layout
- Grid layout
- Stack layout
- Wrap layout
- Flex layout

Let's look at each one of them briefly.

Absolute layout

The absolute layout is similar to the absolute positioning that's done in CSS. The child elements are positioned at the top-left coordinates of the page:

```
<AbsoluteLayout>
    <Label text="Start from top left" width="100%" top="10"
     height="90" backgroundColor="yellow"></Label>
    <Label text="Start from below the above element" width="100%"
     top="110" height="90" backgroundColor="red" color="white"></Label>
</AbsoluteLayout>
```

The preceding code will produce the following layout:

In the preceding example, we have two label elements positioned absolutely to each other. The first element starts from the top 10 pixels and 10 pixels from the left. The second element starts 110 pixels from the top and 10 pixels from the left.

AbsoluteLayout is the simplest layout in NativeScript. It will not enforce any layout constraints on its children and will not resize them at runtime when its size changes. Now, let's look at how the dock layout works in NativeScript.

Dock layout

The dock layout docks the children to the left, right, top, bottom, or center of the layout. It uses the dock property to specify the position of the element. In order to position an element at the center, we need to pass it as the last child and set stretchLastChild on the dock layout to true:

```
<DockLayout width="210" height="210" backgroundColor="lightgray"
  stretchLastChild="true">
```

```
    <Label text="left" dock="left" width="60"
     backgroundColor="red"></Label>
    <Label text="top" dock="top" backgroundColor="green"></Label>
    <Label text="right" dock="right" backgroundColor="blue"></Label>
    <Label text="bottom" dock="bottom" backgroundColor="yellow"></Label>
</DockLayout>
```

The preceding code will produce the following layout:

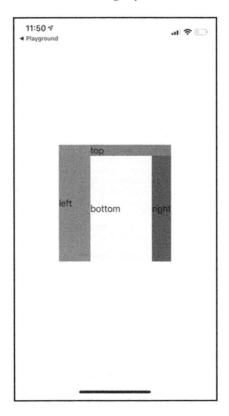

In the preceding example, we pass four label elements inside `DockLayout`, with the `stretchLastChild` property set to `true`. Though the bottom element is docked to the bottom, it stretches all the way to the top since `stretchLastChild` is set to `true`.

Now, let's look at how the grid layout works.

Grid layout

As its name suggests, `Gridlayout` arranges the children in a table structure of rows and columns. `GridLayout` has one row and one column by default, but we can add additional rows and columns by passing them to the layout:

```
<GridLayout columns="auto, *" rows="auto, *" width="210" height="210"
    backgroundColor="lightgray">
    <Label text="Label 1" row="0" col="0" backgroundColor="red"></Label>
    <Label text="Label 2" row="0" col="1" colSpan="2"
     backgroundColor="green">                    </Label>
    <Label text="Label 3" row="1" col="0" rowSpan="2"
     backgroundColor="blue">                         </Label>
    <Label text="Label 4" row="1" col="1" backgroundColor="yellow"></Label>
</GridLayout>
```

The preceding code will produce the following layout:

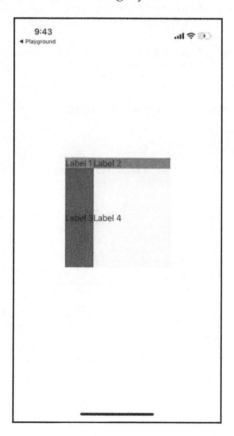

Columns and rows can be either absolute numbers, auto, or *. A number indicates the width in pixels, auto makes it as wide as the widest child, and * takes up all the available space. rowSpan or colSpan gets or sets a value that indicates the total number of rows or columns that the child content spans within a GridLayout.

Now, let's look at how the stack layout works.

Stack layout

StackLayout stacks its child elements below or beside each other, depending on its orientation. It is very useful for creating lists.

Use the following code to check how StackLayout works:

```
<StackLayout orientation="vertical">
    <Label text="Label 1" height="100" backgroundColor="red"></Label>
    <Label text="Label 2" width="150" height="100"
     backgroundColor="green"></Label>
    <Label text="Label 3" width="50" height="50"
     backgroundColor="blue"></Label>
</StackLayout>
```

The preceding code will produce the following layout:

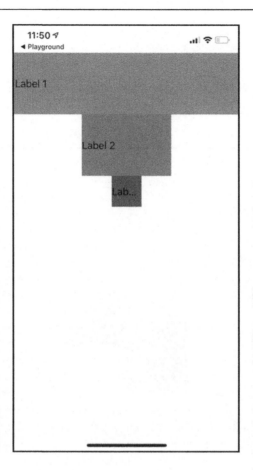

In the preceding example, we have three labels stacked vertically.

Now, let's look at how the wrap layout works.

Wrap layout

`WrapLayout` is similar to `StackLayout`, except it doesn't stack all the child elements in one column/row; instead, it wraps them to new columns/rows if no space is left. `WrapLayout` is often used with items of the same size, but this is not a requirement:

```
<WrapLayout orientation="horizontal" width="200" height="200">
    <Label text="Label 1" width="100" height="70"
     backgroundColor="red"></Label>
    <Label text="Label 2" width="100" height="70"
     backgroundColor="green"></Label>
```

```
        <Label text="Label 3" width="100" height="70"
        backgroundColor="blue"></Label>
    </WrapLayout>
```

The preceding code will wrap the three labels into one column. Since the width exceeds the width of `WrapLayout`, it wraps the third label onto a new column and produces the following layout:

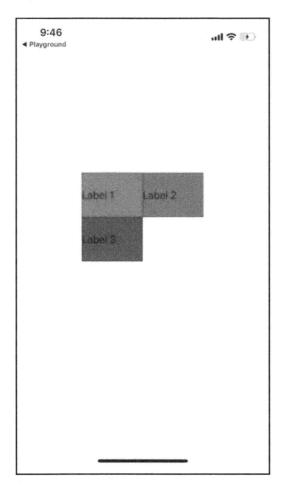

In the preceding example, `WrapLayout` has a width of 200 pixels, but the children need 300 pixels to be stacked horizontally. `WrapLayout` creates a new row to accommodate the third child.

Now, let's look at how the flex layout works.

Flex layout

`FlexboxLayout` is a non-conforming implementation of the CSS flexible box layout and is based on an existing Apache 2 licensed flexbox implementation:

```
<FlexboxLayout width="300" height="200" flexDirection="column"
 flexWrap="wrap">
 <Label text="Label 1" width="70" height="70"
  backgroundColor="red"></Label>
 <Label text="Label 2" width="70" height="70"
  backgroundColor="green"></Label>
 <Label text="Label 3" width="70" height="70"
  backgroundColor="blue"></Label>
 <Label text="Label 4" width="70" height="70"
  backgroundColor="yellow"></Label>
</FlexboxLayout>
```

In the preceding example, `FlexLayout` has a height of 200 pixels, but the children need 280 pixels to be stacked vertically. The preceding code will produce the following layout:

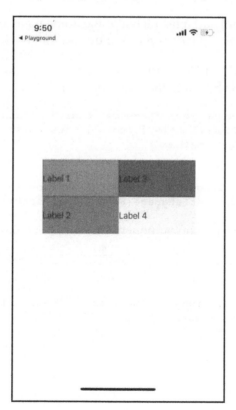

In the preceding example, we have a `FlexboxLayout` with four labels, each of which are `70` pixels in terms of width and height. The `flexWrap` property wraps the children and adds a new row or column as needed. The `flexDirection` property stacks the children either row-wise or column-wise.

Now that we have understood the different layouts that are available in NativeScript, we will implement some of them by creating a new Angular app.

Creating the application

The NativeScript core team works with the Angular team at Google to ensure that NativeScript and Angular are seamlessly integrated. If you know Angular, you're already ready to develop amazing native mobile apps with NativeScript. With NativeScript and Angular, a single code base (and skillset) can be used to create web apps and native mobile apps with 100% native performance and power. Buttery smooth animations, direct access to 100% of the native platform APIs, it's pretty amazing. Let's get started:

1. Let's go ahead and add a list picker to the home page for language selection, along with an action header on top so that we can navigate between pages.

Replace the HTML with the following, that uses `ListPicker` and `ActionBar` in our `home.component.html` file by using the following code:

```
<ActionBar title="Choose your language" class="action-bar">
    <ActionItem [nsRouterLink]="['/news']" ios.position="right"
     text="Next"></ActionItem>
</ActionBar>

<ListPicker [items]="languages" [(ngModel)]="languageSelected"
(selectedIndexChange)="setLanguage($event)"></ListPicker>
```

Let's initialize the languages in our component by using the following code in `home.component.ts`:

```
...
class HomeComponent {
    languages: Array<string> = ['English', 'Spanish'];
    languageSelected: number = 0;
    setLanguage(e) {

    }
}
```

Our languages are declared in a variable inside our component. We fetch them and bind them to the list picker.

Save the changes and let the app update. You should see the following on success:

Add the router link to the action bar to direct it to the news page after clicking on **Next**. We also need to set the index of the selected item in the service so that we can use it to load our news in the selected language.

Let's create the service using the Angular CLI by using the following command:

```
> ng g s app
```

The purpose of `AppService` in our application is to achieve the following:

- Storing the language that's been selected
- Making calls to our mocked APIs
- Storing all the news that we wish to display on the details page (avoid multiple calls)

We can achieve this by adding the `getNews` function and saving the response from the API in the `news` property. Let's create a property so that we can store the language that's selected by the user by using the following code in `AppService`:

```
...
import { HttpClient } from '@angular/common/http';
import { tap } from 'rxjs/operators';
...
const API_URL = 'https://demo7831153.mockable.io';
export class AppService {

    language = 'English';
    news;

    constructor(private http: HttpClient) { }
    getNews() {
        return this.http.get(this.getUrl()).pipe(
            tap((resp: any) => this.news = resp.articles),
        );
    }

    getUrl() {
        if (this.language === 'English') {
            return `${API_URL}/en`;
        }

        return `${API_URL}/es`;
    }
}
```

Our service will default the language to `English` until the user changes it from the line picker. We will be using the `HttpClient` from Angular to make the API call. Since we are using `HttpClient`, do not forget to import `HttpClientModule` in our `AppModule`. Create a `getNews` method that accepts a URL and returns the `news` object.

In the `home` component, we will be adding a `setLanguage` method to set the index of the language that's selected:

```
...
import { AppService } from '../app.service';
...
export class HomeComponent {
    constructor(private appService: AppService) {}

    setLanguage(e) {
        const selectedIndex = e.object.selectedIndex;
        this.appService.language =
            this.languages[selectedIndex];
```

```
    }
  }
```

Now, let's go ahead and create the news page to display the news headlines.

Creating the news page

Here, we are going to create one more component that's similar in nature to our home page. This page will be loading all the news posts and showing us their headlines:

```
> ng g c news
```

Let's define the news route in our app-routing module:

```
{ path: 'news', component: NewsComponent },
```

Let's start by fetching the news from our mocked API:

```
. . .
import { AppService } from '../app.service';
. . .
export class NewsComponent implements OnInit {
    public data;

    constructor(private appService: AppService) { }

    ngOnInit(): void {
        this.getData();
    }

    getData() {
        this.appService.getNews()
            .subscribe((response: any) => {
                this.data = response.articles;
            });
    }

}
```

On the `home` component's initialization, we are going to call the `getData` method, which fetches the URL of the mocked API and calls the `getNews` method inside the app service. The `getNews` method returns an observable, which, on subscription, gives us access to the response. On getting the response, we need to set the data inside the home component.

Let's go ahead and add some HTML to display the news. We will add the following code:

```
<ActionBar title="News Report" class="action-bar"></ActionBar>
<GridLayout>
    <ListView [items]="data">
        <ng-template let-data="item">
            <GridLayout class="list-item" [nsRouterLink]="['/detail',
            data.source.id]">
                <Image [src]="data.urlToImage" class="image"
                 stretch="aspectFill"></Image>
                <Label [text]="data.title" class="item-title"
                 textWrap="true"></Label>
            </GridLayout>
        </ng-template>
    </ListView>
</GridLayout>
```

We will use `GridLayout` to display all the news posts. Each news post will be a `GridLayout` in itself. The posts will be listed in `ListView`. The data that's fetched from our response is bound to `ListView` and looped through to display each post.

Now, let's add some CSS to our page by using the following code:

```
.list-item {
    margin-bottom: 2;
    height: 25%;
}

.item-title {
    background-color: rgba(0,0,0,0.4);
    color: white;
    vertical-align: bottom;
    padding: 16;
    font-size: 14;
}
```

Now, you should see the **News Report** page styled, as shown in the following screenshot:

Each post that's a `GridLayout` has a router link bound to it that points to the specific post's detail page.

Now that our news page is ready, we will create a details page to display the description.

Creating the details page

The details page is going to display the description of the news post that's clicked on the news page.

Let's create a new component similar to the other two components we created previously:

```
> ng g c detail
```

Let's define the detail route in our app-routing module:

```
{ path: 'detail/:id', component: DetailComponent },
```

Now, let's use ActivatedRoute to get the id from the route, and AppService to get the detail of the current news that is going to be displayed on the details page. We need to initialize ActivatedRoute and AppService inside the constructor method of DetailComponent, which we can do by using the following code:

```
...
import { ActivatedRoute } from '@angular/router';
import { AppService } from '../app.service';

...
export class DetailComponent implements OnInit {
 currentNews = {};

    constructor(private route: ActivatedRoute, private appService:
    AppService) {

    }
    ngOnInit() {
        this.route.params.subscribe(params => {
            this.getNews(params.id);
        });
    }

    getNews(id) {
        const data = this.appService.news;
        this.currentNews = data.find(item => id == item.source.id);
    }
}
```

Fetch the id from the route params to display the specific news details on the details page.

After successfully fetching the post's `id`, we want to call the `getNews` method. This method will filter out a specific post from all of the posts on the news page:

```
<StackLayout class="main" orientation="vertical">
    <Image row="0" col="0" height="300" stretch="aspectFill" class="card-
      img" [src]="currentNews.urlToImage"></Image>
    <Label class="description-text" [text]="currentNews.description"
      fontWeight="bold" textWrap="true">
    </Label>
    <Label [text]="currentNews.content" textWrap="true"></Label>
</StackLayout>
```

We can use `StackLayout` for the details page as we will be stacking the content vertically:

Now that our details page is ready, let's look into how we can implement our app in different languages using the Angular Translate library.

Implementing internationalization using ngx-translate

When developing multi-language Angular applications, it is very important that all the text on a page can be translated. There are many ways of supporting such a feature, one of which we will use in this chapter, called ngx-translate. ngx-translate lets you use the same app for multiple languages, instead of creating multiple apps for different languages.

So far, we have used different APIs for each language, but in this instance, we need to translate text that doesn't come from the API, such as the headings and button text. Let's get to it:

1. Let's go ahead and install the ngx-translate module using the following command:

```
> npm install @ngx-translate/core --save
```

2. Now, we need to add TranslateModule in the imports of our AppModule, as follows:

```
import { TranslateModule } from '@ngx-translate/core'
...
@NgModule({
    imports: [
        ...
        TranslateModule.forRoot(),
    ]
})
export class AppModule {

}
```

3. Let's add the translated text in the constructor of our AppComponent and set the default language to English, as follows:

```
...
import { TranslateService } from '@ngx-translate/core';
...
export AppComponent {
    constructor(translate: TranslateService) {
        translate.setTranslation('en', {
            TITLE: 'Title',
            DESC: 'Description',
            CHOOSE_LANG: 'Choose your language',
```

```
            NEWS: 'News',
            NEXT: 'Next'
        });

        translate.setTranslation('es', {
            TITLE: 'Título',
            DESC: 'Descripción',
            CHOOSE_LANG: 'Elige tu idioma',
            NEWS: 'Noticias',
            NEXT: 'Siguiente'
        });

        translate.setDefaultLang('en');
    }
    ...
}
```

4. In the `HomeComponent`, where we are setting the language on top of the next button, we will be setting the language to translate service using the `setDefaultLang` method, as follows:

```
...
import { TranslateService } from '@ngx-translate/core';
...
const LANGUAGE_MAPPER = {
    English: 'en',
    Spanish: 'es'
}
...
export class HomeComponent {
    ...
    constructor(private appService: AppService, private translate:
    TranslateService) {}
    setLanguage(e) {
        const selectedIndex = e.object.selectedIndex;
        this.appService.language = this.languages[selectedIndex];
    this.translate.setDefaultLang(
            LANGUAGE_MAPPER[this.languages[selectedIndex]]
        );
    }
}
```

5. Let's add the `translate` pipe to our HTML details page:

```
<StackLayout class="main" verticalAlignment="top">

    <Image row="0" col="0" height="300" stretch="aspectFill"
```

```
class="card-img" [src]="currentNews.urlToImage"></Image>

    <Label col="1" class="tile" [text]="'TITLE' | translate"
     fontWeight="bold" textWrap="true"></Label>
    <Label col="1" class="description-text"
    [text]="currentNews.title" textWrap="true"></Label>
    <Label editable="false" textWrap="true" [text]="'DESC' |
     translate" fontWeight="bold">
    </Label>
    <Label editable="false" class="description-value"
     textWrap="true" [text]="currentNews.description"></Label>
    <Label editable="false" textWrap="true"
    [text]="currentNews.content"></Label>
</StackLayout>
```

Angular's `translate` pipe uses the string's `id` pass in the expression and binds the rendered translated string inside the `label` element. Now, you can see that the labels are properly displayed in the application, along with correct internationalized labels, as shown in the following screenshot:

Now that we have translated the whole application, including the static strings, let's try to use one of the NativeScript plugins in our application.

Adding a NativeScript plugin to our application

NativeScript plugins are npm packages with some added Native functionality. Therefore, finding, installing, and removing NativeScript plugins works a lot like working with the npm packages you might use in your Node.js or frontend web development. You can find all the available NativeScript plugins at the NativeScript Marketplace: https://market.nativescript.org/.

Let's go ahead and add a NativeScript plugin to our application. The plugin we will be adding is called snackbar. We can add the plugin to our application by using the following code:

```
> npm i nativescript-snackbar
```

To use our snackbar plugin, we will initialize the Snackbar in our HomeComponent and call it on the setLanguage method:

```
import { SnackBar } from 'nativescript-snackbar';

export class HomeComponent {
    ...
    setLanguage() {
        const selectedIndex = e.object.selectedIndex;
        const snackbar = new SnackBar();

        this.appService.language = this.languages[selectedIndex];
        this.translate.setDefaultLang(
            LANGUAGE_MAPPER[this.languages[selectedIndex]]
        );
        this.translate.get('LANG_UPDATED').subscribe(val => {
            snackbar.simple(val, 'red', '#067ab4', 3, false);
        });
    }
}
```

Now, we should be able to see a Snackbar every time we set a language.

 NativeScript plugins do not run on NativeScript playground app, as it does not include the native packages. You need to run the application in the emulator using `npx -p nativescript tns run <platform>`. The platform could be either iOS or Android. If the emulator is not setup on your machine, the command will let you configure for local builds, which will take you to a step by step installation process to be able to run the application on the emulator.

This completes our NativeScript application's implementation. In the next chapter, we will be creating a Reusable Component library and publish it to npm and wrap a Angular Component as a Web Component using Angular Element.

Summary

In this chapter, we used our Angular knowledge to create a Native mobile application using NativeScript Angular. We created a multi-language news application and successfully used `ngx-translate` to add internationalization to our application. We also added a NativeScript plugin from the NativeScript marketplace so that we can add a Snackbar whenever the language is switched.

Now, you can create Native mobile applications using NativeScript Angular, and also use third-party Angular modules such as `ngx-translate` to add internationalization to your app. We learned about different layouts that can be used to create layouts in our NativeScript app.

In the next chapter, we will create a reusable component library and publish it to npm. We will also create an Angular component and convert it into an Angular element that can be used in any application, with or without the Angular framework.

Questions

Test your knowledge of this chapter by answering the following questions:

- What is NativeScript? How does it differ from Ionic?
- What is the NativeScript Playground app?
- What are the different layouts in NativeScript?
- What is `ngx-translate`, and why should we use it in our application?
- What are NativeScript plugins?

Further reading

The following reading material will provide you with more information about NativeScript, layouts, `ngx-translate`, and NativeScript's `snackbar` plugin:

- Quick Setup guide for NativeScript Angular: `https://docs.nativescript.org/angular/start/quick-setup`.
- NativeScript layouts: `https://docs.nativescript.org/ui/layouts/layout-containers`.
- ngx-translate: `https://github.com/ngx-translate/core`.
- NativeScript Marketplace: `https://market.nativescript.org/`.
- NativeScript Snackbar plugin: `https://market.nativescript.org/plugins/nativescript-snackbar`.

10
Building a Component Library Using Angular CDK and Elements

In this chapter, we will build a component library that can be used not only in our applications but can also be published on npm so that it can be used by any other applications that want to use our component library. Reusable component libraries are something that make teams build awesome applications super fast. We will be building a drop-down reusable component library that will be so flexible that it can be used multiple times in the application.

The following topics will be covered in this chapter:

- Understanding Angular CDK
- Creating drop-down functionality
- Adding accessibility support
- Publishing a library on npm
- Introducing Angular elements

Technical requirements

This chapter's code can be found in this book's GitHub repository, https://github.com/ PacktPublishing/Angular-Projects, under the Chapter10 folder. The code has been provided for you so that, whenever you are stuck, you can verify whether you've done something different and play with the working project in the repository.

We want you to follow the sections in this chapter in the order in which they appear and learn as much as you can about different aspects of Angular development.

Understanding the Angular CDK

The Angular **Component Development Kit** (**CDK**) is a set of tools that are provided by the Angular Material team for implementing common interaction patterns. This was primarily built for the Angular Material component library, but it can be used by any other component library or project so that you can implement common patterns in web development, ranging from accessibility, bi-directionality, drag and drop, and responsive layouts, along with reusable generic components such as steppers, tables, and trees.

The Angular CDK makes it easy for developers to create high-quality component libraries for their projects. In this chapter, we will be using the Angular CDK to manage the focus of the drop-down component when the user interacts with it.

Project overview

In this chapter, we will be using **Nx** to create a workspace and a `demo` app, as well as a library of reusable components. Then, we will create one reusable component, a drop-down, using the **Bulma CSS** framework. Finally, we will add accessibility for keyboard users by using the Angular CDK.

The following screenshot shows what our drop-down will look like:

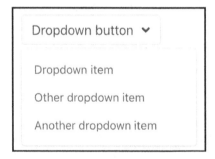

When the `Dropdown button` is clicked, the drop-down options are toggled.

Afterward, we will create an application that will create an Angular element, which can be used in any web application. We will create a simple web application without a framework/library and run our Angular element in it.

Getting started

We will be using Nx here, which we already used in Chapter 8, *Building an Enterprise Portal Using Nx, NgRx, and Redux*, in order to create our workspace. Previously, we converted our existing Angular CLI application into an Nx workspace, but in this chapter, we will use `create-nx-workspace` to create a new Nx workspace for this project.

Let's use `npx`, along with `create-nx-workspace`, to create our project. We will use the following command to do so:

```
> npx create-nx-workspace@latest bulmas --npmScope <<YOUR-UNIQUE-NPM-
SCOPE>>
? What to create in the new workspace angular [a workspace with a sing
le Angular application]
? Application name demo
? Which stylesheet format would you like to use? SCSS
```

In the above command replace <<YOUR-UNIQUE-NPM-SCOPE>> with a unique string, which defines a unique organization in `npmjs.org`. To make sure no one else have used it, login to `https://www.npmjs.com/` and try to create an organization using `https://www.npmjs.com/org/create`.

Let's generate a `library` that is `publishable` and has a prefix of `ba`:

```
> ng generate library bulma --publishable --prefix=ba
? Which stylesheet format would you like to use? SASS(.scss)   [
http://sass-lang ]
```

Now, let's include our `BulmaModule` from our library in the `AppModule` of the demo application so that we can run the components from it in our demo application:

```
...
import { BulmaModule } from '@<<YOUR-UNIQUE-NPM-SCOPE>>/bulma';

@NgModule({
    ...
    imports: [BrowserModule, BulmaModule],
    ...
})
export class AppModule {}
```

Let's install all of the dependencies that are required for this library. We will be using the Bulma CSS framework, Lodash, and the Angular CDK in this project. We can install the dependencies by using the following command:

```
> npm install --save bulma lodash-es @angular/cdk
```

Let's include the Bulma CSS file for our `demo` application in our Angular configuration, `angular.json`:

```
{
    ...
    "projects": {
        "bulma": {
            ...
        },
        "demo": {
            ...
            "architect": {
                "build": {
                    "builder": "@angular-devkit/build-angular:browser",
                    "options": {
                        ...
                        "styles": [
                            "apps/demo/src/styles.scss",
                            "./node_modules/bulma/css/bulma.min.css"
                        ],
                        ...
                    },
                    ...
                },
                ...
            }
```

Let's also include Font Awesome's CSS file in the `index.html` file of our `demo` application:

```
<link rel="stylesheet"
href="https://use.fontawesome.com/releases/v5.6.3/css/all.css"
integrity="sha384-
UHRtZLI+pbxtHCWp1t77Bi1L4ZtiqrqD80Kn4Z8NTSRyMA2Fd33n5dQ8lWUE00s/"
crossorigin="anonymous">
```

Now, let's use the drop-down components' HTML from Bulma's documentation, `https://bulma.io/documentation/components/dropdown/`, in `app.component.html`. Replace its content with the following code:

```
<div class="dropdown is-active">
    <div class="dropdown-trigger">
        <button class="button" aria-haspopup="true" aria-
        controls="dropdown-menu">
            <span>Dropdown button</span>
            <span class="icon is-small">
                <i class="fas fa-angle-down" aria-hidden="true"></i>
            </span>
        </button>
```

```
        </div>
        <div class="dropdown-menu" id="dropdown-menu" role="menu">
            <div class="dropdown-content">
                <a href="#" class="dropdown-item">
                    Dropdown item
                </a>
                <a class="dropdown-item">
                    Other dropdown item
                </a>
                <a href="#" class="dropdown-item">
                    Another dropdown item
                </a>
            </div>
        </div>
    </div>
</div>
```

Now, serve the demo application by using the following command:

```
> ng serve demo
```

You should see the following output:

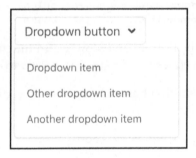

Since we've only added HTML and CSS, you will see that clicking on the dropdown button does not close the drop-down. It is currently open because we've used the is-active class, along with the dropdown class.

Now, we have a basic drop-down that is styled using Bulma's CSS, but it currently doesn't function. In the next section, we'll add the necessary functionality so that our drop-down works.

Creating dropdown functionality

Let's create some drop-down functionality by using directives. You could have also chosen some components to create it, but in a few cases, directives provide more flexibility. In this chapter, I have chosen directives since drop-downs can be used in various ways. Not only can the drop-down trigger be applied to a button—it can also be applied to other elements, such as anchors.

Let's create four directives: `dropdown`, `dropdown-toggle`, `dropdown-menu`, and `dropdown-item`. The `dropdown` directive will be the parent directive that will control whether the drop-down is open and not, while `dropdown-toggle` will be used to toggle the state of the drop-down. `dropdown-menu` will be the parent of all `dropdown-item` we add. We'll also export them as they are in the library. By doing this, they will be able to be imported. We can do this by importing `BulmaModule` into any application.

Let's run the following commands in the Terminal to create four directives:

```
> ng g d dropdown/dropdown --project bulma --export
> ng g d dropdown/dropdown-toggle --project bulma --export
> ng g d dropdown/dropdown-menu --project bulma --export
> ng g d dropdown/dropdown-item --project bulma --export
```

Now, let's go from the top to the bottom and slowly add functionality to each one. First, let's just use the directives to add specific classes to each element.

Let's make sure that any element that has `baDropdownItem` directives has a class of `dropdown-item`:

```
import { Directive } from '@angular/core';

@Directive({
    selector: '[baDropdownItem]',
    host: {
        'class': 'dropdown-item'
    }
})
export class DropdownItemDirective {

    constructor() { }

}
```

Similarly, any element that has `baDropdownItem` directives needs to have a class of `dropdown-menu` and a role of `menu`:

```
import { Directive } from '@angular/core';

@Directive({
    selector: '[baDropdownMenu]',
    host: {
        'class': 'dropdown-menu',
        'role': 'menu'
    }
})
export class DropdownMenuDirective {

    constructor() { }

}
```

Any element with `baDropdownToggle` will have the `aria-haspopup` attribute on it:

```
import { Directive } from '@angular/core';

@Directive({
    selector: '[baDropdownToggle]',
    host: {
        'attr.aria-haspopup': 'true'
    }
})
export class DropdownToggleDirective {

    constructor() { }

}
```

Finally, let's add the class of `dropdown` and `is-active` to the `baDropdown` directive:

```
import { Directive } from '@angular/core';

@Directive({
    selector: '[baDropdown]',
    host: {
        'class': 'dropdown is-active'
    }
})
export class DropdownDirective {

    constructor() { }
}
```

Now, in our `demo` application, we'll need to remove the `dropdown`, `dropdown-item`, and `dropdown-menu` classes and replace them with our new directives in the `app.component.html` file. Also, make sure that we remove the role from `dropdown-menu`, as well as the `aria-haspopup` attribute from the drop-down toggle button:

```html
<div baDropdown>
    <div class="dropdown-trigger">
        <button class="button" baDropdownToggle aria-controls="dropdown-
        menu"
            <span>Dropdown button</span>
            <span class="icon is-small">
                <i class="fas fa-angle-down" aria-hidden="true"></i>
            </span>
        </button>
    </div>
    <div baDropdownMenu id="dropdown-menu">
        <div class="dropdown-content">
            <a href="#" baDropdownItem>
                Dropdown item
            </a>
            <a baDropdownItem>
                Other dropdown item
            </a>
            <a href="#" baDropdownItem>
                Another dropdown item
            </a>
        </div>
    </div>
</div>
```

Now, when you check your `demo` application, you should see the same drop-down component and no toggling functionality. This is because we haven't touched any logic to toggle whether the drop-down is open or not.

Let's start with our parent directive, `DropdownDirective`. Here, we'll create the class properties menu and toggle what we will set from their respective directives by getting the host, that is, `DropdownDirective`. We will also create an `open` property and then create a `get` property to get the open status so that it can be used in host binding. Let's remove the `is-active` class from the `HostBinding` class and add its own `HostBinding`, depending on the open status:

```typescript
import { Directive } from '@angular/core';
import { DropdownMenuDirective } from './dropdown-menu.directive';
import { DropdownToggleDirective } from './dropdown-toggle.directive';

@Directive({
```

```
    selector: '[baDropdown]',
    host: {
        class: 'dropdown',
        '[class.is-active]': '_open'
    }
})
export class DropdownDirective {
    open: boolean;
    menu: DropdownMenuDirective;
    toggle: DropdownToggleDirective;

    get _open() {
        return this.open;
    }

    constructor() { }

}
```

Now, let's use the `Host` decorator to get the instance of our parent directive `DropdownDirective`, and set the `toggle` property to the instance of `DropdownToggleDirective`. Let's add a click event to our `Host` object. Then, in the `toggle` method, toggle the `DropdownDirective` open property:

```
import { Directive, Host } from '@angular/core';
import { DropdownDirective } from './dropdown.directive';

@Directive({
    selector: '[baDropdownToggle]',
    host: {
        ...
        '(click)': '_toggle($event)'
    }
})
export class DropdownToggleDirective {

    constructor(@Host() private dropdown: DropdownDirective) {
        this.dropdown.toggle = this;
    }

    _toggle(event) {
        this.dropdown.open = !this.dropdown.open;
    }

}
```

Let's also set the instance of `DropdownMenu` in `DropdownMenuDirective` to the `DropdownDirective` class property menu. We need to make sure that, when the drop-down menu is clicked, the drop-down closes:

```
import { Directive, Host } from '@angular/core';
import { DropdownDirective } from './dropdown.directive';

@Directive({
    selector: '[baDropdownMenu]',
    host: {
        class: 'dropdown-menu',
        '(click)': '_close()'
    }
})
export class DropdownMenuDirective {

    constructor(@Host() private dropdown: DropdownDirective) {
        this.dropdown.menu = this;
    }

    _close() {
        this.dropdown.open = false;
    }

}
```

Now, let's check our demo application. You should see that the drop-down is closed in the beginning, but when you click on drop-down button, the menu opens up. If you click on any item inside the menu or drop-down button, the menu should close.

Next, let's try to add accessibility support to our component.

Adding accessibility support

Accessibility is very important when it comes to the components library. Our components need to be accessible to all users. Some users may be blind, use screen readers to access our websites, or have a motor disability, which means they can only use the keyboard to access the website.

If you are using Windows, you can use tools such as NVDA to run a screen reader on your machine. If you are using a macOS, then you can use VoiceOver, which is built into macOS.

We've already added `aria-popup` to our `DirectiveToggleDirective`. However, we also need to set the `aria-controls` attribute, which tells the screen reader what element the popup is, which is controlled by this toggle. In our HTML, we have `aria-controls` set to `dropdown-menu`, which is the ID on the drop-down menu element. When we have multiple drop-downs, these IDs need to be different for each element.

Let's use `uniqueId` from Lodash to produce a new unique ID for our `DropdownMenu`. We will be using `HostBinding` and the following code:

```
import { Directive, Host, HostBinding } from '@angular/core';
import uniqueId from 'lodash-es/uniqueId';

...
export class DropdownMenuDirective implements AfterContentInit {
    @HostBinding('id') id = uniqueId('dropdown-id-');
    ...
}
```

Now, let's access `id` so that we can set `aria-controls` on our `DropdownToggleDirective`. We do this by accessing the `id` we just created in `DropdownMenu`, like so:

```
import { Directive, Host, ElementRef, HostBinding } from '@angular/core';

...
export class DropdownToggleDirective {
    ...

    @HostBinding('attr.aria-controls') get ariaControls() {
        return this.dropdown.menu.id;
    }
}
```

Now, when we have multiple drop-downs on our page, this will make sure that each drop-down has a unique ID for accessibility.

Next, let's work on the keyboard accessibility of our component. When you use *Tab* to go to our `Dropdown button` element and click *Enter* or space, you should see that the drop-down opens up. However, there is no way for us to select the items from the menu using the keyboard alone. We want to use the up and down keyboard keys to traverse the menu. When we click *Enter*, we want the focus to go back to `Dropdown button`.

We will be using Angular CDK's focus manager to manage the focus of our drop-down. Let's start by adding the `focus` method to our `DropdownItemDirective`, which will focus on `nativeElement` of the `host` element:

```
...
export class DropdownItemDirective {
    ...
    constructor(private el: ElementRef) { }

    focus() {
        this.el.nativeElement.focus();
    }
}
```

Now, we'll use `ContentChildren` in `DropdownMenuDirective` to access all of the `DropdownItemDirective` that are used inside it. Then, in the `AfterContentInit` life cycle method, we'll initialize our `FocusKeyManager`. We'll also add the `keydown` event and call the `onKeydown` method of `keyManager`.

Let's make these changes in `DropdownMenuDirective`, as follows:

```
import { Directive, Host, ContentChildren, QueryList, AfterContentInit }
from '@angular/core';
...
import { DropdownItemDirective } from './dropdown-item.directive';

@Directive({
    selector: '[baDropdownMenu]',
    host: {
        ...
        '(keydown)': 'onKeydown($event)'
    }
})
export class DropdownMenuDirective implements AfterContentInit {
    @ContentChildren(DropdownItemDirective) items:
    QueryList<DropdownItemDirective>;
    public keyManager: FocusKeyManager<DropdownItemDirective>;

    ...

    ngAfterContentInit() {
        this.keyManager = new FocusKeyManager(this.items).withWrap();
    }

    onKeydown(event) {
        this.keyManager.onKeydown(event);
    }
```

```
    ...
}
```

Now, we need to make sure that, when the drop-down opens, the first item is selected in the menu. We do this by updating the `_toggle` method in `DropdownToggleDirective`, like so:

```
...
export class DropdownToggleDirective {
    ...

    _toggle(event) {
        this.dropdown.open = !this.dropdown.open;
        if (this.dropdown.open) {
            setTimeout(() =>
                this.dropdown.menu.keyManager
                    .setFocusOrigin('keyboard')
                    .setFirstItemActive()
            );
        }
    }
}
```

Let's try `demo` once again. Now, you should be able to use the following code:

```
import { Directive, Host, ElementRef } from '@angular/core';
...

export class DropdownToggleDirective {
    ...

    constructor(
        @Host() private dropdown: DropdownDirective,
        public el: ElementRef
    ) {
        this.dropdown.toggle = this;
    }
}
```

Now that we have `ElementRef` `el` available on `DropDownToggleDirective`, let's use it in `DropDownMenuDirective` to focus on `nativeElement`, as follows:

```
...
import { ENTER } from '@angular/cdk/keycodes';
...
export class DropdownMenuDirective implements AfterContentInit {
    ...
```

```
onKeydown(event) {
    if (event.keyCode === ENTER) {
        this.dropdown.toggle.el.nativeElement.focus();
    } else {
        this.keyManager.onKeydown(event);
    }
}
...
}
```

Now that we have our component ready to be used in our project, let's try to publish the library on npm so that anyone can consume it in their project.

Publishing a library on npm

npm is the world's largest software registry that JavaScript developers use to share and use millions of packages. In this book, we have installed a lot of different packages for our projects.

Let's go ahead and publish our first npm package, which other developers can install and use in their projects. Before we build our application, make sure that you know the version of the library that we will be publishing. The version can be found in the package.json file of the Bulma library folder:

```
{
    "name": "@<<YOUR-UNIQUE-NPM-SCOPE>>/bulma",
    "version": "0.0.1",
    "peerDependencies": {
        "@angular/common": "^7.2.0",
        "@angular/core": "^7.2.0"
    }
}
```

Whenever you want to update a new version of the library, you need to make sure to update this version. The version is divided into three parts: major . minor. patch.

The major version needs to be updated when the whole library is rewritten or a major update occurs. The minor version needs to be updated whenever you add a new feature to your library. Whenever you have fixed bugs, simply update the patch version.

First, let's build the library by using the following code:

```
> ng build bulma
```

This should `build` your library with different configurations, such as `esm5`, `esm2015`, `fesm5`, `fesm2015`, and `umd`, in the `dist/libs/bulma` folder.

Now, let's add a packaging script to our `package.json` scripts:

```
{
    ...
    "scripts": {
        ...
        "package:bulma": "cd dist/libs/bulma && npm pack"
    },
    ...
}
```

Now run the script, using the following `npm` command:

```
> npm run package:bulma
```

This should create the `<<YOUR-UNIQUE-NPM-SCOPE>>-bulma-0.0.1.tgz` file. Now that we have built and packaged our library, let's publish our library on `npm`.

Before we publish our package on `npm`, make sure you have an account on `http://npmjs.com`. We will need to log in to `npm` using the following command:

```
> npm login
```

You need to enter your credentials to log in to the `npm` CLI. Now, let's use `npm publish` to publish our library:

```
> npm publish <<YOUR-UNIQUE-NPM-SCOPE>>-bulma-0.0.1.tgz --access public
```

This should create a library on `http://npmjs.com`, so that anyone can install it using `npm`. Just use the following command:

```
> npm install @<<YOUR-UNIQUE-NPM-SCOPE>>/bulma
```

We have successfully published an Angular reusable component library on `npm`. Next, we will look at what Angular elements are and look at how we can create one.

Introducing Angular elements

Another thing that we can consider while creating a reusable library is Angular elements. Angular elements are nothing but Angular components packaged as web components. Web components are a web standard way of creating custom elements for the web, all of which can be used in any application as simple HTML elements. By converting our components into Angular elements, we can make sure that our components can be used not only in different Angular applications but also alongside other frameworks or libraries or even with Vanilla JS (without any framework or library).

Angular elements project

In order to create an Angular element, we need to have a separate application, and not a library, since an Angular element has to be packaged along with Angular core, polyfills, and so on.

Let's create a new application called `bulma-elements` using the following command:

```
> ng generate application bulma-elements --prefix ba
? Which stylesheet format would you like to use? SASS(.scss)  [
http://sass-lang ]
? Would you like to configure routing for this application? No
```

Now, let's create the component in our project using the following command:

```
> ng g c pagination --project bulma-elements
```

Let's add the functionality to our `pagination.component.ts` file:

```
import { Component, OnInit, Input, Output, EventEmitter, SimpleChanges }
from '@angular/core';

@Component({
    selector: 'ba-pagination',
    templateUrl: './pagination.component.html',
    styleUrls: ['./pagination.component.scss']
})

export class PaginationComponent implements OnInit {
    @Input() pages = 0;
    @Output() change = new EventEmitter();
    currentPage = 1;
    pageList;

    constructor() { }
```

```
ngOnInit() {
    this.makePageList(this.pages);
}

ngOnChange(changes: SimpleChanges) {
    if (changes.pages && changes.pages.previousValue !==
    changes.pages.currentValue) {
        this.makePageList(changes.pages.currentValue);
    }
}

makePageList(value) {
    if (typeof value === 'string') {
        value = parseInt(value, 10);
    }
    this.pageList = new Array(value).fill(0).map((_, i) => i + 1);
}

goTo(page: number) {
    this.currentPage = page;
    this.change.emit({
        page,
    });
}

}
```

Now, we'll use the HTML from the Bulma pagination and use our methods and properties from the `PaginationComponent` class:

```html
<nav class="pagination" role="navigation" aria-label="pagination">
    <button class="pagination-previous" (click)="goTo(currentPage - 1)"
    [disabled]="currentPage === 1">Previous</button>
    <button class="pagination-next" (click)="goTo(currentPage + 1)"
    [disabled]="currentPage === pageList.length">Next page</button>
    <ul class="pagination-list">
        <li *ngFor="let page of pageList">
            <a
                class="pagination-link"
                [ngClass]="{'is-current': currentPage === page}"
                [attr.aria-label]="'Page ' + page"
                [attr.aria-current]="page===currentPage ? 'page' :
                undefined"
                (click)="goTo(page)"
            >
                {{page}}
            </a>
        </li>
```

```
        </ul>
    </nav>
```

You can use the component in `app.component.html`, as follows:

```
<ba-pagination [pages]="3"></ba-pagination>
```

Now, let's `serve` our application using the following command:

```
> ng serve bulma-elements
```

You should be able to use the pagination component. Click on the **Previous** and **Next page** buttons, as well as the individual page buttons.

Now, let's install `@angular/elements` to convert the `PaginationComponent` into a custom element, using the following command:

```
> npm install @angular/elements
```

Next, we need to use the `createCustomElement` function from Angular Elements, as well as `customElements`, to define our new component as an Angular element. We also need to define the `doBootstrap` method, as follows:

```
import { BrowserModule } from '@angular/platform-browser';
import { NgModule, Injector } from '@angular/core';
import { PaginationComponent } from './pagination/pagination.component';
import { createCustomElement } from "@angular/elements";

@NgModule({
    declarations: [PaginationComponent],
    imports: [BrowserModule],
    entryComponents: [PaginationComponent],
    providers: [],
})
export class AppModule {
    constructor(injector: Injector) {
        const el = createCustomElement(PaginationComponent, { injector });
        customElements.define('ba-pagination', el);
    }

    ngDoBootstrap() { }

}
```

Let's also remove `AppComponent` from the imports and declarations of `NgModule`, and delete the `app.component.ts` file, as it will throw an error while compilation, if it didn't find `AppComponent` to be a part of any `NgModule`.

Now, let's build our application by using the following command, with no `output hashing` so that the bundles that are generated do not have a random string attached to them:

```
> ng build --prod --project bulma-elements --output-hashing none
```

Now, let's concatenate `runtime.js`, `polyfills.js`, and `main.js` into one file called `bulma-elements.js` using the `cat` command on macOS or `copy` command on Windows :

```
> cat dist/apps/bulma-elements/runtime-es2015.js dist/apps/bulma-
elements/polyfills-es2015.js dist/apps/bulma-elements/main-es2015.js >
dist/apps/bulma-elements/bulma-elements.js
```

 You can add `ngx-build-plus` to your project using the `ng add ngx-build-plus` Angular schematic and simply use a `singleBundle` flag while building the application, instead of manually concatenating the files after building the application.

Now, outside of our Nx application, let's create an `index.html` file and copy the `bulma-elements.js` file from the `dist/apps/bulma-elements` folder to the folder where you create the `index.html` file. Include the following HTML in the `index.html` file:

```html
<!DOCTYPE html>
<html lang="en">
<head>
    <meta charset="UTF-8">
    <meta name="viewport" content="width=device-width, initial-scale=1.0">
    <meta http-equiv="X-UA-Compatible" content="ie=edge">
    <title>Document</title>
    <link rel="stylesheet"
href="https://cdnjs.cloudflare.com/ajax/libs/bulma/0.7.4/css/bulma.min.css"
>
</head>
<body>
    <ba-pagination pages="5"></ba-pagination>
    <ba-pagination pages="3"></ba-pagination>

    <script src="./bulma-elements.js"></script>

    <script>
        const el = document.querySelector('ba-pagination');
```

```
        el.addEventListener('change', (e) => {
            console.log(e);
        });
    </script>
</body>
</html>
```

Now, when you open the `index.html` file in your browser, you should see that the pagination component works, even in a Vanilla JS application.

Summary

In this chapter, we created a reusable component library so that it can be used in multiple projects. We also published it on npm so that other people can use it in their projects. Then, we created another Angular application in order to convert an Angular component into an Angular element that can run in any application, with or without Angular.

We met our goal in this chapter by creating a library of reusable components and learning how to publish any library to npm for anyone who wants to consume the reusable components. We also learned about what Angular elements are and how to create them so that our reusable components can be consumed by any Angular or non-Angular projects.

In our next and final chapter, we will learn how to test our Angular components with different approaches, from unit testing to integration testing using Jasmine and Karma. We will also look at testing using Jest and writing end-to-end testing.

Questions

Test your knowledge of this chapter by answering the following questions:

- What is the importance of the component library in application development?
- Why is accessibility important in our application?
- What is the Angular CDK?
- What is npm?
- How do you publish a library on npm?
- What are Angular elements?

Further reading

The following reading material will provide you with more information about component libraries, the Angular CDK, and npm:

- Angular resources: `https://angular.io/resources`.
- Angular CDK: `https://material.angular.io/cdk`.
- Contributing packages to the npm registry: `https://docs.npmjs.com/packages-and-modules/contributing-packages-to-the-registry`.
- Angular elements: `https://angular.io/guide/elements`.
- ngx-build-plus: `https://github.com/manfredsteyer/ngx-build-plus`.

11
Testing an Angular Application Using Jasmine, Jest, and Protractor

In this chapter, we will cover one of the important topics in software development, that is, testing applications, and why it is important. We will start with an existing application that was built using the Angular CLI and we will make sure that all the existing tests pass. Then, we will add a new isolated test case and some deep integration testing to our application. We will then move on to running a code coverage report and setting thresholds for our coverage report. Afterward, we will move on to updating our tests, using Jest as the test runner to make the testing experience delightful. We will end this chapter by adding some **end-to-end** (**e2e**) tests to test the application.

The following topics will be covered in this chapter:

- Why test our web applications?
- Isolated unit testing
- Deep integration tests
- Deep integration tests for the component
- Deep integration tests for the service
- Understanding code coverage
- Using Jest with the Angular CLI
- Snapshot testing
- End-to-end testing
- Custom error handling

Technical requirements

This chapter's code can be found in this book's GitHub repository, `https://github.com/PacktPublishing/Angular-Projects`, under the `Chapter11` folder.

The code has been provided for you so that whenever you are stuck, you can verify whether you've done something differently and play with the working project in the repository.

We want you to follow the sections in this chapter in the order in which they appear and learn as much as you can about different aspects of Angular development.

Why test our web applications?

Software testing is the process of evaluating the functionality of the application and checking whether the expected results match the actual results of the software. There are a lot of different ways software can be tested, varying from unit testing, integration testing, end-to-end testing, manual testing, accessibility testing, and so on.

The main purpose of testing applications is to reduce bugs. The more the application is tested, the more confidence the development/project team has about the software. It makes sure that the users write better code, which, is testable and follows a better structure. It also adds documentation for the application so that the new developers of the application can see what is being tested.

All the projects have a unique way of testing the application, and they can introduce testing at different points in the development cycle:

- **Test before they write the code**: In some projects, the test cases are written before development starts. In this method, what kind of result is expected is decided beforehand, and so it's easier for the development team to move forward knowing the rigid requirements.
- **Test while they write the code**: In this method, some developers prefer to write test cases during the development process. In this case, the methods are written first, and then the test cases are written to verify whether the methods are passing.
- **Test after the whole software is complete**: In some projects, the team prefers to test the whole application after the development team has finished developing the feature. An example of this is manual testing.

Project overview

In this chapter, we will take an already existing application built from the Angular CLI, which has no tests written for it, except for the default test files that were generated by the Angular CLI while generating different files. This is a simple application that uses the Behance API to display a collection of design projects (`https://www.behance.net/dev/api/endpoints/5`). When you click on a particular project, it takes you to the details page:

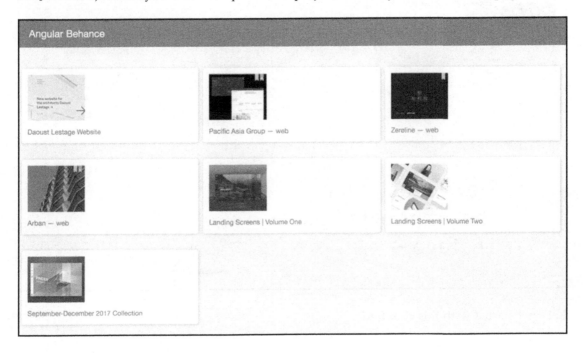

The details page has more details about the design project. The following screenshot shows an example design we clicked on, where we have the option to click on the **Add To Favorite** button to add the image to our favorites:

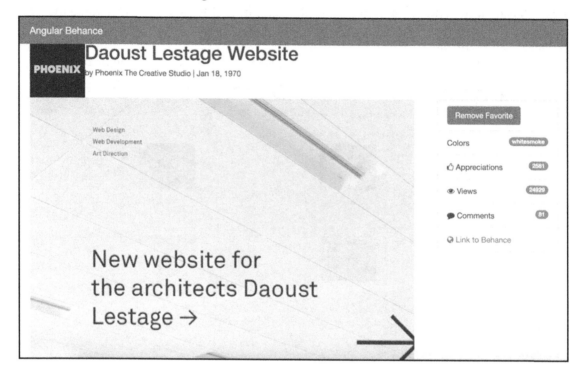

Let's get started with this chapter.

Getting started

In this chapter, we will be learning about the initial steps of testing, and we write a simple test case to demonstrate how testing works. Let's get started by cloning the project.

Please run the following command in your favorite command-line program. This will clone the repository on your local machine:

```
> git clone https://github.com/mohammedzamakhan/ngx-behance
```

Before we run our test, let's open up a test and understand some basics about Jasmine testing. Let's look at the `behance.service.spec.ts` file, which looks as follows:

```
import { TestBed } from '@angular/core/testing';
import { BehanceService } from './behance.service';
import { HttpClientTestingModule } from '@angular/common/http/testing';

describe('BehanceService', () => {
    beforeEach(() => TestBed.configureTestingModule({
        imports: [HttpClientTestingModule]
    }));

    it('should be created', () => {
        const service: BehanceService = TestBed.get(BehanceService);
        expect(service).toBeTruthy();
    });
});
```

The `describe` function is used to group multiple test cases. Here, we will group all the tests that are related to `BehanceService` in our `describe` block. The next thing we will see is `beforeEach`, which is inside the `describe` block. The function inside `beforeEach` runs before all the test cases in `describe` run. Similarly, Jasmine provides the `afterEach`, `beforeAll`, and `afterAll` methods. The `afterEach` method runs after each test block runs. If you want to speed things up, you can use `beforeAll` and `afterAll` if all the test blocks run some common code before all the tests. We need to be careful when we use `beforeAll` and `afterAll` as we cannot reset behavior between multiple tests. We then have the `it` function, which is used to define a single test case. In our test case, we can use `expect` to test the expected behavior with the actual behavior. In the preceding code, we have used a matcher called `toBeTruthy` to check whether the service value is available. There are a lot of different matchers that can be used, some of which are described here, in the Jasmine documents: `https://jasmine.github.io/api/edge/matchers.html`.

Now that we understand some of the basics of Jasmine testing, let's run the default tests that are generated by the Angular CLI using the following command:

```
> ng test
```

This should compile the application and open a browser to run all the test cases. The tests of the application can be found in the `*.spec.ts` files in the application. After the command finishes running in the browser, you should see that a total of **7 specs** (test cases) ran, and that **5** of them failed. This is because the Angular CLI added test cases for the code and then we modified the code for our application but never updated the test cases:

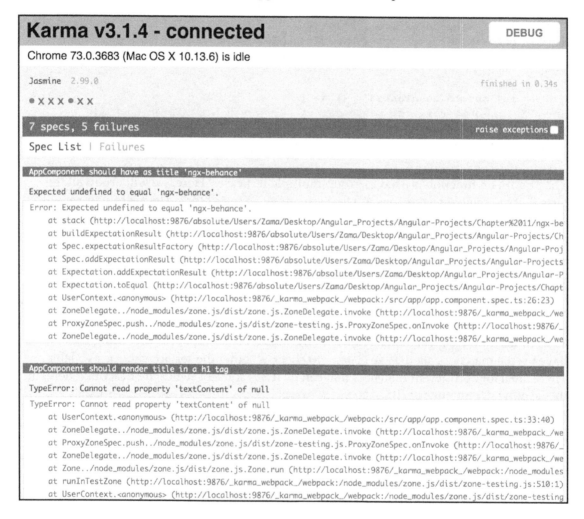

Let's fix all of the errors first, either by changing the tests to pass or by completely deleting that test case. Let's go from top to bottom.

The first test that failed says, **AppComponent should have as title 'ngx-behance'**. Let's check the test case first before fixing it. We will see that the failure happened because of the following code in the `app.component.spec.ts` file:

```
it(`should have as title 'ngx-behance'`, () => {
    const fixture = TestBed.createComponent(AppComponent);
    const app = fixture.debugElement.componentInstance;
    expect(app.title).toEqual('ngx-behance');
});
```

In this test case, it's getting an instance of the component and saving it in the `app` variable, checking whether the `title` property is equal to `ngx-behance`. However, when we check our `app.component.ts` file, we don't have any properties or methods in it. So, let's go ahead and delete this test case altogether.

Let's move to the next test case which says, **AppComponent should render title in h1 tag**. This test failed because of the following code:

```
it('should render title in a h1 tag', () => {
    const fixture = TestBed.createComponent(AppComponent);
    fixture.detectChanges();
    const compiled = fixture.debugElement.nativeElement;
    expect(compiled.querySelector('h1').textContent).toContain('Welcome to
    ngx-behance!');
});
```

In this test case, we use `debugElement` to get access to `nativeElement`, and then we use `querySelector` to get access to the `h1` tag's `textContent`, which contains `'Welcome to ngx-behance!'`. However, when we check our `app.component.html` file, we don't find any `h1` tags—but we do find an `anchor` tag that has a `textContent` of `'Angular Behance'`. Let's update our test case to consider that:

```
it('should render title in a h1 tag', () => {
    ...
    expect(compiled.querySelector('a').textContent).toContain('Angular
    Behance');
});
```

Now, when you check the browser that runs your test cases, you should see that out of 6 tests, **3** of them failed.

Let's look at the next failed test, that is, **BehanceService should be created**. Now, if we see an error, we should also see the reason for its failure:

```
Error: StaticInjectorError(DynamicTestModule)[HttpClient]:
StaticInjectorError(Platform: core)[HttpClient]:
    NullInjectorError: No provider for HttpClient!
```

From this, we can see that it failed because it could not find the `HttpClient` service, which should have been injected into the service when it was being created in our test file. In our application, we provide `HttpClientModule` to our `AppModule`, but since test cases have to run individually, we need to inject a module into it. We will be injecting `HttpClientTestingModule` here, which is provided by the Angular team for testing the `HttpClient` module, in `behance.service.spec.ts` file:

```
import { TestBed } from '@angular/core/testing';
import { HttpClientTestingModule } from '@angular/common/http/testing';

import { BehanceService } from './behance.service';

describe('BehanceService', () => {
    beforeEach(() => TestBed.configureTestingModule({
        imports: [HttpClientTestingModule]
    }));

    . . .
});
```

This should result in reducing the test failure count to **2**. Now, let's check the next failure:

```
HomeComponent should create
Failed: Template parse errors: Can't bind to 'routerLink' since it isn't a
known property of 'a'. (" <div class="row">
```

This test failed because we used `routerLink`, which is part of `RoutingModule`. Similar to `HttpClientModule`, we need to include a module that can understand `routerLink`. Again, Angular provides a `RouterTestingModule`, which we can include in the spec file of our `HomeComponent`:

```
. . .
import { RouterTestingModule } from '@angular/router/testing';

describe('HomeComponent', () => {
    let component: HomeComponent;
    let fixture: ComponentFixture<HomeComponent>;

    beforeEach(async(() => {
        TestBed.configureTestingModule({
```

```
        imports: [ RouterTestingModule ],
            declarations: [ HomeComponent ]
        })
        .compileComponents();
    }));
    ...
});
```

Now, when we check the browser, we will still have two test failures; the HomeComponent test case failed again because of HttpClient. This happened because HomeComponent uses BehanceService, which in turn uses HttpClient. Let's include HttpClientTestingModule in our HomeComponent, along with RouterTestingModule. Once added, you should only see one test case failing.

This time, our PostComponent failed upon creation because of the following error:

```
Failed: Template parse errors: The pipe 'colorNamer' could not be found
("of post.colors"> <span class="label label-default label-pill pull-xs-
right">{{[ERROR ->]color | colorNamer}}</span> </span>
```

That means that we have used a pipe called colorNamer, which it couldn't find. Let's declare the pipe in TestingModule and include RouterTestingModule and HttpClientTestingModule since our PostComponent uses routerLink as well as BehanceService:

```
import { ColorNamerPipe } from '../color-namer.pipe';

beforeEach(async(() => {
    TestBed.configureTestingModule({
        imports: [HttpClientTestingModule, RouterTestingModule],
        declarations: [ PostComponent, ColorNamerPipe ]
    })
    .compileComponents();
}));
```

Now, our Karma spec should show all of our test cases passing:

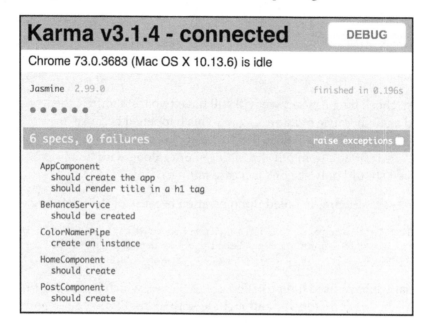

Now that we have understood the basic structure of Jasmine, how it works, and all our existing test cases have passed, let's focus on testing all of the classes and functions/methods.

Isolated unit testing

In this section, we will be looking at isolated unit testing. Isolated unit testing is the process of isolating a class or function and testing it as regular JavaScript code. In such test cases, we don't worry about the framework-specific stuff. We will be doing isolate unit testing for our `ColorNamerPipe` class, which looks as follows:

```
import { Pipe, PipeTransform } from '@angular/core';
import * as colorNamer from 'color-namer';

@Pipe({
    name: 'colorNamer'
})
export class ColorNamerPipe implements PipeTransform {

    transform(value: any, args?: any): any {
        return
```

```
colorNamer(`rgb(${value.r},${value.g},${value.b})`).html[0].name;
      }
}
```

We will test this code without worrying about the decorator on the class, that is, `ColorNamerPipe`. What this pipe takes is an object with r, g, and b values and uses an npm module to return the name of the color.

The Angular CLI already initializes the test files for pipes as isolated unit tests. In the following code, we can see that Angular has prepared a basic test to check whether the pipe has been created:

```
import { ColorNamerPipe } from './color-namer.pipe';

describe('ColorNamerPipe', () => {
    it('create an instance', () => {
        const pipe = new ColorNamerPipe();
        expect(pipe).toBeTruthy();
    });
});
```

Let's write our new test case, which will pass various values and check whether the pipe returns the correct value or not:

```
...
describe('ColorNamerPipe', () => {
    ...
    it('should return current color', () => {
        const pipe = new ColorNamerPipe();
        let transformedValue = pipe.transform({
            r: 255,
            g: 255,
            b: 255
        });
        expect(transformedValue).toEqual('white');
        transformedValue = pipe.transform({
            r: 255,
            g: 0,
            b: 0,
        });
        expect(transformedValue).toEqual('red');
        transformedValue = pipe.transform({
            r: 0,
            g: 255,
            b: 0,
        });
        expect(transformedValue).toEqual('lime');
```

```
      });
   });
```

In the preceding code, we are testing a particular block of code only. This is why it is called an isolated test case—because our test case is isolated only to one single feature. In this particular test case, we are testing whether the transformed value is returning as expected or not.

Deep integration tests

Isolated unit tests are good when we are testing a class without depending on the integration of the framework that we are using. But when it comes to testing a class alongside the framework, then we need to use integration testing. In the integration test, we test the behavior of a class/function as a whole to ensure that it works cohesively with the framework.

In deep integration tests, we let the framework run all the classes, just like it would do when it runs in its environment (such as a browser). We might want to mock some classes and functions, but overall we let the framework do most of the heavy lifting for us.

Angular uses dependency injection to create different Angular components, and it does so by using @NgModule. For testing, Angular provides TestBed, which can be used to create a TestModule that emulates Angular's @NgModule.

Deep integration tests for the component

In this section, we will be performing an integration test on our component by mocking an observable with an expected type of data. This will help us understand whether the data that's passed is flowing properly in our component and that the expected result is being obtained. We have already successfully configured TestModule for the spec of our HomeComponent. Let's add some data to our HomeComponent and check whether we can find the items that are being displayed by the template:

```
beforeEach(() => {
    fixture = TestBed.createComponent(HomeComponent);
    component = fixture.componentInstance;
    component.posts$ = of([{id: 1, name: 'Title 1', covers: {115: 'image
    1.jpg'}}, {id: 1, name: 'Title 2', covers: {115: 'image 2.jpg'}}]);
    fixture.detectChanges();
});
```

Here, in `beforeEach`, before we call our fixture to detect changes in the component, we've added a couple of posts. Let's add a couple of tests to test whether it has added two cards in the DOM and if the first card's title is like it was in the data we passed:

```
describe('HomeComponent', () => {
    ...
    it ('show have 2 post cards', () => {
        const cards = fixture.debugElement.queryAll(By.css('.card'));
        expect(cards.length).toEqual(2);
    });

    it ('should have the title in the card', () => {
        const cards = fixture.debugElement.queryAll(By.css('.card'));
        expect(cards[0].query(By.css('.card-
        text')).nativeElement.textContent)
            .toEqual('Title 1');
    });
});
```

By doing this, we have performed a deep test, which not only verifies whether the element with the `card` class has been created but also checks whether the title matches in the first element.

Deep integration tests for the service

Our service, `BehanceService`, uses `HttpClient` and has a couple of methods, `getPosts` and `getPost`, both of which call an HTTP call. In our testing, we don't want to call the HTTP call and test the actual API. Instead, we need to mock the HTTP call. We already included `HttpClientTestingModule` in the `BehanceService` spec file, which will help us to mock the API so that the actual HTTP request doesn't go out. Instead, we return a mocked response:

```
describe('BehanceService', () => {
    ...

    it('should call posts api', () => {
        const response = 'response';
        const service: BehanceService = TestBed.get(BehanceService);
        const httpMock: HttpClientTestingBackend =
        TestBed.get(HttpTestingController);

        service.getPosts().subscribe(data => {
            expect(data).toEqual(response);
        });
```

```
        const req = httpMock.expectOne(
            (request: any) => {
                return request.url === environment.api +
                'collections/170716829/projects?per_page=20&page=' + 1 +
                '&api_key=' + environment.token;
            }
        );

        expect(req.request.method).toEqual('JSONP');
        req.flush(response);
    });
});
```

Here, we have got the HTTP mock from `HttpTestingController`. We call the `getPosts` method and expect the data to be returned with a response. Then, we use `httpMock` as we expect a URL to be called and then use `req.flush` to execute the call, which should run the expectation inside the subscription.

Let's also go ahead and test the `getPost` method in a similar fashion:

```
describe('BehanceService', () => {
    ...

    it('should call post api', () => {
        const id = 'id';
        const response = 'response';

        const service: BehanceService = TestBed.get(BehanceService);
        const httpMock: HttpClientTestingBackend =
        TestBed.get(HttpTestingController);

        service.getPost(id).subscribe(data => {
            expect(data).toEqual(response);
        });

        const req = httpMock.expectOne(
            (request: any) => {
                return request.url === environment.api + 'projects/' + id +
                '?api_key=' + environment.token;
            }
        );

        expect(req.request.method).toEqual('JSONP');
        req.flush(response);
    });
});
```

In these tests, we are following the preceding concept of doing a deep integration test, but on a service instead of a component. In this case, we are testing whether the response is equal to the mock response that we created. It also checks the type of request that was made. The deeper the integration test goes, the better, because it does a thorough check to ensure no bugs pass through.

Understanding code coverage

Code coverage is a measure we use to describe the degree to which the code has been covered using tests. It gives a degree of confidence based on the percentage of the code that's been tested. Code coverage measures the percentage of lines of code that have been tested, the percentage of functions that have been tested, the percentage of statements that have been tested, and whether all the branches of code have been tested.

The Angular CLI supports code coverage out of the box. We can use the `code-coverage` flag and check the results. Let's run it by using the following command:

```
> ng test --code-coverage
```

After the preceding code runs all the tests, you will see a code coverage report on the console:

```
============================== Coverage summary
===============================
Statements : 89.74% ( 35/39 )
Branches : 100% ( 2/2 )
Functions : 76.92% ( 10/13 )
Lines : 90.63% ( 29/32 )
================================================================================
=====
TOTAL: 11 SUCCESS
TOTAL: 11 SUCCESS
```

All of these percentages give developers confidence about the code they are writing. In addition, we can add thresholds to our code coverage so that if we do not meet any particular percentage for code coverage, our tests fail. This is helpful in the continuous integration and continuous deployment of code. If our test coverage drops, our build fails, and our code does not go into production.

Let's add the threshold in the `karma.conf.js` file to our application's `src` folder:

```
module.exports = function (config) {
    config.set({
        ...
        coverageIstanbulReporter: {
            ...
            thresholds: {
                global: {
                    statements: 80,
                    branches: 80,
                    functions: 90,
                    lines: 80
                }
            }
        },
        ...
    });
};
```

In the preceding code block, we added the `thresholds functions` value as `90`, which is way higher than the code coverage report that we got when we ran the code coverage previously, which was `76.92`:

```
=============================== Coverage summary
================================
Statements : 89.74% ( 35/39 )
Branches : 100% ( 2/2 )
Functions : 76.92% ( 10/13 )
Lines : 90.63% ( 29/32 )
=============================================================================
=====
18 04 2019 22:21:40.189:ERROR [reporter.coverage-istanbul]: Coverage for
functions (76.92%) does not meet global threshold (90%)
TOTAL: 11 SUCCESS
TOTAL: 11 SUCCESS
```

Here, we need to set reasonable thresholds for our code coverage so that it does not fail. If you change it back to `75` and run it, the build will not fail. Different projects will need to have different thresholds. Open source projects and libraries need to have very high code coverage, for example, over 95%. However, enterprise applications and other applications might have around 75-85% code coverage, which is a good percentage.

We may also want to update the Karma config so that it runs in `ChromeHeadless` instead of the Chrome browser. Let's update the settings in the `karma.config.js` file, like so:

```
module.exports = function (config) {
    config.set({
        ...
        browsers: ['ChromeHeadless'],
        ...
    });
};
```

The preceding code helps in running the test on the CLI itself, and not open in the browser, which makes it simpler to test. Unless the user wants to debug the test, this is a better option.

Using Jest with the Angular CLI

The Angular CLI comes with Karma and Jasmine so that it can run unit test cases out of the box. Jasmine has been out there longer, but apart from Jasmine, there are other test runners in the JavaScript community. Some of the most popular ones are Mocha and Jest. Jest is one of the latest test runners and comes from Facebook. It is not only fast and easy to configure but also delightful to test with. It also allows you to perform a new kind of testing known as snapshot testing.

Let's configure `jest` using the `ng add` command:

```
> ng add @davinkevin/jest
```

This is one of the many community-provided schematics that adds Jest support, though others can add support too, such as `@briebug/jest-schematic`, `@itrulia/jest-schematic`, `@ockilson/ng-jest`, and so on.

Now, let's run the `test` command using the new script that we added to `package.json`:

```
> npm run test:watch
```

This should give you various options for running the test:

> **Press o to run only run tests related to changed files.**
> **Press a to run all tests.**
> **Press p to filter by a filename regex pattern.**
> **Press t to filter by a test name regex pattern.**
> **Press q to quit watch mode.**
> **Press Enter to trigger a test run.**

This allows you to select the way you want to run the tests.

We can also run the code coverage process by using the following command:

```
> ng test --coverage
```

Use the `vscode-jest` extension in your VS Code editor. It will tell you whether the test passed or failed within the spec file, and show the error on the line that failed.

Now we understand how Jest levels up our testing process. The base Angular CLI test is good but doesn't have a user-friendly interface that shows the tests that have passed; instead, it simply lets us know how *many* tests have passed.

Snapshot testing

Snapshot testing is mostly done on the reusable components of our application or parts of UI that do not change unexpectedly. Running snapshot testing is as easy as adding an `expect` using the `toMatchSnapshot` method.

Let's add a snapshot test to our `home.component.spec.ts` file. The following code is a simple test that mocks and generates the snapshot file of the component:

```
it('run snapshot', () => {
    expect(fixture).toMatchSnapshot();
});
```

Now, when we run the test, we will see that a new file has been created inside the `home` directory, `__snapshot__/home.component.spec.ts.snap`, which has the snapshot of the HTML rendered inside it. Now, any changes that are made to our template will make the snapshot test fail.

In this section, we have covered how and why snapshot testing helps us. Let's move on to e2e.

End-to-end testing

The Angular CLI also provides end-to-end testing for applications out of the box and uses Protractor to do so. e2e testing is used to test the application by running the application in a browser and testing whether everything works as expected end-to-end. Protractor uses Selenium behind the scenes to run the application and does testing by using JavaScript.

Let's run the e2e test case for the application using the Angular CLI command:

```
> ng e2e
```

This should open the browser and navigate to the home page. It should fail:

```
****************************************************
* Failures *
****************************************************
1) workspace-project App should display welcome message
 - Failed: No element found using locator: By(css selector, app-root h1)
Executed 1 of 1 spec (1 FAILED) in 2 secs.
[23:35:36] I/launcher - 0 instance(s) of WebDriver still running
[23:35:36] I/launcher - chrome #01 failed 1 test(s)
[23:35:36] I/launcher - overall: 1 failed spec(s)
[23:35:36] E/launcher - Process exited with error code 1
An unexpected error occurred: undefined
```

The test cases are found in the e2e folder. Currently, there is only one spec file, app.e2e-spec.ts, which has one test in it:

```
it('should display welcome message', () => {
    page.navigateTo();
    expect(page.getTitleText()).toEqual('Welcome to ngx-behance!');
});
```

page is the object that was created using AppPage using the app.po.ts file. Po stands for page objects here. Let's update the getTitleText function in the app.po.ts file to get the new text on the home page:

```
export class AppPage {
    ...
    getTitleText() {
        return element(by.css('app-root .navbar-brand')).getText();
    }
}
```

Then, we need to update the test case:

```
it('should display welcome message', () => {
    page.navigateTo();
    expect(page.getTitleText()).toEqual('Angular Behance');
});
```

We need to be aware that the e2e test cases are being run in an actual environment. There might be delays when the click event occurs and we may have to wait for an element to become visible. Let's add some helper functions to our e2e application using Protractor.

Let's create a new file, `action.ts`, in a new folder called `shared` in the `e2e/src` folder. In this file, we are asking the browser to wait for a period of time so that the content on the view is rendered, and then perform the tests:

```
import {
    browser,
    ElementFinder,
    ExpectedConditions as waitFor,
    ExpectedConditions,
    ElementArrayFinder,
} from 'protractor';

export function click(locator: ElementFinder, title: string, errorString?:
string, timeout: number = 1000) {
    console.log(`Clicking ${title}`);
    browser.wait(ExpectedConditions.presenceOf(locator));
    browser.wait(
        waitFor.elementToBeClickable(locator),
        timeout,
        errorString || `timed out waiting for ${title} to be clickable`);
    locator.click();
}

export function count(locator: ElementArrayFinder, title: string) {
    console.log(`Counting ${title}`);
    return locator.count();
}

export function wait(locator: ElementFinder, title = '', time = 10000) {
    browser.wait(waitFor.visibilityOf(locator), time, `timed out waiting to
    select ${title}`);
}
```

Let's use the `count` method to assert that more than one card is being displayed. To do that, let's create a page object to get the count of cards in `app.po.ts`:

```
export class AppPage {
    ...
    getCards() {
        return element.all(by.css('.card'));
    }
}
```

Now, we will add a new expectation to our test so that we can check whether there's more than one card.

Chapter 11

The following test case navigates to the page, checks whether the page title is as expected, and also verifies whether there's more than one card on the page. Simple, right?

```
it('should display welcome message and cards', () => {
    page.navigateTo();
    expect(page.getTitleText()).toEqual('Angular Behance');
    expect(count(page.getCards(), 'behance
    cards')).toBeGreaterThanOrEqual(1)
});
```

In our next test case, let's test that, when the user clicks on a card, they will be taken to the details page. To do this, we need to create a couple of page objects; first to get the first card item and, second to get the heading of the details page:

```
export class AppPage {
    ...
    getFirstCardTitle() {
        return element.all(by.css('.card-text')).first();
    }

    getBehancveDetailsPageHeading() {
        return element(by.css('.media-body h1'));
    }
}
```

Now, let's use these page objects in our new test case to test its functionality:

```
it('clicking on a card should show details', () => {
    page.navigateTo();
    const title = page.getFirstCardTitle().getText();
    click(page.getFirstCardTitle(), 'first card');
    const heading = page.getBehancveDetailsPageHeading();
    wait(heading, 'Behance details page header');

    expect(heading.getText()).toBe(title);
});
```

With this, we've learned how e2e tests help us. e2e tests are heavily emphasized since they help in automating the process, and in some cases remove the requirement for manual testing.

Custom error handling

Adding custom error handling can be helpful for projects. Let's suppose you forget to test your application—custom handling can help you detect the errors that users face. You can save the error log to a backend system, where you can view the errors that were faced by your customers, and fix the errors or start fixing the errors before the customers report them. This will help in keeping the product bug-free, or at least keep us aware of the bugs our customers are facing.

You can create a server that saves all of these errors, but you can also use some error-tracking software to track the errors for you. There are tools such as Sentry (`https://docs.sentry.io/clients/javascript/integrations/#angular`), Rollbar (`https://docs.rollbar.com/docs/angular`), Keen (`https://keen.io/docs/api/`), TrackJS (`https://docs.trackjs.com/browser-agent/integrations/angular2/`), and so on that you can use, all of which have varying pricing models. We will be using Sentry in this section, which has a very good free usage tier for small projects with fewer error logs.

Let's create a service that implements `ErrorHandler` by running the following command:

```
> ng g s global-error-handler
```

Now, let's implement the `ErrorHandler` interface in the new service, `GlobalErrorHandlerService`:

```
import { Injectable, ErrorHandler } from '@angular/core';

@Injectable({
    providedIn: 'root'
})
export class GlobalErrorHandlerService implements ErrorHandler {
    constructor() { }

    handleError(error) {
        console.log('custom logic should run here when an error is
        thrown!');
    }
}
```

Now, let's provide our `ErrorHandler` instead of the default `ErrorHandler` in our `AppModule.ts` file:

```
...
import { NgModule, ErrorHandler } from '@angular/core';
...
import { GlobalErrorHandlerService } from './global-error-handler.service';
```

```
import { environment } from 'src/environments/environment';

@NgModule({
    ...
 providers: [{
        provide: ErrorHandler,
        useClass: environment.production ? GlobalErrorHandlerService :
        ErrorHandler,
    }],
    ...
})
export class AppModule { }
```

Let's throw an error in our post page. This will be triggered when we click on the `toggleFavorite` button:

```
...
export class PostComponent {
    ...
    toggleFavorite() {
        throw new Error('TOGGLE FAVORITE');
        ...
    }
}
```

Now, when you build your application with the `prod` flag, run the application, and click on the toggle **Favorite** button, you should see a log in the browser's console, which we added to `handleError` method of our `GlobalErrorHandlerService`.

Now that we have added a custom error handler, let's get Sentry set up. You need to create an account on `https://sentry.io/` and create a new project, selecting `Angular` when asked.

Now, let's wire up the setup, as mentioned in the documentation. Here, we will make changes to `GlobalErrorHandlerService`.

Let's install `@sentry/browser` using npm:

```
> npm install @sentry/browser --save
```

Now, let's use it in our `ErrorHandler`:

```
...
import * as Sentry from '@sentry/browser';

Sentry.init({
    dsn: 'https://56a508d8c2df42f199435717d5ce8725@sentry.io/1443406'
```

```
});

@Injectable({
    providedIn: 'root'
})
export class GlobalErrorHandlerService implements ErrorHandler {
    ...
    handleError(error) {
        const eventId = Sentry.captureException(error.originalError ||
        error);
        Sentry.showReportDialog({ eventId });
    }
}
```

Then, we need to build our application with the `prod` flag, with our Sentry setup in place.

Now, when you click on the toggle **Favorite** button, you should see a dialog box where you can enter more details about the error you encountered:

It looks like we're having issues.

Our team has been notified. If you'd like to help, tell us what happened below.

NAME

> Jane Doe

EMAIL

> jane@example.com

WHAT HAPPENED?

> I clicked on 'X' and then hit 'Confirm'

Submit Crash Report   Close   Crash reports powered by ⚡ SENTRY

If we check the Sentry.io application, we should get more details about the error, even if the user didn't want to submit a crash report.

This should show the whole stack trace of the error, along with the breadcrumb, which allows developers to understand what steps triggered this error:

BREADCRUMBS		Q Search breadcrumbs...	
ui.click	`div#navbar-header.collapse.navbar-toggleable-xs.container > a.navbar-brand`		15:29:04
navigation			15:29:04
to	`/snaps`		
from	`/`		
ui.click	`div.album.text-muted > div.container > div.row > div.card > a`		15:29:05
ui.click	`app-home > div.album.text-muted > div.container > div.row > div.card`		15:29:06
ui.click	`div.row > div.card > a > img.img-responsive[alt="Card image cap"]`		15:29:07
navigation			15:29:07
to	`/snaps/52472961`		
from	`/snaps`		
ui.click	`div.col-md-3 > ul.list-group > li.list-group-item > button.btn.btn-primary`		15:29:07
exception	`Error: TOGGLE FAVORITE`		15:29:10

This will help us find the errors and fix them in our active development or support cycles. This is the brilliance of using custom error handling. More often than not, when the customer complains, someone from the support team has to coordinate with the customer and track down the bug. This avoids all the fuss and provides a much better experience, both for the customer and the development team.

Summary

In this chapter, we used an application that we created using the Angular CLI, added tests to it by using Jasmine, and ran it using Karma. We saw how we can test our application using isolated unit testing, integration testing, and end-to-end testing. We also measured the code coverage of our application and measured the percentage of code that's covered using our tests. We also replaced our Jasmine and Karma setups with Jest and ran a snapshot test of one of our components.

After completing this chapter, you should be writing code that is very close to being bug-free. Often, developers have the opinion that, since manual testing has already been done on the feature code, it's not required to write tests, but more often than not, they usually end up getting bugs in it. There are possibilities that a very minute change ends up breaking the application. This can end up being a huge loss for the company when it is being used by customers. This is why large organizations emphasize so much on writing tests – so that they can be sure that their application is working properly and is less prone to errors.

With this chapter, you should be able to write various kinds of tests that help you verify that your code is running expectedly, and automate your application with just a few commands.

This completes our journey for *Angular Projects*. I hope you have learned and experienced the power of the Angular ecosystem and gained a lot of knowledge about it. You should now have a good grasp of adding new capabilities to your applications, and also supporting different platforms using NativeScript or Ionic.

I wish you all the best for your future projects. Keep learning and exploring!

Questions

Test your knowledge of this chapter by answering the following questions:

- What are the different types of testing strategies?
- What is isolated unit testing?
- What is deep integration testing?
- What is shallow integration testing?
- What is code coverage?
- What is Jest and what are its advantages?
- What is end-to-end testing?

Further reading

The following reading material will provide you with more information about Angular testing:

- **Angular testing guide:** https://angular.io/guide/testing.
- **Code coverage:** https://en.wikipedia.org/wiki/Code_coveragex.
- **Jest:** https://jestjs.io/.
- **Protractor:** https://www.protractortest.org/#/.

Other Books You May Enjoy

If you enjoyed this book, you may be interested in these other books by Packt:

Learn WebAssembly
Mike Rourke

ISBN: 978-1-78899-737-9

- Learn how WebAssembly came to be and its associated elements (text format, module, and JavaScript API)
- Create, load, and debug a WebAssembly module (editor and compiler/toolchain)
- Build a high-performance application using C and WebAssembly
- Extend WebAssembly's feature set using Emscripten by porting a game written in C++
- Explore upcoming features of WebAssembly, Node.js integration, and alternative compilation methods

Web Development with Angular and Bootstrap - Third Edition
Sridhar Rao Chivukula, Aki Iskandar

ISBN: 978-1-78883-810-8

- Develop Angular single-page applications using an ecosystem of helper tools
- Get familiar with Bootstrap's new grid and helper classes
- Embrace TypeScript and ECMAScript to write more maintainable code
- Implement custom directives for Bootstrap 4 with the ng2-bootstrap library
- Understand the component-oriented structure of Angular and its router
- Use the built-in HTTP library to work with API endpoints
- Manage your app's data and state with observables and streams

Leave a review - let other readers know what you think

Please share your thoughts on this book with others by leaving a review on the site that you bought it from. If you purchased the book from Amazon, please leave us an honest review on this book's Amazon page. This is vital so that other potential readers can see and use your unbiased opinion to make purchasing decisions, we can understand what our customers think about our products, and our authors can see your feedback on the title that they have worked with Packt to create. It will only take a few minutes of your time, but is valuable to other potential customers, our authors, and Packt. Thank you!

Index

Auth0 (Auth zero)
  about 221
  registering 240, 241, 242
  signing in 240, 241, 242
authentication library
  adding 229
  adding, Nx used 229, 230
  Auth0, registering 240, 242
  Auth0, signing in 240, 242
  callback route, adding 237, 238
  interceptor, used for adding authorization token to
    header 244, 245
  NgRx auth action, updating 230, 232
  NgRx Auth effect, updating 234, 235, 237
  NgRx Auth reducer, updating 232, 234
  NgRx state, generating 230
  routes, creating in application 238, 239
  routes, securing with route guards 243, 244
authorization token
  adding, to headers with interceptor 244, 245

B

Backend as a Service (BaaS) 166
Behance API
  URL 301
built-in actions
  adding 107, 108, 109, 110, 112, 113, 114
Bulma CSS framework
  using 278
Bulma's documentation
  reference link 31
  URL 280
Bulma
  reference link 30
bundle
  optimizing 114, 115, 116

C

callback route
  adding 237, 238
Clarity Angular
  URL 89
Clarity
  URL 92
class and property decorators

  about 9, 10
  examples 10
client application
  creating, Nx used 225, 226
client
  state, transferring to 194, 195, 196, 198
code coverage 313, 314, 315
Color Generator tool
  reference link 165
Create, Read, Update and Delete (CRUD) 85
Cross-Origin Request Sharing (CORS) 123
custom error
  handling 320, 321, 322, 323
custom validations
  adding 107, 108, 109, 110, 112, 113, 114

D

D3 library
  URL 245
D3 visualization
  ngx-charts, using 245, 246, 247, 248, 249
Database as a Service (DBaaS) 166
deep integration tests
  about 310
  for component 310
  for service 311, 312, 313
dock layout 255, 256
dropdown functionality
  creating 282, 283, 284, 286
dynamic forms
  creating, from ngx-formly 176, 178, 179, 180,
    182, 183

E

electronic-store application
  creating 223
end-to-end (e2e) test cases 11
end-to-end (e2e) testing 316, 317, 318, 319
es-api 223

F

Facebook
  reference link 206
feature module 73
Fira Code